MW01010420

A TREASURY OF
BUSINESS OPPORTUNITIES

by

DAVID D. SELTZ

. . . Featuring Over 400 Ways To Make A
Fortune Without Leaving Your House!

FARNSWORTH PUBLISHING COMPANY, INC.
Rockville Centre, New York 11570

© 1976, David D. Seltz.
All rights reserved.
First printing, January 1977.
Second printing, March 1977.
Third printing, October 1977.
Fourth printing, March 1978.
Fifth printing, October 1978.
Sixth printing, May 1979.
Seventh printing, May 1980.
Published by Farnsworth Publishing Co., Inc.,
Rockville Centre, New York 11570.
Library of Congress Catalog Card No. 76-47103.
ISBN 087863097X.
Manufactured in the United States of America.
No part of this book may be reproduced
without the written permission of the publisher.

To Doris, Anne, Laurie, and David John, my primary success motivators. And to Nat and Lautia, my primary success advisors.

Table of Contents

1.

SECRETS OF SELF MASTERY

Yes, it's possible to earn money ... lots of money. And it can be accomplished, in many instances, in your own home, spare time, and with little capital (as little as five hundred dollars or less).

This book will endeavor to show you how. First, through case histories of how others have done it. Second, by relating my own experiences covering some twenty years.

Throughout most of these years I've been a "business consultant" to both individuals and corporations.

For individuals, I would point out the basic "ingredients" considered important to success. First, the things needed to organize themselves and, second, the things needed to organize their selected business.

For corporations, my advice would be very similar (and it's amazing how similar the two are!). Many businesses, like many individuals, are floundering, directionless, unable to envision and to profit from their own capabilities, thus attaining only a small portion of their potential growth.

I have been privileged to advise some of the country's largest corporations, many in the billion-dollar class. I have also been privileged to advise many thousands of individuals, doing this both on a one-to-one basis and in large "groups" (as many as five hundred and more) through my worldwide lectures, and through my extensive writings and cassettes.

I have authored some fifteen books and over two thousand articles. I have been engaged by foremost governmental agencies, chambers of commerce, industrial associations (both in this country and overseas) to lecture on the general subject of "business opportunities." I have also officiated each year as chairman of the International Franchising Congress in Zurich, Switzerland.

During the course of this extensive experience, I have been able to observe first-hand the things that often cause failure and the things that help to achieve success. For this evaluation, I was fortunate to occupy a "box office" seat . . . being privy to information that was not normally obtainable.

I could see numerous examples of how individuals with a million-dollar potential eroded their lives with constant defeats . . . kept slicing away their assets into small bits until there was very little left.

I have also seen individuals (and companies, too) with seemingly minimal capabilities and potential who had been able to zoom into the million-dollar class, achieving this by effectively marshalling and utilizing their available capabilities to attain maximum growth.

Within the pages of this book, I will endeavor to present the essence, the distillation, of this experience. Hopefully, it can save you years of frustrating, expensive "trial and error," and magnify your opportunities to succeed.

In doing so, I'll endeavor to convey the benefits of my own experiences that have enabled me to earn substantial consultant fees for similar advice. The two main subjects discussed will be: first, the "personal YOU" . . . how to achieve personal success; second, the "business YOU" . . . how to achieve business and financial success. Each in itself is vital; both are interlinked. They form a necessary "team" to help achieve your goals.

I will also strive to describe possible businesses for you to enter . . . simple-to-operate businesses that can fit practically every aptitude and need. And, finally, I will provide a list of possible financing sources—both governmental and private—to assist in your financing needs.

And, to help assure your continuing success, I will discuss "how to think up ideas"—practically at will—to help achieve the "innovativeness" that is so vital for the successful operation of any business venture.

To start off, I'd like to present my "Cardinal Rules" for success.

CARDINAL RULE #1: *Expel Negatives*

Has this happened to you?

You start something, get halfway into it, and then suddenly doubt your ability to finish it. You now try something else. And then something else. Each project fails to get done, or to get done right. And now you virtually expect defeat . . . and everything you do thereafter gets stained with this expectation.

It happens to most people. As a consequence, plans go unresolved, capabilities go unused, and failure follows failure. It has also happened to me many times in the past.

I remember the time I almost drowned. I was swimming across a narrow river. I had done this many times before, with no problems. But this time, an alien thought crept into my mind just about when I was half across: "What if I couldn't swim any further?" The thought had barely crossed my mind when it happened: I simply couldn't swim another stroke. There was a sudden, inexplicable paralysis of my muscles. Try as I might, I couldn't lift my arms. Fortunately, I was rescued at the last moment. But not until I had gone down twice. A cramp? Possibly. But more in the mental sense than the physical. I succumbed to my own fears. I *thought* defeat . . . and so I *met* defeat.

It's happened to me in various other ways, too. For example, the time I had to make an important business presentation. I was thoroughly prepared for it. However, a negative thought arose: "What if I forgot my pitch and found myself at a loss for words?" You guess it—it happened. I did forget, I groped for words, and I did lose the sale.

Then there was another time. I was called upon to make a speech before a large audience. Thought I: "What if I become stagestruck?" And, of course, it happened—and the speech was a dud.

What does this all prove? A number of things . . .

. . . the paralyzing effect of those words: "What if";

. . . the erosive effect of negative suggestions;

. . . the importance of belief in oneself.

Your mind works like a computer. Feed it a negative input and it starts working that way.

Thereafter, you're helpless. You don't plan right . . . you don't work right. You procrastinate. You think of hundreds of "what if" reasons why the project will not work . . . even though you spent months preparing it. What's more, if you don't have enough reasons of your own, you can generally depend on other reasons from friends, relatives, and associates who are only too happy to add their own negatives to your collection. Saying "no" comes easier than saying "yes."

More tragedies are caused . . . more failures are accelerated . . . more successes (about to be achieved) have turned into failure . . . because of one basic factor: self-doubt.

You "anticipate" defeat, and thereafter your life becomes a succession of half-starts, near-misses, and constant frustrations. And each defeat leaves a set of new emotional shambles in its wake . . . making it all the more difficult to achieve a new start.

Which, incidentally, reminds me oi a story. I call it my "million dollar" story . . . I feel it's been easily worth that much to me.

It's about a miner who worked for months digging for gold, but to no avail. Finally, in disgust, he hurled his axe with such force that it embedded itself in the ground, where he left it, exclaiming: "I've had enough—I'm getting out of here."

An hour later another miner passed by. He noticed the axe sticking in the ground and decided he'd retrieve it. Pulling it out of the ground, he exposed— directly beneath it—a rich vein of gold that eventually reaped millions of dollars!

The moral, of course, is that if the first miner had had a little more faith in himself and his project, and had persevered just a few minutes more, he would have achieved riches beyond his fondest dreams!

I profited from this story. I now *forced* myself to "believe" in myself . . . to stick with things until they were properly completed.

As a result, I reaped rich dividends—getting more things accomplished, and accumulating many of the artifacts that are normally associated with leading a "good" life.

The story can help you, too. Try.

CARDINAL RULE #2: *The Magic of Positive Attitude*

Determine that a project *can* get done . . . vow that you *will* succeed . . . and you unfailingly will! It's as simple as that. You have detoured a defeat momentum into a winner momentum. You become charged up with the excitement of triumph, the thrill of being a winner. Soon—instead of dawdling and brooding—you're afire with a sense of achievement and accomplishment.

So much for attitude and determination, which are of primary importance. Now let's continue on your road to success.

CARDINAL RULE #3: *List Your Assets*

Have you looked at a Business "Balance Sheet"—either your own or others'? It chronicles debits and credits of a business. It exposes weaknesses and strengths—areas that are over-burdened and pull down assets . . . earning potentials not realized . . . leakages that erode capacities. Perhaps your balance sheet shows too many employees, too large an overhead, under-capitalization, or possibly concentration on a business that is outdated or over-competitive . . . or other factors.

Similarly, a *personal balance sheet* is important . . . a way to measure your own assets and liabilities . . . to expose your strengths and weaknesses, and to determine which areas should be expanded and which should be reduced or eliminated. For example:

ASSETS	LIABILITIES
• get along with people	• no endurance
• am creative	• lack of purpose
• generate trust, confidence	• vacillate
• am ambitious	• waste time
• have stick-to-it-iveness	• over-complacent
• have friendly, genial manner	• insincere
• am perceptive	• self-doubt
• good judgment	• lack thoroughness
• purposeful	• switch to many different things
• sincere	• think small
• efficient	• over-preoccupied with others' opinions
• dedicated	• over-sensitive to criticism
• self-confident	• non-cooperative
• thorough	
• decisive	

CARDINAL RULE #4: *Avoid These Pitfalls*

1. Self-Defeatism: Do you *assume* defeat? . . . *fear* success? View them as your number one enemies. They are the prime "shatterers" of plans, any plans.

2. Hop-Skipping: Do you have so many things to do that you don't do any, because you can't decide what to start first? Thus, you hop-skip from one thing to another, each becoming marginally done or superficially finished . . . but rarely thoroughly done. Plan to concentrate on one project at a time . . . ignoring others until this is adequately completed.

3. Not enough advice: Few people can operate successfully as "loners." Ideas need a bounce-back on others.

4. Too much advice: Bounce your idea among enough people and it will perish in its infancy. You'll get a plethora of negatives—"reasons why it won't work." On one hand, seek the advice of others qualified to give sincere advice. On the other hand, stand above it. Sift it carefully. Select that which you deem pertinent. If, after careful consideration, you still doubt it, wait awhile. Don't be discouraged in going ahead on your project.

5. Poor self-discipline: Do you do the things you resolve to do . . . or do you procrastinate? Develop good working habits.

6. Running scared: Fear of failing prevents "attempting"! The thought, "what if I fail," will unfailingly conduce failure. Once you undertake something, embark on it with complete self-confidence.

7. Determination: Do you give in easily? To become a winner you must "go for the guts" in any project. Life is competitive . . . as in baseball, it's the player who's truly competitive, the man who'll argue and fight for every point, who normally comes out way ahead.

8. Lack of perspective: Do you involve yourself with trivial details—the "nitty gritties" of life—so that you constantly find yourself on a treadmill? Remember: The thing that counts is the "project" you've *completed*, not how busy you appear to be. Many people get so involved with meaningless details, they lose perspective on their true, meaningful, aspired goals.

9. Self-pity: You can spend so much time pitying yourself, that—suddenly, ten years have flown past and you wonder where they went, and where were you all this time?

10. Procrastination: It's always easy to find reasons why one should wait for tomorrow. And then tomorrow . . . and tomorrow . . . somehow it becomes a succession of tomorrows that never come. Procrastination is a deceiver that comes to you as a seeming ally and ends up as an implacable foe.

Now that you have absorbed the "not-to-do" things, let's look at the "to-do" things.

CARDINAL RULE #5: *Set "Realizable" Goals*

People must have a purpose. There must be a goal. Otherwise you tend to end up with hundreds of deferred, or partially completed plans that become yellowed with the years. Many people have closets full of such incompleted projects. You'll notice that the person who gets places sets a goal for one accomplishment at a time . . . and sticks with it until it's done.

Follow these rules for setting goals:

1. Establish one goal at a time. Set strict completion schedules.

2. Start with small, "do-able" things. Feel the thrill of small accomplishments; they'll open the door to bigger and bigger ones!

3. Constantly "upgrade" your goals; look ahead to bigger and bigger accomplishments. Say: What will I do in six months that will advance me from where I am now?

The subject of "upgrading" reminds me of the experience of George Waddel. He told me: "I started my career as a writer. I was paid two cents a word and I experienced hectic competition from persons who, in many instances, had far greater talent than myself. So I thought: How can I better utilize my talents to earn more money? I decided to enter the advertising field, where I averaged five cents a word. And still later, in the sales promotion field, I was able to earn ten cents a word. Finally I broke into the marketing field where the price per word was virtually unlimited."

The secret was that the more "different," the more "non-competitive" George became—and the more "mystique" involved in what he did—the bigger the fees he could command. Nevertheless, George was still, basically, the same writer who had first been able to earn only two cents a word, and with plenty of competition.

Prepare Goal Cards: Write out your goals on index-sized cards: your short-range goals and your long-range goals. Give yourself firm schedules. Also give yourself rewards (things that "pamper" you) as an incentive to meeting these schedules.

Take Chances: Better try ten things and fail in nine of them than to try none . . . and achieve nothing. Each failure has its own benefits . . . as you've learned valuable lessons in how to reduce chances for the next failure. The important thing is: you've tried!

Dr. Conant, former president of Columbia University, said: "The only time a turtle makes progress is when he sticks his neck out."

Are You a Yo-Yo? Many people have a yo-yo syndrome. The yo-yo keeps going up and down and ends up nowhere. The same with moods. If uncontrolled, they'll also go up and down—ranging from depression to exhilaration, from confidence to despair, and you, too, gradually will end up nowhere. Learn to control your moods . . . make little conquests of your moods and, in time, you'll become a virtual "conquistador"!

Cut Your Losses: Not all goals are valid. You figured it was good, yet it turned out to be a flop. Don't hang on to a loser—"cut it" and go on to more constructive pursuits.

Mail order firms will first "test" before plunging. If they succeed, they double and triple their next commitment. If they fail, revise. Companies of many types (and particularly franchise companies) will first set up prototypes, prove out their success potential, *before* committing the bulk of their capital and energies. Hence, with your own goals, make your own "tests," establish your own "prototypes." If they appear inadvisable, fruitless, waste no more time with them. Cut your losses, quick!

CARDINAL RULE #6: *Develop Appealing "Self-Image"*

No doubt you have seen it happen in your own community, and have wondered about it. There are two stores, in very equivalent locations—in some cases almost side by side. The services they offer are virtually identical, and the prices, too, are just about the same. Yet one store is generally empty, while the other is crowded with customers. And you just can't help but wonder what is the reason for the difference.

By the same token, you see the same situation in people. In appearance and in their capacities, they seem so alike. Yet one person will be a success in everything he does—everything he touches will turn to gold, everyone he meets will sing his praises . . . while the other person just can't seem to click and must constantly struggle for acceptance.

The essential difference between store number one and store number two, and between person number one and person number two can be summed up in one simple word—and that word is *"image."* And while that may be a simple word, its meaning is far from simple. *Image* is an *impression* created in the mind of the viewer. The popular store had succeeded in creating an image that appealed to people and made them *want* to come in and buy. The image of the second store was one that discouraged patronage.

With people it's the same thing. One person conjures up an image of success; he is warm, outgoing, decisive and people sense this and like it, and are attracted to him because they like a winner. The other person creates quite the opposite image. People see in him a wavering picture of indecision, irresolution, and aimlessness. They tend to avoid him because they just don't want to be bothered with a loser.

How does one achieve the proper image? How does one create an aura of success? Why is it that some people—just like some stores—have it, and others don't? It is something that must come from within—something that sets one person apart from another, and causes that person to be in demand, while the other is virtually ignored.

Create the proper image in your own mind's eye, and that image will come through and be discerned by others. The image you create is based on your own belief in yourself, and your own determination. It isn't necessarily something you can build overnight. It's something you must work at.

As previously stated, "self-image" is your conception of yourself. Set it low and you will think in terms of the "nitty-gritties" of life, and will become afraid of larger accomplishments. Set it high and you will think *big*. You will set high goals for yourself and will aim for *big* achievements. You'll gain self-assurance and an aura of success—and in most instances, you *will* succeed!

Al Bruno, for example, received a "top" fee of fifteen hundred dollars for his services. John Fisher performed similar services for another client and received only seventy-five dollars. Yet Al's client was happier to pay the fifteen hundred dollars to him, whereas John Fisher's client begrudged him his fee. Why? He "bought" the high value that Bruno placed on himself and his services. Fisher's client, on the other hand, sensed the low value that Fisher placed on himself and his work and paid him accordingly, considering that he was being generous in paying the amount he did.

Franklin D. Roosevelt turned the country around by declaring: "We have nothing to fear but fear itself." Eliminate fear from your vocabulary. Think in success words and terms and phrases. In every word and thought, accentuate the positive. Fill your mind with such words as purpose, courage, determination. Think optimism, progress. Act in a manner that's warm, friendly, keen, and alert.

CARDINAL RULE #7: *Re-Computerize Yourself?*

Each of us, like a computer, is the sum of the input that we have received from infancy. We react accordingly. The quality of this input is exposed by the quality of our "output." It is necessary to take a close, hard look at *your* computer . . . your input. Perhaps it should be re-computerized . . . .

For example . . . does your computer input comprise:

- Sure to fail.

- Put off till tomorrow.

● Has happened before—defeat will repeat itself.

● Don't have capabilities to do it.

● Will fail anyway, why complete it.

● Lack of capital—why not wait until I have more.

It requires re-structuring your HABITS—your thoughts and reactions. This is not done overnight. It is accomplished step-by-step . . . *trickle-by-trickle*.

Trickle #1—Start At Once! Set a goal . . . and work your goal. For example, Ed Tabor would plan his day by writing "To Do," and beneath that would list a barrage of things—often as many as twenty. At the end of the day, nothing was accomplished. In planning his day in this manner, he almost expected that nothing would be accomplished. They were "fragments" of plans, with no purpose or expectation of attainment. He changed to: "What do I want to accomplish today." This now required his thinking in terms of "projects" rather than "pieces." It suddenly cleared his mind, gave him purpose, and made his day resultful.

Trickle #2—Avoid Deflections! Stick to your project, don't let anything distract you. Hundreds of rational "reasons why" will come to your mind . . . reasons why you shouldn't do it at that time—or that day—and should put it off for another time. FIGHT THESE! Determine that you'll stick to it and finish it according to schedule.

Have you noticed, for example, that when doing work for someone else, especially a business client, no matter how extensive the task and brief the deadline, you manage to complete it. Why? Because you knew you would be held strongly accountable to meeting the schedule (otherwise you would lose the client and not get paid). YOU HAD TO . . . hence, you did.

Why not develop the habit of thinking of your own projects as "assign-ments" accountable to a tight schedule. Become your own strict client. It achieves wonders in getting projects finished, and on time.

Trickle #3—Meeting Your Biggest Adversaries Head On! Don't give them a chance to gain a foothold. They are:

a. Pretending there is no problem
b. Running from your problem
c. Waiting for someone else to solve your problem
d. Always blaming someone else
e. Criticizing other people constantly

Decision and success are the results of:

a. Making sure of what you want
b. Recognizing its value
c. Believing you can do it
d. Taking one step at a time
e. "Committing" yourself by making your intentions known
f. Beginning a pattern of achievement . . . persistence
g. Avoid wasting time
h. Do not accept criticism from others . . . man's greatest enemy is negative thinking

Trickle #4—Be "Different"! Nat Sherman, the renowned tobacconist, achieved extraordinary success in an "ordinary" field . . . by being *different*. Hence, his business has shown great growth each year, and is considered the foremost of its type in the country. The original business was an "ordinary" tobacco store . . . however, he filled it with different, extraordinary products —cigarettes of unusual shapes, sizes, quality, imprints. People went out of their way to patronize his store. It became a status symbol . . . they were proud to show the Sherman "label." What is different about what you're doing?

Trickle #5—Value Your Time! The other day a person asked me what time it was. I said, "Three o'clock." His watch was fifteen minutes fast, showing 3:15. He exclaimed: "Isn't that wonderful. I've just added fifteen minutes to my life!"

His comment jolted me into a realization of the value of time . . . and how we normally take it for granted, squander it. Every minute you've properly utilized . . . that you've saved . . . you've practically added to your years, extended your own life.

NEED TO BANISH "HATE"

We often go through life "hating." We can "hate" at the drop of a hat, and on any subject—trivial or colossal, fancied or real. Our hates cover a multitude of things: the fellow who accidentally bumped into you; the fellow worker you believe seeks your job. And so on.

You tend to "hate," and your entire personality becomes choked up. You no longer think or act freely, constructively! The emotion of "hate" sends its poisons through your system . . . causes frustrations, stops solutions. Your whole being is obsessed with unresolved broodings, resentments, plans for revenge.

Ed Johnson told me how he banished hate. "It was simple," he said. "I merely reversed the emotion, instead of hating my enemies, I resolved to *'forgive'* my enemies. It's interesting how the rancor suddenly exited from my system. Because of this new outlook, I was now able to see my 'enemy' objectively, in perspective . . . rather than as emotional 'blotches.' I could now see points of view, justifications, that I'd previously locked out."

"At the very least," he continued, "I now felt superior to my problems, and unleashed from my tethers. My mind could start re-functioning constructively, creatively. The advantages of 'forgiving' thus brought greater, and immediate rewards, far beyond the emotion of hating (even if I was justified in hating!)."

HOW THIS BOOK CAN HELP YOU

There is no magic elixir. It is the aim of this book to point out the goldmine of "riches" that *now* reside with *you*, and to help you put them to best use. They're there, right now . . . waiting to be unleashed!

It reminds me of a well-known parable. It's about the convict who was in prison for twenty-five years. Escape seemed hopeless. One day he fell against his cell door, quite by accident. It opened. He then realized that it could have been opened at any time . . . he just never tried!

People make their own prison doors. Great attainments lie before them . . . if they only tried!

Ed Greenley discusses how he "escaped" from *his* "prison." "I attribute much of my success to the ability I've developed to eliminate the negative. Every time a negative thought tries to invade my mind, I sense it and I dismiss it by thinking a positive thought. As a result, my self-confidence has grown by leaps and bounds, and I find that I can concentrate on the positive and can adhere to a single purpose and idea until I'm ready to go on to my next goal. I've become the master of my mind and do not permit it to drift into worthless, negative channels."

Ed is living proof that the road to success is a matter of decision followed by action. And the action must be positive.

- If there's a predicament, admit it. But face it in a positive, not a negative, way.

- Don't run away from the problem. Act courageously.

- Don't always blame somebody else.

- Don't criticize others.

Rules for decision and action are as follows:

- Make sure of your goal and know exactly what you want.

- Understand and appreciate the value of what you're after.

- Have faith in your ability to achieve it.

- Outline the steps required and take one step at a time.

- Assume responsibility by making your intentions known.

- Follow through toward achievement.

Goals help you in pacing yourself. By pacing yourself properly, you'll find that you attain your goals more easily and more quickly. Goals are the milestones on your road to success. These milestones help you measure your progress. *If your goal is small, you'll never make it big!*

2.

DOORWAYS TO BUSINESS SUCCESS

When I was young, I set out to change the world. When I grew a little older I perceived that this was too ambitious so I set out to change my state. This, too, I realized as I grew older was too ambitious, so I set out to change my town. When I realized I could not even do this, I tried to change my family. Now as an old man I know that I should have started by changing myself. If had I started with myself, maybe then I would have succeeded in changing my family, the town, or even the state—and who knows, maybe even the world!

(Words of a Chasidic Rabbi on his deathbed.)

In deciding on a business, many factors should be taken into consideration:

1. Your life style—what kind of work will give you comfortableness, and self-satisfaction . . . and also meet with the approval of your family?

2. Your economic needs—how much must you earn to cover your normal overhead expenses?

3. Permanence—is your outlook long-range or short-range? Are you seeking a business that offers the potential of a "quick lump sum" (which usually doesn't materialize), or one that offers smaller sums, seems more plodding in nature, and provides dependability and permanency?

4. Investment capability—never enter any business with so-called "running scared" capital. This is one of the chief architects of business failure.

5. Risk factor—decide on how much risk you want to take . . . how much you can afford to take. Hence, weigh all facts solidly and carefully, avoid speculative, promotional ventures.

6. Timely—is it the kind of opportunity that conforms to present-day needs . . . demand?

7. *You*—are you qualified to conduct a business of your own or should you, instead, consider taking a job, and work for someone else?

In entering *any* business you should ask these basic questions:
- What business should you choose?
- What are your chances of success? What will be your return on investment?
- How much capital will you need?
- Where can you get the money?
- Should you share the ownership of your business with others?
- Where should you locate?
- How will you price your products or services?
- What are the best methods of selling in your proposed business?
- What management problems will you face?
- What records should you be prepared to keep?
- What laws and regulations will effect you?
- What tax and insurance problems will you have?

CHECKLIST FOR STARTING A BUSINESS

The U.S. Department of Commerce has suggested a check list of things to consider in entering a new business, inclusive of:

a. *Are You The Type?*

- Have you rated your personal qualifications using a scale similar to that presented in this book?
- Have you had some acquaintances rate you on such scales?
- Have you carefully considered those qualities in which you are weak and taken steps to improve them or to get an associate whose strong points will compensate for them?

b. *What Business Should You Choose?*

- In what business have you had previous experience? In what business do you know the characteristics of the goods or services you will sell?
- Do you have special technical skills, such as those needed by a pharmacist, plumber, electrician, or radio repair man, which may be used in a business?

- Have you studied current trends to be certain the new business you are planning is needed?
- Have you considered working for someone else to get more experience?

c. *What Are Your Chances For Success?*

- Are general business conditions good or bad?
- Are business conditions in the city and neighborhood where you are planning to locate good or bad?
- Are current conditions in the line of business you are planning good or bad?

d. *What Will Be Your Return On Investment?*

- How much will you have to invest in your business?
- What will be your probable net profit?
- Will the net profit divided by the investment result in a rate of return which compares favorably with the rate you can obtain from other investment opportunities?

e. *How Much Capital Will You Need?*

- What income from sales or services can you reasonably expect in the first six months? The first year? The second year?
- What is the gross profit you can expect on these volumes of business?
- What expenses can you forecast as being necessary?
- Is your salary included in these expenses?
- Are the net profit and salary adequate?
- Have you compared this income with what you could make as an employee?
- Are you willing to risk uncertain or unregular income for the next year? Two years?
- Have you made an estimate of the capital you will need to open and operate this business until income equals expenses, in accordance with the suggestions outlined in this book?

f. *Where Can You Get The Money?*

- How much have you saved which you can put into the business immediately?
- How much do you have in the form of other assets which you could, if necessary, sell, or on which you could borrow to get additional funds?
- Have you some place where you could borrow money to put into the business?
- Have you talked to a banker? What does he think about your plan?
- Does he think enough of the venture to lend you money?

- Do you have a financial reserve available for unexpected needs?
- How does the total capital, available from all sources, compare with the estimated capital requirements?

g. *What Reserves Should You Be Prepared To Keep?*

- Have you planned a bookkeeping system?
- Have you planned a merchandise control system?
- Have you obtained any standard operating ratios for your type of business which you plan to use as guides?
- What additional records are necessary?
- What system are you going to use to keep a check on costs?
- Do you need any special forms or records? Can they be bought from stock? Must they be printed?
- Are you going to keep the records yourself? Hire a bookkeeper? Have an outsider come in periodically?

h. *What Laws And Regulations Will Affect You?*

- Is a license to do business necessary? State? City?
- Have you checked the police and health regulations as they apply to your business?
- Are your operations subject to interstate commerce regulations?
- Have you received advice from your lawyer regarding your responsibilities under Federal or State statutes or local ordinances pertaining to such matters as advertising, pricing, purity of product, royalties, labeling, trade practices, patents, trademarks, copyrights, brand names?

i. *What Tax And Insurance Problems Will You Have?*

- Have you worked out a system for paying the withholding tax for your employees?
- Have you worked out a system for handling sales taxes? Excise taxes?
- Has fire insurance been purchased? Windstorm? Use and occupancy?
- Has fire insurance protecting against damage suits and public liability claims been purchased?
- Has workmen's compensation insurance been provided?
- Has burglary and hold-up insurance been considered?
- What other hazards should be insured against?

j. *How Will You Keep Up To Date?*

- How do you plan to keep up with improvements in your trade or industry?

k. *How Will You Price Your Products And Services?*

- Have you decided upon your price ranges?

- What prices will you have to charge to cover your costs and obtain a profit?
- How do these prices compare with prices of competitors?
- Have you investigated possible legal restrictions on your establishment of prices?

l. *What Are The Best Methods Of Selling In Your Proposed Business?*

- Have you studied both the direct and indirect sales promotional methods used by competitors?
- Have you outlined your promotional policy?
- Why do you expect customers to buy your product or services—price, quality, distinctive styling, other?
- Are you going to do outside selling?
- Are you going to advertise in the newspapers? Magazines?
- Are you going to do direct mail advertising?
- Are you going to use handbills?
- Are you going to use radio advertising?
- Are you going to use television?
- Are you going to use displays?

m. *How Will You Select And Train Personnel?*

- Will employees supply skills you lack?
- What skills are necessary?
- Have you written job descriptions for prospective employees?
- Are satisfactory employees available locally?
- What is the prevailing wage scale?
- What do you plan to pay?
- Would it be advantageous or disadvantageous to hire someone now employed by a competitor?
- What labor legislation will affect you?
- Have you planned your training and follow-up procedures?

n. *What Other Management Problems Will You Face?*

- Are you going to sell for credit?
- Do you have the additional capital necessary to carry accounts receivable?

o. *Should You Share The Ownership Of Your Business With Others?*

- Do you lack needed technical or management skills which can be most satisfactorily supplied by one or more partners?
- Do you need the financial assistance of one or more associates?
- If you do (or do not) share the ownership with associates, have you

checked the features of each form of organization (individual proprietorship, partnership, corporation) to determine which will best fit
your operation?

p. *Where Should You Locate?*

- Should you locate nearer to your source of material supply, your labor,
  or your market, measured by relative freight, labor, distribution,
  power, and other costs?
- Which is more desirable, a city, suburban, or country location,
  measured by cost and availability of labor, transportation, power, etc.?
- Where will you find an adequate supply of labor of the types you
  require?
- What transportation, power, water supply, fuel, do you need, and
  where will you find them adequate?
- Are climatic conditions important to your product or process?
- How do tax rates compare, allowing for differences in municipal
  services?
- What type of building will you need?
- How much space do you need?
- What provision are you making for future expansion?
- What special features do you require, such as particular types of light-
  ing, heating, ventilating, air conditioning, or dust collecting facilities?
- What equipment do you need?
- If proper equipment is not in the building site you have selected, where
  can it be obtained?
- If you are planning a manufacturing plant, what structural strengths
  are required in the building you select to support the machinery and
  other equipment? Have you complied with the building code in this
  regard?
- After selecting a location on the basis of the above factors, are you and
  the members of your family satisfied that the community will be a
  desirable place to live and rear your children?
- If the proposed location does not meet nearly all your requirements, is
  there a sound reason why you should not wait and continue seeking a
  more ideal location?

Success is dependent chiefly on how you manage the business. Keep up to
date. Some sources of information are:

- Commercial and industrial banks
- Chambers of commerce
- Trade associations and trade papers
- Better Business Bureaus
- Credit bureaus
- Merchandise and equipment suppliers with whom you deal

- Business sections of libraries
- The United States Small Business Administration

Visit your nearest United States Small Business Administration field office to consult with the business specialists. Use the business library facilities which are available in the principal offices.

HOW TO ASSURE YOURSELF OF THE CONTINUING "BUSINESS HEALTH" OF YOUR BUSINESS

One fallacy of business is that, often, the small businessman thinks he is doing well because he has been very busy all year (working as many as twelve hours a day). Imagine his consternation when, at the end of the year, he discovers that he has actually lost money. He pathetically asks why.

The reasons are usually based on the lack of arithmetic control of his business. He has not properly assessed expenses versus income to determine that he is making a profit (at every step). He has failed to give himself a month-by-month awareness of exactly how he is doing—to assure himself that he is in profitable momentum, and to promptly correct any weakness—before it's too late!

In most instances, for example, small businessmen have no idea as to the Break-Even point of their business—what it is and how it safeguards their business.

Within the scope of this chapter, we will endeavor to explain the things you should know to give you adequate, continuing control of the business phases of your operation. This section comprises:

a. Proper record keeping systems

b. Knowing the Break-Even point of your business

c. Knowing your business ratios

Record Keeping For Your Business:

As a general rule, most people shun the arithmetic aspects of their business. These are considered necessary "negatives" which they prefer not to see—in fact, such figures are shoved under some hypothetical carpet to be ignored.

This reminds me of a story about newlyweds I knew. Seems that the bride had prepared her first meal for hubby. He registered disapproval, and kept registering it several times. "I wish you would stop bringing up that meal again," his wife exclaimed with great exasperation. "I would like very much not to," the husband replied coyly, "however, it keeps coming up—all by itself!"

The same with your business arithmetic. You can similarly forget—shove it under the carpet—however, it will "keep coming up—all by itself." When it does come up, its reaction may be explosive. You may suddenly discover:

- You are not in adequate control of what you're doing.
- You may be over-paying for certain things where, in actuality, you can avoid as much as half the cost without impeding your business progress. For example: rent, personnel, advertising, etc.
- You may be under-paying for certain things that can help to expedite business expansion.
- You may be over-inventoried . . . or under-inventoried (both of which can prove damaging to your business status).
- You may be under-paying on taxes (subjecting you to severe penalties), or you may be over-paying on these taxes (again throttling your business progress or earning potential).
- You may have a series of wasteful leakages in your business—enough of them to permanently sink your ship.

What are the things that a proper record keeping system should show a businessman? Below is a partial list:

1. How much total business is he doing?
2. How much cash does he have in the bank and on hand?
3. Is the latter amount sufficient?
4. Is there any cash shortage?
5. How much inventory does he have on hand?
6. How much merchandise is he taking out of the business for personal or family use?
7. How much money does he owe to wholesalers and others?
8. How much gross profit does he earn?
9. How much were his expenditures for any given period?
10. How much net profit is he making?
11. How much is he obligated to pay in taxes?
12. What is his net worth; that is, what is the value of his proprietorship?
13. What are the trends in his sales, expenses, profits, net worth? How is his business progressing from month to month each year?
14. How does this business compare with those of similar type businesses?

The answers to the above questions are, in effect, directional signals. They tell the small businessman where he is going and whether he should do something to change the direction and course of the business. Once he understands the conditions which exist, the franchisee can take the necessary action to improve his position.

Basic requisites of a successful record keeping system are as follows:

- It should be simple.
- It should be quickly and easily implementable.
- It should provide easy procedures for day-by-day figure compilation.
- It should provide a periodic summation—enabling an at-a-glance perspective of your business.
- It should require very little time on your part to transcribe pertinent figures, usually during the evening.
- It should be so simple that you can control the system . . . irrespective of any professional accountant you may use.

A number of such simplified systems are available—making quick transcription, easy awareness, and continuing control of his business arithmetic. In most instances these services will also—as part of their overall service to small businessmen—go as far as to prepare their tax statements. This would include related data, estimates of income, Social Security figures, and the profit-and-loss statement.

Knowing The Break-Even Point In Your Business

One of the most vital factors in assuring the continued health of your franchise is constantly knowing the Break-Even point of your business. As the term implies, it is that particular spot in your business operation where you neither lose nor make money, but have just covered the expenses.

To make that still clearer, it is the particular point where your gross profits exactly equal the total of your fixed plus your controllable expenses.

Let us assume for example, that you have a shop with a potential for doing a maximum business of $5,200 a month, and you wanted to determine your Break-Even point. This, of course, is a hypothetical figure—to enable us to convey an understandable "for instance." Most franchise operations are expected to gross much more.

Here is what you would do:

FIRST: Ask yourself, what are your FIXED EXPENSES? They would include your rent, utilities, insurance, depreciation, various taxes you must pay—all the items that remain constant and do not change no matter what amount of business you do. Let us jot down your fixed total expenses, let us say, as being eight-hundred a month.

SECOND: Jot down your maximum sales potential per month. That, as previously stated, is $5,200.

THIRD: Figure out your VARIABLE EXPENSES—in other words, the expenses that usually increase as your sales volume increases. These would include gross wage, outside labor, operating supplies, advertising, bad debts, repairs and maintenance, car and delivery, administrative, legal, and miscellaneous expenses.

Now, let us assume that your records indicate that your average sales for the month should amount to 80% of your maximum potential—in other words, about $4,200. Then further determine your variable expenses at, let us say, 67% of $4,200—or about $2,800.

FOURTH: Add together your fixed expenses ($800) plus your variable expenses ($2,800) and you arrive at a total expense of $3,600.

Knowing these figures, you are now ready to make up your Break-Even chart. This should show you the point where your business will reach a Break-Even spot—neither making nor losing money—under a given set of conditions.

Instructions For Preparing Your Break-Even Chart

1. Draw a blank chart like that shown on page 35, with equal horizontal divisions numbered 0, 10, 20, 30, 40, and so on to 100—these figures representing 0% to 100%.

2. Your vertical divisions, in this case, run from $0 to $5,200. So let's decide to make the vertical division represent sales in hundreds of dollars, with the bottom line representing $0, the next line $400, the next line $800, then $1,200, $1,600, etc.

3. Rule a diagonal line running from $0 in the lower left corner, to $5,200 in the upper right corner, the line we show as A-B. Label this line SALES.

4. Now rule a horizontal line across at the $800 mark. This indicates your fixed expenses, which remain approximately the same every month, no matter what your sales. This line is shown here as line C-D and is labeled FIXED EXPENSES.

5. We stated above that the average expected sales would be 80% of maximum potential and that total expenses would amount to $3,600. So run your finger up the vertical line at 80%, and another across the horizontal line at $3,600. Place a dot at the point where these two lines meet. This we show as point E on our chart.

6. Now draw a line from $800 at 0% diagonally up to point E. This is indicated as line C-E, and we label it TOTAL EXPENSES.

7. Now, where lines A-B and C-E intersect, that is your Break-Even point. This we show as point X.

8. Point X in our example falls at $2,400—which is a little better than 45% of maximum sales potential. This signifies that you must do $2,400 worth of business in order to break even. At this point you are neither making nor losing money, but just covering your expenses.

BREAK-EVEN POINT CHART

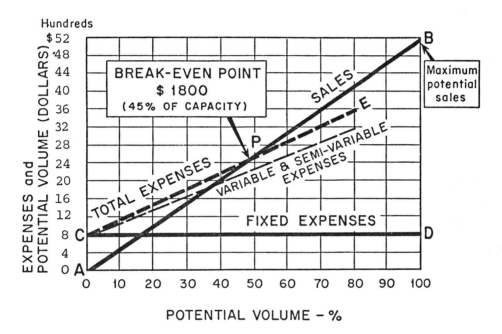

How Your Break-Even Chart Can Help You

You can see from this particular chart, for example, that for any month, in order to make a profit, you must do a sales volume of more than $2,400. The chart can help you control your budget by indicating changes that may be necessary in order to bring expenses into line with income.

When your sales aren't all they should be, the chart will indicate this, too, telling you that you should do something about your sales methods, your merchandise, or your staff.

Here are some other things the Break-Even chart can show you:

- How much business you can afford to lose before you run the risk of disappearing profits.
- What would take place if you increased or reduced prices.
- Whether you can afford to incur the added expense of making improvements.
- Which lines and items you should push and which you might be wise to drop.

Before the start of each month, learn how much business you must do that month by making a Break-Even chart. This will help you plan your way to bigger, more consistent profits, and will tell you which way you are heading at all times.

What Are Your Business Ratios?

Many businessmen often tell us that they would appreciate some yardstick that will help give them a valid, continuing picture of their business progress.

The RATIO is one proven method to help you judge the financial condition of your business, and financial changes that may occur. In most cases, you will be able to detect the start of any small trouble and stop it before it has a chance to do your business genuine financial harm. The ratio will show you the relationship between two items; usually between a complete item and one or more of its parts, or between two or more parts of the same item.

When you apply the ratio to your balance sheet or your profit and loss statement, you can compare items that are part of the same statement or compare various items from different statements. You can also use this method to compare your business status with others in the industry—for there are available standard ratios for most types of business.

Below are listed examples of ratios and how they can be applied to your business. In all examples, use the largest number that will divide each number evenly.

1. CURRENT RATIO: A comparison between current assets and current liabilities, sometimes known as the working capital ratio.

Current assets are those which flow into cash during a normal business cycle. They include: cash, notes, and accounts receivable, inventory, and other assets intended to be converted in normal business procedures. Current liabilities will include bills due within a short period of time, notes, accounts payable for merchandise, bank loans, and taxes.

For example: a grocer has current assets totaling $3,600 and total current liabilities of $3,000. The ratio would be found by computing as follows: $3,600/$3,000 *or* 6/5. Therefore, his ratio would be 6 to 5, meaning that for every $6 of assets, he has $5 of liabilities.

2. OPERATING RATIO: Compares net profits to total net sales.

A druggist has monthly net sales of $1,800 and the net profit from these sales is $600. Comparison may be made as follows: $1,800/$600 equals 3/1. In this example, then, the operating ratio would be 3 to 1, $3 of sales for every $1 of net profit.

When a comparison of your ratio is made with those of other firms in the same business, results of ratios of a few years back can often be as useful as very recent ratios. The important thing is to get started with a comparison standard. Profit margins do not ordinarily vary widely from year to year.

3. GROSS EARNINGS RATIO: Comparison of total net sales to gross earnings (mark-up).

In the last example, we have assumed that the druggist's total net sales were $1,800. If his gross earnings were $1,200, this ratio would be $1,800/$1,200 *or* 3/2. This ratio shows that for every $3 of net sales, there are $2 of gross earnings.

Your cost of goods may effect this, as well as other ratios. Costs of goods may seem high simply because of a low selling price. For example: If sales are $10,000 and cost of goods is $8,000, then your gross profit on your sales is 20% and the cost of goods sold is 80%.

Now, if your gross profit was increased to 25% and the cost of the goods remained the same, your sales would be $10,666 and the $8,000 figure would represent only 75% of sales.

4. UNIT COST RATIO: Comparison of the costs of production and the physical volume produced.

If a manufacturer finds that his actual production costs come to $300 for every 1,500 cases of merchandise sold, the example can be compared as 1,500/$300 *or* 5/1. Therefore, for every five cases of merchandise, the manufacturer has production costs of $1.

5. CAPITAL EMPLOYED RATIO: Comparison showing how much capital was invested to produce net profits.

In example 2, the net profits were $600. If this businessman invested $500 to obtain these profits, the ratio can be figured as: $600/$500 *or* 6/5. Thus, $6 of profits are received for every $5 of invested capital.

If you compare your ratio to that of another business in the same line and you find that the gross profit should be 25%, this does not mean that you must average 25% gross profit for every single item you sell.

Your competition may force you to lower your profit margin on some items. There may be other excellent reasons in your business for your company to be higher or lower than your competitor on certain items or ratios. However, a sound and well-balanced pricing policy will enable you to obtain the same margin of profit on your over-all business.

6. FIXED PROPERTY RATIO: Fixed assets (furniture, fixtures, property) compared to total net sales.

A plumber has fixed assets totaling $3,600. His total net sales are $12,000. Therefore, to find how much was invested to produce each dollar of net sales, the example would be $12,000/$3,600 *or* 10/3. Thus, the plumber finds that $10 of sales are produced for each $3 invested in fixed assets.

Knowing fixed assets ratios can become very useful to a businessman because it answers these questions: (a) How much business is being generated by every dollar invested in equipment? (b) Can I increase business by further investment in fixed assets?

The application of the ratio, for comparing various items connected with the operation of your business, can be most helpful. You will be able to spot any weak points of your business with these comparisons. You can check back on possible leakages or inefficiencies if you find that your sales figures come too close to production costs. You will be able to re-adjust any items that you find are becoming costly in the operation of your business.

Because the operating ratio is such an important one, here is a list of some classifications usually covered by operating ratios:

MANAGEMENT WAGES: In most small businesses it is often the practice to compute profits before allowing any compensation to the owner or owners. After all other deductions are made, the earnings left usually represent their compensation. However, it is recommended that the business allot a salary to the owner for his services—as a more valid yardstick for measuring his business progress.

EMPLOYEE WAGES AND SALARIES: Wages and salaries vary, depending on the type of business. In grocery stores, for example, it's as low as 2.5% of gross receipts. In laundry plants it's as high as 40%. To assure that you are not overpaying—or underpaying—it's advisable to study basic rates paid by others in your line.

OCCUPANCY COSTS: Rent or occupancy costs are an important factor in your financial statement. It's advisable not to overpay. It's equally advisable not to underpay. Often low-rent locations require commensurately large outlays in advertising to draw traffic so that, in effect, you are paying a penalty for a low-rent location. Analyze: Do you have the type of business that depends on passerby-impulse traffic . . . or will customers ordinarily seek you out?

ADVERTISING: As you know, advertising is a powerful factor in attracting customers. As a rule of thumb, the larger the number of turnovers in your business, the more you should spend on advertising. Set aside a definite portion of your budget and increase it as your business volume increases. Check with other people in the same line of business as to what percentage of expenditures is spent on advertising.

CREDIT: Most small businesses must extend some credit to realize their maximum sales potential. Properly controlled, credit can stimulate sales, encourage large orders and build good will. A recent survey showed that over 75% of small businesses extend credit. Credit requests range from occasional "charges" to regular installments or budget sales. In setting up a credit program, it is vital that it be organized methodically and carefully maintained. A good program can hold credit losses to 1% or less.

Here are some steps that should be taken to set up an effective credit program:

First: At the time an account is opened, inform the customer clearly of your collection policy—exactly when payment is expected. Do not vary your procedures.

Second: Send out statements promptly. Follow up with additional statements if the account is not paid promptly.

Third: Set a specific credit limit for each customer and do not exceed this limit at any time.

Fourth: If you deal with people who are transient, and unknown to you, have them fill out a financial statement. This lists personal and financial references. Check the references carefully in advance.

Fifth: Maintain proper credit records.

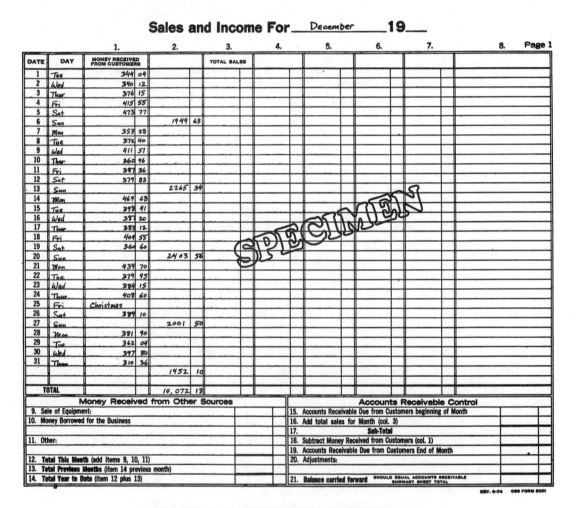

1. MONTHLY RECORD OF SALES AND INCOME

Indicates daily cash receipts from business plus all additional funds received from other sources.

The record-keeping charts contained on this and subsequent pages have been furnished through courtesy of Bernard Browning, President of General Business Services, 51 Monroe Street, Rockville, Maryland.

These simple do-it-yourself charts, comprising part of a Business Management System offered by this company, have helped thousands of small businesses to keep proper records, to control day-by-day business progress, and to achieve a net profit rather than unexpected losses.

Business Expenses For December 19___

Page 2

(1a) BUSINESS TAXES LICENSES			(1b) EMPLOYER'S SHARE SOCIAL SECURITY (FICA)			(2) RENT		(3) REPAIRS AND MAINTENANCE		(4) GROSS EMPLOYEES SALARIES		(5) INSURANCE		(6) PROFESSIONAL FEES	
607	County Lic.	58 40				599	650 —	618	41 50	ENTER MONTHLY TOTALS FROM PAYROLL SUMMARY		626	56 —	604	25 —
619	State Lic.	73 40	(1c) UNEMPLOYMENT					1	36 11	31	1040 —				
TOTAL		131 80	TOTAL			TOTAL	650 —	TOTAL	77 61			TOTAL	56 —	TOTAL	25 —

(7) COMMISSIONS	(8) INTEREST AND BANK CHARGES		(9) ADVERTISING		(10) AUTO - TRUCK		(11) DUES AND SUBSCRIPTIONS			(12) OFFICE SUPPLIES		(13)
	601	37 —	614	111 17	613	107 11	605	25 —		2	1 85	
			17	10 —	624	103 07	625	12 —		3	5 —	
					1	3 —				18	3 —	
					5	3 —				632	87 06	
					9	3 —						
TOTAL	TOTAL 37 —		TOTAL 121 17		17	3 —	TOTAL 37 —		TOTAL 1040 —			

(14) TELEPHONE	(15) UTILITIES		(16)	21	3 —	(17) OPERATING SUPPLIES		(18) TRAVEL				
				24	3 —							
603	47 50	621	91 47			612	193 59					
	622	123 62				3	6 40					
						26	10 12					
TOTAL 47 50	TOTAL 215 09		TOTAL	TOTAL 231 18					TOTAL 96 91	TOTAL		

(19) LAUNDRY AND UNIFORM	(20) Trading Stamps		(21) ENTERTAINMENT		(22) CONTRACT SERVICES		(23) MISCELLANEOUS ITEM		(24)
1	3 30	602	85 —	11	4 —	617	86 —		
8	3 30			2	5 —				
14	3 30			14	2 —				
22	3 30			18	5 —				
29	3 30			28	2 —				
TOTAL 16 50	TOTAL 85 —		TOTAL 4 —		TOTAL 100 —	TOTAL 210 11	TOTAL		TOTAL

REV. 5-73   GBS FORM 5001

2. MONTHLY BUSINESS EXPENSE

All payments are listed by expense category.
Provides an immediate check on comparative expense items.

Monthly Summary For _December_ 19___   Page 3

WITHDRAWALS & PERSONAL EXPENSES OF PARTNERS OR OWNER					OTHER PAYMENTS Loans — Notes — Fixtures — Equipment — Deposits		
CHECK # OR DATE	J. Jones	CHECK # OR DATE	B. Smith	CHECK # OR DATE	ITEM		AMOUNT
2	230 -			601	C.D. Bank		200 -
9	230 -			616	Add. Mach		100 -
16	230 -			623	Auto		500 -
23	230 -						
30	230 -						

SPECIMEN

1,150 -	← Total This Month →	800 -
10,810 -	← Total Previous Months →	2,200 -
11,960 -	← Total Year To Date →	3,000 -

MONTHLY PROOF & BALANCE

TOTAL MONEY AVAILABLE THIS MONTH:

1. Beginning of Month: CASH (Including Receipts not yet deposited in bank) — 50 —
   CHECK BOOK BALANCE — 2,117 82
2. Total received from customers this month (Column 1, Page 1) — 10,072 13
3. Money received from other sources (Item 12, Page 1)
4. Total (Sum of Lines 1, 2, 3) — 12,239 95

TOTAL MONEY SPENT THIS MONTH:

5. Total Business Expenses this month — 3181 87
6. Less: Employees Taxes & other items withheld — 258 —
7. Net Business Expenses — 2923 87
8. Total Purchases (For Resale) — 5435 76
9. Total other Payments on Loans, Notes, Fixtures & Equipment — 800 —
10. Total Withdrawals and Personal Expenses of Partners or Owners — 1150 —
11. Payment of Payroll Deductions Withheld
    Ck. #   State W/H Tax
    Ck. #   Federal W/H & S.S. Tax — 247 —
    Ck. #   Other — 247 —
12. This Month's Expenditures (Sum of Lines 7-11) — 10,556 63
13. Total Money Which Should be Available End of Mo. (Line 4 minus Line 12) — 1,683 32
14. Actually Available End of Mo.: CASH (Including Receipts Not Yet Deposited in Bank) — 310 36
    CHECK BOOK BALANCE — 1,372 96 / 1,683 32
15. Overage or Shortage — Difference Between 13 and 14

PROFIT AND LOSS

ITEMS	TOTAL THIS MONTH		TOTAL PREVIOUS MONTHS		TOTAL YEAR TO DATE		%
BUSINESS INCOME:							
a. Money Received from Customers	10,072	13	115,829	67	125,901	80	100
b.							
c. Purchases (For Resale)	5,435	76	63,809	55	69,245	31	55
d. GROSS PROFIT (a. minus c.)	4,636	37	52,020	12	56,656	49	45
BUSINESS EXPENSES:							
1a. BUSINESS TAXES, LICENSES	131	80	581	60	713	40	.6
1b. EMPLOYER'S SHARE SOCIAL SECURITY			684	32	684	32	.5
1c. UNEMPLOYMENT			393	12	393	12	.3
2. RENT	650	00	7150	00	7800	00	6.2
3. REPAIRS AND MAINTENANCE	77	61	826	39	904	—	.7
4. GROSS EMPLOYEES SALARIES	1040	—	13,520	—	14,560	—	11.6
5. INSURANCE	56	-	904	—	960	—	.7
6. PROFESSIONAL FEES	25	—	275	—	300	—	.2
7. COMMISSIONS			520	—	520	—	.4
8. INTEREST AND BANK CHARGES	37	—	409	80	446	80	.4
9. ADVERTISING	121	17	1372	97	1494	14	1.2
10. AUTO - TRUCK	231	18	2724	38	2955	56	2.3
11. DUES AND SUBSCRIPTIONS	37	—	338	40	375	40	.3
12. OFFICE SUPPLIES	96	91	1079	45	1176	36	.9
13.							
14. TELEPHONE	47	50	486	70	534	20	.4
15. UTILITIES	215	09	2101	79	2316	88	1.8
16.							
17. OPERATING SUPPLIES	210	11	2027	58	2237	69	1.8
18. TRAVEL			338	20	238	20	.3
19. LAUNDRY AND UNIFORM	16	50	180	90	197	40	.2
20. Trading Stamps	85	—	795	—	880	—	.7
21. ENTERTAINMENT	4	—	268	15	272	15	.2
22. CONTRACT SERVICES	100	—	1340	—	1440	—	1.1
23. MISCELLANEOUS			49	23	49	23	.1
24.							
f. Total Business Expenses	3181	87	38,366	98	41,548	85	33
g. NET PROFIT (d. minus f.)	1,454	50	13,653	19	15,107	64	12

REV. 9-74   GBS FORM 9405.8

3. MONTHLY SUMMARY

Shows on one page, all income, expense, and withdrawals and provides a monthly and "total-to-date" profit and loss analysis. Also includes a Proof and Balance form for reconciling cash.

Above chart reprinted through courtesy of General Business Services, Rockville Maryland.

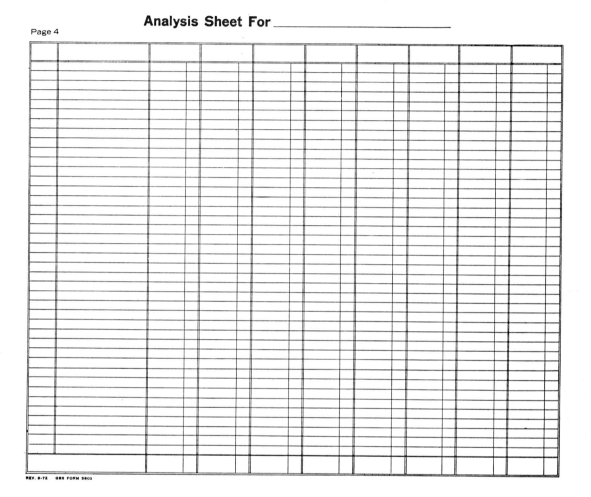

Analysis Sheet For _____

REV. 9-72   GBS FORM 3802

4. ANALYSIS SHEET

Allows for the analysis of additional business breakdowns, i.e., retail and wholesale
sales, cash and credit sales, etc.

Above chart reprinted through courtesy of General Business Services, Rockville, Maryland.

3.

154 PROFITABLE SPARE-TIME BUSINESSES

Tutoring Service

Good at teaching any subject? Offer "tutoring." First, locally, and thereafter in surrounding communities. There's a constant demand for tutoring on a variety of subjects, both to individuals and to groups. You can subsequently expand your business by hiring teachers on a per-hour basis who seek to amplify their income (and you'll find many in this category!). A substantial multi-community business can thus be achieved.

"Wholesale" Media Space

Build a flourishing communications business with practically no investment. Here's how: Contact local radio and TV stations and obtain a "wholesale" price (often as much as 50% below regular price) for use of these stations' "time." Resell this time to local merchants at regular time rates. Prepare a "sales theme"; for example, one entrepreneur called himself "Best Buy Real Estate Selector" and each day headlined another "good buy" in homes in that area. Real estate firms participated as advertisers buying thirteen-week "insertions." Another individual used the theme of "Career Advancement," with vocational schools participating as advertisers, etc.

Newspaper Co-Op Advertising

Ronald P. prepared a weekly newspaper "column" that publicized "best buys" among merchants in his area. He paid two hundred dollars (usual rates) for this advertising space, and received as much as eight hundred dollars in advertising fees, a neat profit of six hundred dollars!

45

Photo Blowups

Offer to "blow-up" photos to sizes as large as 11 x 17. There are literally thousands of people who seek to avail themselves of this service; they use these "blowups" for decoration, for commercial exhibits, as well as personal egotistical objectives. A profit of five dollars each is often obtainable on each such blowup.

Prepare Financial Prospectuses

Many businesses have constant need for "financial prospectuses" to show current financial status, plus future potential. This is vital to obtain bank and commercial loans, as reports to shareholders, etc. Even companies that have their own accountant use an outside "financial consultant" for this specialized service. James P. publicized this service, stating that the prospectuses he prepared would accurately reflect both actual existent financial status and future prospects. He charged as high as two thousand dollars for each prospectus and was surprised at the immediate business "flow" that he achieved.

TV Repair

This is a simple business, operated from the home, in many instances. John T., handy in TV repair, advertised his services throughout his community, and received continual patronage. Horace H. also did well, even though he was not "repair" oriented. He hired people to do needed servicing.

Bicycle Repair

Bicycles have increased in popularity in recent years. It is now a multi-billion dollar industry. This offers a splendid opportunity to profit from bicycle repairs, as this is often unavailable and the need for such services is frequent. Usual charge is seven dollars an hour. Added profits are obtainable from the sale of bicycle parts.

Legal Forms

Most attorneys use a constant flow of imprinted legal forms in addition to customary stationery. Howard G. recognized good earning possibilities of this field. He offered specialized printing for lawyers and sent a "catalog" itemizing the various types of legal forms, etc., that he made available. He achieved a profitable "growth" business.

Collections Systems For Medical Field

Doctors, dentists, optometrists, etc., have a continuing problem with delinquent accounts, often totalling hundreds of thousands of dollars. Albert H. offered a collection service, specialized to the needs of the medical field, and it was highly successful. He received a constant flow of accounts year 'round and achieved a 70% "collection record."

Water Conditioners

This is a big profit item. It is also a very urgently needed item in many "hard water" areas. John L. tied in with a manufacturer who supplied him with the product at a wholesale price. He then contacted the various homes throughout the area, demonstrating the benefits of the water conditioner. He averaged sales of one a day, with profits averaging one hundred fifty dollars per water conditioner. Subsequently, he engaged several salesmen, thus expanding his potential.

Antique Exhibits

There are literally millions of antique buffs in this country, who attend the dozens of antique exhibits that are constantly being held in most communities. Elizabeth T. kept apprised of these exhibits, and arranged to set up a "sales table" in these exhibits containing an assortment of antiques. She was able to acquire her antique products on "consignment" from antique dealers. She resold the products for an average of 50% profit. Elizabeth conducted two exhibits a week with an average profit of two hundred dollars per exhibit.

Research Service

Various types of research is constantly needed by many types of businesses, by newspapers, and also by individuals. Carole H. profited from this need. She advertised her services offering to obtain research information of any type. She soon received a constant flow of interesting assignments. As a collateral service, she also conducted personal interviews and community "polls."

Flea Markets

John H. profited from vacant spaces in his community. He organized "flea markets," conducted on Saturdays and Sundays in the parking areas or vacant lands which were not in use. He charged fifty dollars per exhibit and had as many as two hundred exhibitors for each of his localities.

Women's Thrift Shop

In most communities, well-to-do people dispose of their clothes after minimal use while still relatively new and in excellent condition. In most instances, this apparel was initially expensive and style-oriented. Theatrical people also are accustomed to discarding apparel (often very luxurious and costly), after minimum use. Joan H. contacted these sources offering to purchase these items, and received a flow of customers. She then resold them at a profit from 50% to 75%. Eventually she opened her own women's thrift shop.

Social Get-Togethers

Do you desire to meet other people under congenial, relaxed conditions? Herbert T. arranged "get acquainted" socials in his home, each weekend. He charged six dollars admission and served refreshments and arranged to introduce people to each other, conformant to their particular interests. He now has a continuing, profitable operation that earns him an average of two hundred dollars a week.

Affinity Tours

Mildred G. contacted transportation sources—airlines, cruises, trains, even buses—and obtained a "group price" for travel to various appealing places. She then contacted societies, clubs, associations, and specialized interest groups (e.g., sewing clubs, fishermen's clubs, etc.) offering a discount "package" fee for travel. She has now achieved a flourishing business.

Picture Framing

Handy? Like to work with your hands? Picture framing can be both fulfilling and profitable. Many types of projects constantly need framing inclusive of photos, art, needlepoint, citations, etc. Good earnings are achievable from both materials and labor.

Needlepointing

Creative Needlepointing, a new rage, can be profitably operated from home. Sell design "kits," wool, etc. Conduct needlepointing classes. "Whole-sale" your own creations to department stores, gift shops, etc. Needlepointing has become a multi-billion dollar industry!

Transportation Co-Op Advertising

Nancy G. advertised products and services of fifteen local merchants on 10 x 18 inch advertising cards—the standard space unit available on buses. The space cost her one hundred fifty dollars a month. She charged each client one hundred dollars, bringing her gross income to fifteen hundred dollars per advertising card. Success in her immediate community led to expanding the service to other communities.

Community Contests

Organize sweepstakes contests in your community by enlisting the participation of local businesses. Each business pays a relatively small sum—e.g., fifty dollars as a participation fee. As many as one hundred or more merchants may participate; this enables a lucrative pot for the winner and a lucrative reward for your own efforts. Merchants may also contribute samples of their merchandise for winners in different categories which will be advertised. Support from the local chamber of commerce can be important to your role as promoter.

Merry-Go-Round Food

The food goes 'round and 'round and the profit flows straight to you in this novel self-service restaurant. A constantly moving belt conveys food along the length of the counter. The customer selects the dish he wants, paying $1.50 for each plate. Appetizingly arranged plates presented in this unusual way has proved very attractive to customers who don't like making snap decisions on cafeteria lines or can't tell what they are getting from reading a menu. Children, of course, will be fascinated.

Telephone Book Covers

Any community with telephone directories—and who can get along without them nowadays?—is a source for thousands of dollars in advertising for you. Directory covers made from durable plastic or canvas cover stock can carry as many as twenty five ads for local businesses. Available free to the public, they are mini-yellow pages for harassed potential customers who don't know where to begin looking for services. With a possible gross sales of twenty five hundred dollars in a single community, your profit margin is substantial.

"Swap" Magazine

There is fascination and universal appeal in "bartering." Bud G. profited from this trend by publishing a "Swap" magazine, issued monthly, that detailed bartering availabilities throughout his area. This publication (inexpensively mimeographed) now has a circulation of eight thousand. He charges fifteen dollars for a year subscription (fifty cents an individual copy).

Do-It-Yourself Center

Michael L. equipped his garage as a tool shop, providing tools and facilities to fulfill the varying needs of weekend do-it-yourselfers throughout his area. He charged a per hour "use" fee. Each Saturday and Sunday an average of ten do-it-yourselfers used his facilities at one time (as many as twenty five throughout the day). The profits were good and he subsequently expanded to other areas.

"Jobs Available" Magazine

Allan S. collected classified "Help Wanted" advertisements from newspapers throughout his area. He had these mimeographed as a tabloid-size publication and charged fifty cents an issue. The publication is issued weekly, so that the "job data" is kept constantly current. His subscription list has steadily grown.

Health And Beauty Aids

Barbara F. noted the success of Avon in selling beauty products direct to homes. She acquired her own line of beauty products by contacting various manufacturers (listed in trade publication, Thomas Register, etc.). She then appointed women as sales representatives who visited homes, women's clubs, etc., throughout her area, to conduct "home demonstrations" (often known as "hostess parties") for the housewife and a group of her friends, neighbors, etc. Sales for each home demonstration averaged twenty dollars. Her business has been expanding each year.

School Year Books

Michael S. handles "year book" printing for twenty five different high schools and colleges in his area. Each book averages one hundred fifty pages (plus expensive photography, engraving, etc.). Michael found that most school editors were eagerly receptive because of the complexity and specialized graphic knowledge needed for the professional printing of school annuals. There was also the need to organize literally thousands of details and to meet tight deadlines. School editors recognized the value of obtaining expert assistance that could handle production of the entire book as a "single package." This is the type of expertise that Michael provided, and he regularly earns fifty thousand dollars and more each year.

Rent Medical Equipment

Chris F. offered to rent a variety of medical equipment products needed by invalids, people recuperating from illness, the elderly in nursing homes, etc. These items included: wheel chairs, crutches, adjustable beds, etc., items that are usually needed for short periods of time. There is a continuity of this type of business, and the profit margin is good.

Language Transcription

Mary S., fluent in three languages, was called upon to translate letters that local industrial firms received from their overseas customers that were written in foreign languages—French, German, Italian, etc. This gave her the idea of establishing a "Language Transcription Bureau." As her translators, she used the services of individuals versed in a variety of languages. Her charges varied from a fee-per-project to a retainer, depending on the extensiveness of her client's translation needs.

Financial Consultant

Albert M. helped businesses in their quest for financing, sources for planned plant expansion, equipment purchases, inventory financing, etc. He referred them to governmental and private financing sources who were receptive to making viable loans. He received a finder's fee of 5% and often achieved substantial sums.

Rubber Stamps

It's easy to produce rubber stamps of all types containing any type of desired copy. And it can be accomplished with low-cost equipment. Malcolm G. has established a thriving rubber stamp production business servicing hundreds of businesses and individuals throughout his community.

Telephone Dictating Service

John T. "loans" dictaphone machines to his subscribers to use for their dictation needs—letters, reports, etc. The dictated cassettes are picked up daily, and the resultant typing is delivered within twenty four hours thereafter. He now has over one hundred regular subscribing customers who pay two dollars per letter, and a minimum monthly fee.

"Knitting" School

So many friends asked Fran L. for advice on knitting (since she was quite an expert knitter), she decided to open a knitting school. Soon, she expanded to two schools and subsequently to as many as five branch schools. She engaged knitting expert associates to do the teaching. She now has over one hundred fifty "students" and earns good money from both instruction fees and the sale of knitting materials and supplies.

Contests And Incentives

Many companies recognize the benefits of conducting contests and incentive programs for both their personnel (to motivate increased productivity), and for their customers (to help generate increased sales). James P. offered "packaged" incentive programs, inclusive of prizes, travel, promotions, etc. He is now an acknowledged authority in this field.

Conducting Hobby Exhibits

Ted C. rented a hall in his community and conducted an "Exhibit for Hobbyists" throughout his area. He charged two dollars admission, and one-hundred dollars per "booth" to exhibitors seeking to sell supplies to hobbyists. The hall is usually thronged, each year. It has become a profitable annual event.

Long-Term Babysitters' Service

Parents off for a childless vacation, a business trip, or a family emergency far away, need child care—a substitute family, really, for a week or two. You can provide this important service by organizing a pool of housewives, carefully screening and supervising them. Janet R. has a list of one hundred housewives to choose from. Charging one hundred fifty dollars a week for their services (including expenses), and netting a profit of 35%.

Temporary Employment Service

Businesses usually prefer to keep a minimum permanent staff and hire more personnel during a busy season. Providing businesses with temporary skilled and unskilled workers—carpenters, secretaries, file clerks, keypunch operators, sales clerks—can be very profitable. Your satisfied clients usually pay 15% of the worker's salary as your broker's fee.

Gourmet Cooking Classes

The delectable soufflé your friends rave about can earn more than praise for you. Start a cooking school in your own spacious, well-equipped, cheerful kitchen. Perhaps a church or other institution with a large kitchen will rent space to you. Your two hour "gourmet foods" classes can also attract men interested in cutting down entertainment expenses. There's a social side, too, in an after-class tasting session. A charge of one hundred seventy five dollars for six sessions is reasonable, depending on the cost of ingredients and other expenses.

Child Care Center

Working mothers need child care services, and not the kind that plops the child in front of a TV set. Put your backyard and basement to work, filling them with toys and recreation equipment. They needn't be expensive; only safe and interesting. Cut costs by making some yourself from found objects, then advertise in your local paper.

Discount Prescription Service

Bill H. recognized an opportunity in providing "discount" prescriptions, particularly in view of the high prices charged by most prescription druggists. He advertised a twenty-four hour "discount" prescriptions service. Prescriptions would be filled in a central facility by a pharmacist, and thereupon "dropped off" at certain designated locations in each area. Customers could thus save as much as 50%. A profitable, steadily growing business was achieved.

Home-Delivered Beverages

Albert T. earned a nice living making weekly deliveries to residential customers of "regularly needed" household food items—beverages, potato chips, etc. In time, he had accumulated over two-hundred customers and was earning approximately fifteen thousand dollars yearly after all expenses were paid.

Advertising Specialties

Most businesses can benefit from the use of imprinted giveaway items—e.g., calendars, pens and pencils, and literally thousands of other items. They usually buy in large quantities, as many as ten thousand and more. This advertising specialty business can be profitable and enduring; customers will frequently reorder year after year. You can locate advertising specialty manufacturers through such trade publications as *Premium Age,* or by contacting members of the Advertising Specialties Association.

Lawn Mower Sharpening

Inexpensive "sharpener" equipment can put you into business practically at once! With this equipment, you can offer to sharpen lawn mowers, saws, ice skates, etc., for people in your community. This is a profitable, virtually non-competitive type of business that can yield good profits.

Jewelry Counter

Invest in a supply of inexpensive costume jewelry, obtainable from a nationwide list of manufacturers. Next, contact local stores in your area (drugs, boutiques, luggage, etc.) offering to "add a profitable jewelry" department as an adjunct to their regular merchandise, at no cost to them. In addition, they receive 15% on all sales. Many stores will be receptive. This add-on business can bring extra profits and help to increase customer traffic.

One such add-on jewelry "counter" in a New York luggage store, achieves sales in excess of one hundred thousand dollars a year.

Keys, Anyone?

Offer to make duplicate keys. Equipment is purchasable for as little as five hundred dollars, enabling you to start in this profitable business. You may expand by establishing "key-making booths" in other existing stores—e.g., hardware, Five and Ten Cent stores, stationery stores, etc. These stores will usually be glad to provide you with space on a percentage-of-sales basis. You may eventually have as many as ten or more such key-producing, and profit-producing, locations.

"Door Handle" Distribution

Postage costs, today, are high (and threatening to go even higher). As a result, many prospective advertisers are discouraged from sending out their mailings. Henry T. offered to deliver advertising for as little as two cents each and, as you can suspect, was literally "flooded" with orders. He pooled the mailings of an average of ten advertisers into one attractive, colorful plastic bag. This was hooked on to the door handle of each apartment in his area . . . thus covering all "occupants" through his community at low cost. Additionally, this type of mail often received better readership than usual advertising mail (often referred to as "junk" mail). This business grew rapidly. In addition to local clients, Harry eventually obtained national advertisers, too.

Manufacturers Representative

Hundreds of manufacturers constantly seek representatives to market their products in each region. Bill C. represented six manufacturers (selling related, though non-competitive products) and earned forty-thousand dollars a year. To become a manufacturer's representative, consult "Distributors Wanted" ads in metropolitan newspapers for manufacturers actively seeking representatives in your area. It's also effective to send "application" letters, detailing your experience, to other manufacturers whose products you seek to represent.

Escort Service

Marge H., residing in a metropolitan city of six hundred thousand population, recognized that many visitors in town would like to have local female escorts as dinner or theatre companions, or to show them the town's "sights." A profitable escort service was consequently established.

Shoe Repair Kiosks

James F. provided a highly visible, convenient shoe repair service by setting up booths, or kiosks, in shopping center parking lots. Customers could drop their shoes off one day and pick them up the next. Repairs were made at a central plant servicing all twelve kiosks owned by James F. and which employed disabled workers. The decreasing number of shoe repair stores in many communities and their frequent inaccessibility also worked in favor of the kiosks.

Co-Operative Advertising On Book Covers

Contacting both public and parochial high schools in his area, Ben S. offered to supply book covers for students at no charge. Some ten schools with a total student body of twelve thousand, agreed to the offer. He then solicited advertising from merchants. The covers cost him three hundred dollars to print; he grossed four thousand dollars in advertising revenues. He went on to expand his business in surrounding communities with similarly effective results.

Profits From Contacts

Establish a "Contacts Exchange," whereby you bring people who have influential contacts together with individuals in businesses who seek such contacts (to sell their products or services, etc.). This can become a flourishing business and highly profitable. Your earnings will be derived from: a ten dollar enrollment fee (to become a member of your exchange), plus a fee of five dollars for each contact provided.

Obtain Magazine Subscriptions

Offer "club rates" to magazine subscribers in your area who subscribe to a number of varied publications. You will find that most publications are receptive to having localized representation and will allow big discounts. You also benefit from renewals, hence, good ongoing earnings can be achieved.

Shoe Bronzing

Many parents seek to preserve mementoes of their recently born children. Shoe bronzing helps to give them a permanent memento of the child's initial years. It also has decorative value, conserved as a paperweight, etc. Bronzing equipment is fairly inexpensive and a profit margin of 50% can be realized. Obtain customers through hospitals, references to birth announcements, direct mail, newspaper ads, etc.

Upholstering

Are you handy with cutting, designing, carpentry? You may enjoy entering the upholstery business, performing this service for people throughout the area. There is a continual need for this type of work and it can be very profitable.

Records And Cassettes

Establish a "club" whereby subscribers can receive records and cassettes of their selection (based on their favorite performers or composers) on a regular monthly basis. A simple mimeographed sheet is sufficient to describe available titles.

Selling Simulated Diamond Rings

A New Orleans housewife acquired a supply of simulated diamond rings (both men's and women's). She arranged these attractively in velvet covered slots in a special suitcase. She then contacted businesses throughout her area, exhibiting and selling these rings to personnel in the various offices. The popularity of these rings (and they looked scintillatingly beautiful in her carrying case) was gratifying. The profitability of this business exceeded even her expectations.

Lawn Care

John T. offered to trim the lawns of homes in his neighborhood and found that many people were eager to use his services for this necessary but troublesome work. He charged annual fees (average of four-hundred dollars a year) and acquired some sixteen customers in a fairly short time.

Rug And Furniture Cleaning

There is a constant need for the cleaning of furniture, upholstery, rugs, draperies, etc. This is a specialized business that often requires the work to be done at home. It is also a profitable business, with usual earnings of ten dollars an hour. Literally, every home in your area is a prospect for this type of service.

Direct Sale Of Shoes

Alex H. arranged with a shoe manufacturer to obtain shoes at discount prices. Using the manufacturer's catalog, he contacted prospects both in offices and at home, measured their shoe size and obtained their orders. These orders were filled and sent to the prospects direct by the company. In most cases, Alex obtained "multiple" orders from as many as five members of a single family or four or more people in each office. His profits average five dollars per pair of shoes.

Book "Remainders"

Many publishers have large quantities of unsold books (now discontinued) which they are willing to close out at a fraction of their original prices. Horace H. contacted publishers in his area and obtained a list of these discontinued books at greatly discounted prices. He thereupon promoted their sale in his area at a discount of 10%. Since his own discount was as high as 60%, and often higher, the 10% discount was very affordable. By dealing with book "remainders," he constantly achieved a profitable "publishing-type" business that required minimum capital outlay.

Money Management Consultation

Many people are unable to properly "manage" their money, hence, are constantly in arrears. John B. offered "budgeting" and "money management" advice through seminars that were sponsored by local banks and financing institutions. He obtained fees from the sponsors for conducting these seminars. Admission fees were also received from seminar participants.

Eighty-Nine Cent Stores

Everything in the store sells for eighty-nine cents, nothing higher, nothing lower! The value of the various products were usually one dollar fifty cents to three dollars. This type of variety store can be operated profitably in other areas. Merchandise is purchasable at low prices through auctions, job lots, close-outs, etc.

Prepare Speeches

Literally thousands of speeches are constantly being made by individuals representing businesses, associations, etc., throughout the areas. There is a constant need for somebody to write these speeches and, if you are good with words, here's an earnings opportunity to consider.

Tennis Instruction

Teach tennis in ten lessons. It is possible to do this with new instruction techniques. In view of the current tennis craze, this can be a highly lucrative business. Your instruction can be conducted with groups of as many as twenty in a group, and can be conducted indoors (in rented gymnasiums, etc.).

Florist Shops

This is a business that is fascinating, profitable, and challenging. It can be conducted from the home, from a store location, or from a kiosk (an enclosed booth situated on a high-traffic parking lot, or in shopping malls). The profit margin can be quite high, as much as 50% to 75%.

Figure Salons

People have become more and more figure and health conscious. Hence, the unusual opportunity for the operator of a Figure Salon. Often this type of business can be tied in with existing facilities, e.g., the swimming pools in hotels, YMCA, etc. As in any exclusive club an annual membership fee is charged. The profit margin can be substantial; many operators of this type of business earn as much as fifty thousand dollars a year.

Interior Decorating Consultant

This type of business can be entered into with little investment, since it is fundamentally based on your own personal services. It can be conducted from your home, and you can arrange tie-ins with a large variety of supplier sources: manufacturers, showrooms in such fields as furniture, furnishings, wallpapers, carpets, etc. You charge a consultant fee for your services and also make a trade commission on products that are sold.

Business Brokerage

In most instances, a license is not required to become a Business Broker. This type of business can be operated from the home. You will be engaged in accumulating listings of business for sale, merger acquisitions, and thereupon offer them to prospective purchasers. Brokerage fees can be as high as 15% of the total sale price and substantial earnings are thus possible. One source for obtaining clients is from the business opportunities classified section of the newspapers.

Welcome Newcomers

You may have heard of Welcome Wagon; this company has established a flourishing business throughout the country, by welcoming newcomers in each area in behalf of local merchants. Merchants in each community are eager to attract the patronage of these newcomers since they normally need to purchase an abundance of items in moving from one locality to another. Moreover, the merchant who attracts their patronage often has them as a continuing customer practically "forever after." This business can be established with minimum capital and operated from home.

"Vending" Toy Gas Balloons

Vending-type machines are now available that dispense a fully gas-blown balloon by inserting a quarter. Tom J. invested in the purchase of ten of these machines and placed them in high-traffic stores in his area—confectionery, drugs, etc. Gradually he was able to use his profits to invest in an additional twenty machines. Substantial earnings were thus achieved on an "absentee" basis. The participating shops received a commission of five cents for each balloon vended.

Bicycle Rentals

Herbert S. tied in with a local gas station to exhibit and offer "bikes for rent" (Herb provided the bikes). He enjoyed a continuing flow of bike rental business, particularly during summer months. The gas station dealer received a commission of 10%.

Shopping Service

Carol G. conducted a "shopping service" in her city. She offered to visit groceries and supermarkets in behalf of her clients on a regular weekly basis, purchasing their various grocery needs. She covered stores that offered "specials" . . . "coupon savings," and other current sales. The savings achieved averaged as much as 25%, in addition to offering a time and energy saving service to housewives. She charged a fee of five dollars a week for the service per housewife, and now has thirty regular clients.

Hotel Register

John P. provided free, a beautiful counter register pad (inclusive of blotter and pen) to hotels throughout his area. Most hotels gladly accepted. John achieved his earnings from the advertising space (along the rim of this register, conspicuously viewable by guests) that he sold to local businesses. Most local businesses are eager to publicize their services to visitors to their city. He achieved an average profit of eight hundred dollars a community . . . and he had little difficulty in obtaining hotel and advertising participants in each community he covered.

Dentist Equipment

A former Chicago dentist has reaped big profits by selling, via mail, used dental equipment to dentists throughout the country. He obtains a list of available used equipment by advertising in dental publications. He then sends a "bulletin" to dentists describing available equipment. Many dentists, particularly those in smaller towns, are often receptive to purchasing used equipment . . . and are normally unaware of any alternate sources to contact for such needed purchases.

Career Uniforms

Roberta K. designs "career uniforms" for all types of businesses: banks, stockbrokers, institutions, even offices. These are "leased" on a monthly fee basis. She now has some seventy five regular customers. Career uniforms are snappy, attractive, and are becoming more and more popular with banks, industrial organizations, hotels, etc.

"Leasing" Floral Arrangements

A florist prospered with this idea. He "rented" artificial flowers and plants—replacing them monthly—to institutions, businesses, and larger residential buildings. These helped to beautify the facade and promenade areas of the building. He charged an average fee of five dollars per plant per month (and received as much as three hundred dollars a month from a single client). He now has over eighty five regular customers, and can make up to $25,000 per year.

Maps and Charts

Hubert T. established a business preparing maps, charts, and graphs for businesses, advertising agencies, etc. Such specialized service is constantly needed for sales presentations, operations manuals, marketing surveys, etc. He eventually was placed on a retainer fee basis by some forty five clients, and his earnings are substantial.

"Welcome Baby" Service

Druggists often invite the patronage of expectant and recent mothers, as these customers generally purchase a continuing flow of various types of drug products and accessories. Carol H. conducted a "welcome baby" service whereby she would obtain names of mothers-to-be (usually from newspaper notices, local hospitals, and from name list companies). She sent a brochure to each prospect offering a gift if she patronized a designated druggist in her area. The druggist paid a continuing fee for this service. She now services some sixty five drug stores in her area.

Selling "Security"

In view of the escalating crime rate in most cities, both homes and businesses are seeking equipment that help provide security against burglary. Charles T. profited as a "Security Expert." He contacted prospects throughout his area, informing them of his services. He evaluated the security needs of their building, and thereupon installed equipment that could afford maximum protection. Sales often totalled one thousand dollars and over.

Mobile Advertising Trailer

Salesmen for textbook publishers constantly visit schools throughout the country to show and interest them in their list of textbooks. Simon L. reasoned that such sales contacts could be done more economically, and with maximum effectiveness, through use of a "mobile advertising trailer" that exhibited the available textbooks of a number of participating publishers. This type of motor van would, in effect, constitute a "travelling exhibit" covering the entire country, visiting schools everywhere. Advance invitations to view the exhibit were sent to all schools, prior to visits. Michael obtained the participation of twelve textbook publishers to exhibit their books. They covered all costs, plus providing him with a substantial sales commission.

Community-Service Booklets

Hugh S. prepared booklets based on vital community betterment subjects. For example: avoiding use of dope; avoiding bicycle accidents; etc. These would be distributed free to schools, to be given to students. Businesses and institutions in each area would "sponsor" these booklets paying a prescribed fee for each one thousand booklets distributed. These booklets thus performed a worthwhile community service and also achieved satisfactory earnings from sponsor advertising.

Books For Children

"Specialization" offers opportunities, and non-competitiveness, that generalized projects often cannot equal. Lucas H. "specializes." He offers books for "children only" through the mail. He promotes these through direct mail, magazine ads, etc., reaching parents. This "specialization" soon gave him a measure of renown as the "place to send to" to obtain children's books. He eventually acquired some three hundred separate titles, and his sales have increased steadily.

Wholesale Guide

"Can you get it for me wholesale?" is a request that one constantly hears. Ernie K. compiled a list of some two hundred wholesale sources pertaining to many types of products. He sold the catalog for five dollars a copy (guaranteeing that the reader would save at least the amount paid, or he could obtain a complete refund). He has built a thriving business.

Cheese And Wine Shops

This is an easy-to-operate type of business, since your products are limited and specialized—cheeses of all types and a variety of wines. Both these products have great appeal for the public and provide an appetizing go-together. Stores of this type have become very popular in many localities, and the profit margin is substantial. For example, food establishments of this type charge as high as three dollars fifty cents for a serving of two or three cheese varieties and a glass of wine. It is also a distinctive business, virtually noncompetitive in most areas. For collateral earnings, cheeses in bulk and bottled wines can be sold on the premises on a retail basis.

Gourmet Shops

There is an ever-increasing popularity for the kind of products carried by gourmet shops. These include such taste-evoking delicacies as: cheeses of all types, delectable sausages, savory breads (often home-baked), and similar items. This is a specialty food business, with high profit margin, continual appeal, and continuing patronage. This is the type of business that can achieve earnings of twenty five thousand dollars a year and higher. If you are gourmet-oriented, you also will find that it is a "fun" business.

Fund-Raising Program

How would you like to have your business located in one hundred or more high-traffic stores and institutions throughout an area, each having the potential of earning ten dollars or more a week for you? And it can be achieved with a minimum amount of your time and effort, since the brunt of your services is based on collecting deposited money each week and replacing supplies. This is achievable with new, unique equipment, resembling postage stamp dispensing machines. A placard on the machine announces: "Vend-A-Prayer For A 25¢ Donation." There are many other variations. These machines are normally placed in parishioner-owned businesses throughout the town, in hotel lobbies, in bus stations, etc. Each church receives fifteen cents from each twenty five cent donation; you receive ten cents. Operations cost is lower than two cents each resulting in a 500 percent markup. You are assisting in worthwhile causes in your community in addition to establishing a business that can yield unusually high profits.

Do-It-Yourself Ice Cream Shop

The ice cream business has proven profitability, catering to both children and adults. A do-it-yourself type of ice cream business provides a uniqueness and enhanced appeal that can achieve almost instant patronage in any area. This business has a "smorgasbord" format, the customer choosing and combining any flavors that his heart desires (he pays for what he takes). This business can be operated in minimal store space, as little as twelve-foot frontage, or as an add-on department to a store.

Photo Kiosks

You have probably seen photo "kiosks" (booths) located in the parking areas of shopping centers, parking lots, suburban train stations, etc., throughout your area. Their attraction to the public is their ease of patronage, since photo needs can be dropped off in the morning and picked up the next day—often without the necessity of leaving the car. The profit margin in this type of business is unusually ·high, as high as 75% for photo prints and collateral services, and 50% for films and other supplies. This type of business can be established with a minimum investment.

Pretzels

"Hot pretzels" are vended from machines that can be located in many high-traffic locations throughout the community. It is possible to have fifty or more such locations. Minimal expertise and effort is required on your part. You receive a shipment of pretzels in the form of frozen dough which is then inserted in these machines, ready for heating and eating. Pretzels machines are also available on a lease basis. Profit margin is high, often 50% or more.

Miniature Golf

If you have patronized a miniature golf course recently, you may have noted that fees per player are as high as one dollar fifty cents for eighteen holes. Thus, a group of four people will often pay six dollars. And, if you have the proper site, you can enjoy a constant flow of patronage. Many owners of miniature golf courses can net as high as twenty five thousand dollars a year during summer months alone, with even higher earnings potential in localities with year 'round warm climate.

Travel Bureau

The travel business is a field that is both lucrative and fascinating in its potential. There are also attractive "fringe" benefits, inclusive of the opportunity to travel to exotic places practically free, or to receive substantial discounts. Initially, this business can be operated with minimal capital—in many instances it can be operated from your home (particularly at the outset).

Rent-All

As operator of a Rent-All business, you stock and rent needed supplies and equipment to homes and businesses throughout your area. These products fill varied needs. For example: hospital supplies (beds, crutches, wheelchairs, etc.) for the "invalided"; silverware, dinnerware, and folding chairs for those planning parties; certain types of tools for the do-it-yourselfer; and so on. Initially, to conserve your capital, you will stock only one or two categories or products. Subsequently, you can expand to others. The profit margin is substantial. Normally, the cost of a product is "paid off" after the first several months, and thereafter, your rental earnings achieve practically 100% net profit. This business can be started with minimal capital, if your budget is tight. In many instances you can tie in with a local gas station to store and display your products—utilizing its unused bays and frontage. It is the type of business that has continuity of patronage, and fills a vital need in practially every community.

Mobile Auto Parts And Tools

This can be a highly profitable business with repeat patronage that can help you achieve a lucrative growth business. Using a motor van, you deliver auto parts and tools to gas stations, garages, etc., the types of products for which they are in constant need. At a subsequent period, you may also invest in cabinets that are placed in each of your customer's places, as a convenient repository for these products. They also enable you to achieve "visual inventory control," since you can see at a glance (each time you make a visit) items that are missing and need replacement. Many entrepreneurs in this business have been able to establish a "customer route" of as many as two hundred customers and even more.

Dog Grooming

There is a constant need for the grooming of poodles and other "shaggy" types of dogs. Dog owners are accustomed to paying substantial fees, $15 to $20 per grooming. This business can be conducted from one's home, store, or shop. It can also be conducted as a *mobile* dog grooming business. Thus, the dog owner need not travel long distances to patronize a store-type grooming service, where the pet usually has to left overnight. Instead, the grooming is done in your van right at the prospect's home curbside. In certain high rise buildings you may obtain as many as five or more customers at a time, and you can use helpers (available at a per hour fee basis) to increase your output and greatly expand your earnings potential.

Maid Service

Maids are often unavailable today, particularly on a part-time basis. And full-time maids are so expensive that few homes can afford them. That is why a business that offers maid service on a part-time basis can achieve an ongoing demand in practically any community. The customer is charged on a per-hour basis (an average of eight dollars an hour) with a possible profit margin of 50%. This type of business can also be conducted on a "mobile" basis, utilizing high pressure cleaning equipment (contained in a van) that can be brought into the home and can do a thorough job in minimum time. Monthly and annual "contract" accounts, assuring continuing weekly patronage, are also readily achievable with this type of business.

Mobile Exterior Home Cleaning Service

Look around your neighborhood. You will note that practically every home needs some type of exterior cleaning: the driveway, patio, home facade, roof, gutters, and so on. By using a motor van containing high pressure cleaning equipment you are able to perform this service throughout the area. The profits can be extremely high, since the main earnings from this type of service are derived from your services (cost of materials is minimal). Hence, you can clean a roof and charge as much as two hundred dollars (based on a per-footage fee) with actual materials costing as little as twelve dollars.

Pet Food Delivery Service

Practically everyone today has pets in their homes—dogs, cats, fish, even birds. There is a need for a continuing supply of food and other items pertinent to the pets. Indicative of the magnitude of this field, it is estimated that some two billion dollars is spent for pet food each year. There is a good opportunity to establish a business that will supply pet food to homes on a weekly basis. With an average expenditure of three dollars a week a home, and with a potential of literally hundreds of customers within a ten-mile radius, substantial income is achievable. An attractive feature of this business is its "continuity," since the majority of customers will often patronize you year after year. As collateral earnings, you can also supply various needed pet accessories and supplies. Profit margin can be as high as 50%.

Recordkeeping Service

Every business must keep records. This refers to practically every store, every professional person, and even to industries. You can offer and sell a recordkeeping system that enables simplified recording of all vital records, at a cost of two to three hundred dollars a year. You can also link this service to pertinent tax preparation (utilizing the figures that have been recorded on the forms by each client). This business also has continuity; many customers have continued this service year after year for ten years and more. The profit potential is substantial, as high as 80% on each annual sale.

Telephone Answering Service

Telephone answering service is needed by both homes and offices in practically every area. In conducting this business, you arrange with the telephone company to tie in your telephone line with that of your various clients. Thus, when their phone rings, so will yours, enabling you to answer it promptly. This type of service has built-in continuity, and many clients will stay with you for many years. Normal fees range from ten to twenty five dollars per month, and it is possible to obtain as many as two hundred customers or more. As you can see, the profit potential for this type of business can be quite substantial.

Art Gallery

There is an ever-increasing appreciation for art in both business and homes —from an artistic and decorative point of view. This includes oil paintings, watercolors, etc. Many talented local artists will gladly have you "broker" their art on a contingent basis: that is, you need pay no advance money, they receive a percentage of actual sales only. **Thus,** you can commence this business with a substantial inventory of beautiful art originals and reproductions at minimal cost. This business can be operated from your home, particularly at the outset. It is promotable as a fund-raising vehicle, in cooperation with churches, women's clubs, other associations and institutions in your area. Your profit margin can be as high as 50%, and you will find this type of business to be challenging and fascinating, bringing you in contact with influential people in your area.

Limousine Service

This type of business can be operated from your home. One entrepreneur in New Jersey, operating a similar business, has been netting as high as fifty thousand dollars a year. The business is based on providing "chauffeurs" who will drive a client *in his car* to the airport, shopping trips, etc., and picks him up (also using his car) at scheduled times. Thus, this business has no required investment for offices, autos, and other expensive equipment. A fee of ten dollars to twenty dollars is charged for each trip to the airport. As owner of this type of business, you will gradually accumulate an "inventory" of many drivers, mainly people in your area (usually presently employed) who seek to earn additional income from "moonlighting"; these often comprise policemen, firemen, teachers, etc. Normal cost per trip (based on payments to your drivers, etc.) is as low as five dollars, thus leaving you with a profit of five dollars or more per trip. Insurance costs to operate this type of business are comparatively low.

Cards And Gifts Store

In owning a cards and gifts store, you can carry maximum inventory, with high profit margin, in minimum space. There are literally hundreds of greeting cards applicable to almost any type of occasion, thus it is the type of business that appeals to the general public and can achieve continuing patronage.

Reading Improvement Schools

Faster reading, and better reading comprehension, are desired by many people today. Reading improvement schools that have been established in various parts of the country have become highly successful. They cater to business executives, and to the general public. Also, students on both high school and college levels have enrolled in this specialized course of instruction. Fees are as high as three hundred dollars per student for each course. The profit margin is unusually high. These courses can be conducted within the facilities of existing institutions: church, temple, school, YMCA, etc. Many classes are held simultaneously in various parts of the locality through use of affiliated instructors (former or current school teachers who seek part-time employment). A comparatively small investment is required to enter this business; earnings in excess of twenty five thousand dollars a year are frequently possible.

Care For The Elderly

Many elderly (also invalided) people prefer being cared for in their own homes rather than in a hospital or institution. A profitable business can be established providing care for the elderly in their homes. As owner of this business, you will deliver two meals daily (conformant to their dietary require-ments) and also provide once a week home cleaning services. A weekly fee is charged, with a profit margin of approximately 50%. In some instances, private or governmental health and medical plans will assist in reimbursing these services. Many hospitals often cooperate in referring clients, since your services enable them to release high-priced beds for other patients in addition to restoring the patient to his or her home environment (aiding recuperation).

Stop Smoking!

Operate a business that helps people stop smoking. In view of the prevalent cancer warnings, there is an ever-increasing number of people who seek ways to discontinue this habit. It is a gratifying, congenial type of business. Minimal capital is needed since, in most instances, you can operate from existing facilities rentable on a per-evening basis. Profit margin is large.

Sell "Discount" Certificates From Local Merchants

Will your local merchants allow a discount of, say, 10% to attract new customers? In most cases, yes! It generally costs them more in other forms of advertising. Here's how you can capitalize on this fact. Enlist the participation of twenty merchants in your community, each of whom agrees to allow a discount of one dollar on any purchase of ten dollars or more. Type their names and addresses on a sheet of paper; xerox a quantity of these, say one hundred. Affix your signature or some other symbol, that identifies the certificates as being genuine and "authoritative."

Sell these certificates for two dollars each to friends, relatives, and others. They are receiving potential value of twenty dollars for the small sum of two dollars, hence, it represents a "good buy" to them. You, on your part, can earn a quick two hundred dollars from the sale of the one hundred. And you can repeat the process each six months. Each time a discount purchase is made, the local merchant cancels out his name on the slip.

Home Catering

Ideal "man and wife" business that can be operated from the home. Like puttering around the kitchen, preparing a variety of tasty morsels? Turn your likes into dollars by offering to "cater" to your community's needs. Include: parties, club meetings, churches, institutions (hospitals, nursing homes), etc. We know one family in Connecticut that has built up a thriving business, having many clients on a continuing "contract" basis. All the materials are prepared in their home kitchen (recently, through expansion, they have also utilized the basement). They prepare hors d'oeuvres, sandwiches, and more extensive meals. There is a profit margin of approximately 50%. My friend indicated a profit of nearly twenty thousand dollars the previous year on sales of forty five thousand dollars. Since they have practically no overhead . . . and profit is clear . . . such a large "net" is understandable.

Wake-Up Service

Here's a money-making, part-time service which requires only a telephone and the will to wake yourself up an hour or so earlier in the morning. Advertise your Wake-Up service in your local shopping newspaper. Offer to phone daily, at whatever hour your customer wishes, to say "Hello. This is your Happy Hour Wake-Up Service. It's just seven a.m.," or whatever time your customer wanted you to wake him. At five dollars per month billing per customer, based upon five calls a customer a week, you'll earn a profit of approximately $2.75 a customer. And with twenty five customers to call each day during that one hour of sleep which you've resolved to do without, you can earn yourself an extra sixty or seventy dollars a month.

Write Short Fillers For Pay

Weekly newspapers, shopping and entertainment guides, house organs, and many other types of publications are continually seeking filler material (jokes, recipes, brief information bits) to fill the blank spaces in their printing layouts. You can start a filler service, which many printers and local publishers will be glad to subscribe to on a weekly or monthly basis. Simply keep track of interesting materials which you find in other publications, or hear from outside sources. Then rewrite, type, and xerox the items which you then send to your subscribers on an annual subscription basis.

Profiting From Your Telephone

Your telephone can be your key to profit in dozens of ways. You can act as a message center, permitting friends, neighbors, and others to give your number out for use at times when they are unreachable. Naturally, you charge for accepting such calls and delivering the messages. You can offer your help on the basis of a monthly service charge or a monthly minimum of, say, one hundred calls at ten cents per call which, of course, would amount to a minimum of about ten dollars per month per customer. And, with just a few such customers, you're on your way to developing a regular telephone answering service which, today, is a very useful and profitable adjunct of the business world.

Why Not Try Mail Order?

Confined to home? Live on a farm? Stuck in suburbia...away from possibilities of getting a job? Are you a semi-invalid? Thousands of individuals in similar positions are earning good livings through mail order. Hundreds of mail order companies will be pleased to pay you commissions, based upon sales from catalogs which you have supplied to friends, neighbors, and other acquaintances. Check the ads of mail order companies in your local newspapers and magazines. Talk over the possibilities with your family and friends and chances are you'll soon be making money by staying at home.

Record And Sell Local Speeches

Your community is a beehive of amateur performers, seeking outlets for self-expression. Just as people become enthusiastic photographers of their family and friends or, for special occasions, hire professional photographers, they are equally interested in capturing their voices on cassettes which can be played back on tape recorders. All you need in the way of equipment to become a professional recorder in your community is a portable tape recorder. List yourself on bulletin boards and with the affair-arranging authorities of your local social clubs, political organizations, schools, meeting halls, and restaurants. Often, you'll be called upon to record events such as wedding ceremonies, speeches by local politicians, talks by community authorities on various subjects, local performances by outside celebrities, or even the first efforts of a baby to talk. You can sell the tape cassettes of such performances for prices varying from five to fifteen dollars each, while your own cost is approximately two dollars a cassette or tape. Allow a discount on the purchase of two or more tapes.

Profit From "Party Plans"

It's an old sales axiom that the more prospects you see, the more you sell. What better way, then, to reach a lot of prospects at one time, than to throw a party at which you can reach five, ten, fifteen or as many people as you wish with just one demonstration. There are numerous products . . . cleaning products, cosmetics, costume jewelry, health foods, and many others, listed in various sales opportunities magazines, which are highly adaptable to party sales. You can start with a 35% profit as a new distributor of certain items and, with patience and conscientious effort, grow to a profitable 40% or 50% profit earning position plus an additional profit-sharing interest in the supplier's firm.

Good At Organizing Parties? Here's How To Profit From It!

Have people remarked about the originality of your parties? The novel way you prepare invitations . . . arrange the theme and decor . . . the whole bit. You can profit, substantially. Offer a complete party "package" for parties of all types—children's parties, graduation, confirmation, Sweet Sixteen, or any-occasion parties of any description. You'll find many takers. Charge a blanket fee of, say, fifty dollars, expenses extra. In many instances you'll also receive commissions from caterers, party ornament makers, etc. We know of one person who has developed the entire package, covering various party formats, and sells it for as high as two hundred dollars profit, after expenses.

Trophies, Plaques, And Awards

Trophies frequently are offered as incentives by companies, churches, institutions, etc., to commemorate various types of achievements. This can constitute a profitable business. Tie in with a trophy manufacturer (you'll find one or more in most cities), obtaining his catalog and becoming his distributor in your area. Trophy items include: plaques, engraved cups, medals, ribbons, desk sets, cups and bowls, clocks, silver trays, pewter mugs, diplomas. Profit margin can often be as high as 50%.

Dial-A-Lunch

Contact business firms throughout your area. Offer to deliver "diet" lunches to personnel in their offices at a fixed, moderate price. Enclose a menu covering a specific meal available for each day of the week. Associate yourself with a restaurant in your area that will prepare and package these meals. Offer discounts for continuity, and for multiple patronage in the same office. This plan has been implemented in the New York area and has achieved immediate success.

Electric Appliance Repairing

Most homes have electric appliances that constantly "break down." Where to go for repair? Here is where you can come in and achieve good profits, particularly so if you are handy in repairing things. It's a business that you can operate from your own kitchen, basement, or garage and can earn as high as ten dollars an hour.

Operating A "Sharpening" Device

In every home (and in many businesses, too) there is a constant flow of items that can be sharpened. These include: saws, lawn mowers, cutlery, etc. Once you have developed customers, you can also anticipate repeat patronage, so that you can, in time, achieve a flourishing growth business. This type of business can earn as much as one hundred dollars a day and more.

Aluminum Awnings

This is a specialty business and you can be noncompetitive in your area. Awnings are used by practically every store, and also for homes (porches, patios, etc.). Aluminum awnings have distinct advantages; they are both attractive and more durable than the usual type of cloth awnings. There are many aluminum awnings manufacturers who would be glad to have you represent them in your area. Profit margin ranges from 35% to 50%.

Greeting Cards Business

This constitutes a fine earnings potential. Contact stores in your area (drug stores, confectionery, gifts, etc.), offering to furnish them with a continuing supply of greeting cards, inserted in attractive racks that occupy minimum space. They will usually be glad to cooperate since this represents an add-on business with add-on earnings, and one that can also attract added patronage to the store. Replace "sold" cards each week with new ones. The merchant gets 15%, and you get 25%. Earnings from ten good locations can yield as much as one hundred dollars a week in spare time.

Auto Purchase Information

John L. inserted this ad: "Buying a new or used car? Protect yourself with a check list." He sold this check list for five dollars; it enabled the prospective auto purchaser to compare deals, breakdown of the optional costs, new and used car charges and financing terms with John's Car Buyer's check list. His sales nationwide were in scope, and he published a new check list annually.

Make Costume Jewelry

This business can be operated in spare time from the home. Make newest, beautiful jeweled earrings, necklaces, bracelets, pins, cufflinks, tieclips, etc. The component parts are obtainable at low cost from jewelry suppliers in practically any area. The products are sold to homes, churches, women's groups, etc., and can bring good sales and profits.

Buy At Wholesale

Everyone seeks to buy things "wholesale." This includes, brand appliances, tools, watches, cameras, phonographs and stereo equipment, sewing machines, jewelry, housewares, sporting goods, typewriters, etc. By checking the Thomas Industrial Directory, you can obtain names of companies that have printed catalogs offering these products at wholesale. (There are a number of them, for example, in both the New York and Chicago areas.) Arrange for them to imprint a number of catalogs with your name and address and to appoint you as their sales representative in your area. Your commissions range from 10% to 15% and you can obtain multiple orders from a single purchaser. It is also a business that has contiuity.

Cabinet Making

Are you handy with tools? Do you enjoy working with your hands? Then you will find the field of "cabinet making" as enjoyable as it can be profitable. Become a skilled woodworker. There are literally hundreds of potential finished wood products that can be made with hand and power tools. Practically every home is a prospect, and many businesses, too.

Plastic Laminating

A simple, inexpensive machine enables you to do plastic sealing and laminating. In addition to lamination of important documents, many products can be laminated, inclusive of: costume jewelry, cigarette boxes, trays, candlesticks, coasters, lamp bases, bookends. It can also be done in colored plastic. A good business can be achieved.

Auto Upholstery Cleaning

Offer this service to both used car dealers and to individual auto owners. Equip yourself with an electric, automatic machine to do this work thoroughly and quickly. The work is done on the customer's premises. One source for this equipment is: Von Schrader Manufacturing Company, Racine, Wisconsin.

Invisible Reweaving

In most communities, qualified reweavers are scarce, and this service is often unavailable. Reweaving helps to make cuts, tears, holes disappear from all fabrics—suits, coats, dresses, etc. There is minimum overhead expenses and material needed for this type-of work, and a normal twelve-hour job can be done in about one-half hour by an expert reweaver.

Establish A Venetian Blind Laundry

It is difficult to clean venetian blinds, hence, there is a good market for this service for home, offices, and factories. It is practically a noncompetitive business, too, since it is normally unavailable in most communities. You may be called to do as many as twenty (and even more) venetian blinds in a single home or business, and can earn as high as fifteen dollars an hour.

Restringing Tennis Rackets

Particularly in view of the current tennis craze, there is a potentially "bustling" market for expert tennis racket restringing. Your expertise will be needed by literally hundreds of tennis buffs in your area, many remaining steady customers. In addition, you can obtain "volume" business from schools, colleges, tennis clubs, etc.

Hobby Shop

Do you have a hobby? Are you interested in other people's hobbies? If so, you would enjoy opening a hobby shop. You sell the various types of artifacts that hobbyists seek (for practically any type of hobby) ranging from handicrafts to woodwork. You can also exhibit and sell hobbyists' creations. This business can be quite profitable.

Research For Advertising Agencies

Before launching an advertising campaign, advertising agencies usually want to know exactly who and where their market is. You can provide this market research data—interviewing prospective customers, doing competitor research, market receptivity evaluation, library research, and more. Since each new account will need some background, you could possibly arrange to work for a busy local advertising agency on a continuing retainer.

Booking Agency

An annual income of fifty thousand dollars a year—now *that's* entertainment, but not an impossible figure for booking agents who match night club, theatre, television talk shows, or commercial ads with the right personality, talent, play, or face. Booking agents (who could even run their business from a phone booth) earn from 10% to 15% of the fee a client pays.

Sell Local Products

It's folksy, it's fun, and eminently profitable in these days when just about everything seems mass-produced and indistinguishable from everything else. Look around your community or region and find indigenous specialties, such as cheeses, crafts, hams, fabric, a pie, furniture. Not only can you earn a healthy income getting these regional specialties to a larger market, but you can save them from extinction by creating a demand and encouraging young people to learn traditional crafts from their elders.

School Advisory Service

Students need advice, and schools need students. On this basic principle, you can help potential private school and college students choose the institution best suited for them, guide them in seeking financial aid, and prepare them for entrance examinations. At the same time you're both encouraging enrollment in local schools, and lessening the selection process the school itself has to perform. Most schools allow a commission of 10% of a year's tuition for such referrals.

Model Agency

The lithe young things that swirl through showrooms in high fashion clothes don't meet all business requirements. Models come in all sizes and shapes and in both sexes for advertising, displaying products, or serving hors d'oeuvres at business meetings, or posing for artists and photographers.

Advertising On Dry-Cleaning Hangers

Advertising can reach a large and affluent audience that use dry cleaners. Ronald P. counted two hundred cleaning establishments in his city, each delivering an average of five hundred clothing items a week—all neatly hung on hangers. All told, one hundred thousand hangers could be circulating advertisers' messages to potential buyers. Attracted by the large circulation, businessmen bought this advertising service for twenty dollars a thousand hangers. Participating dry cleaners received a 15% commission on the number of hangers they used.

Rental Library

Supply the business library many communities lack, by renting books and cassettes relating to local businesses. Begin with general areas—management, cost reduction, personnel motivation, accounting, sales, training. Requests for material too specialized for you to stock can be met by contacting rental services in large business areas.

Rack Merchandising

Install a bright display of inexpensive toys within arm's reach of the impulse buyer visiting drug, stationery, grocery, or confectionery stores. Offer the participating merchant a 10% commission on each toy sold from your compact, attractive rack. Obtain your merchandise from odd-lots dealers or wholesalers.

4.

12 SPECIALLY SELECTED, READY-TO-START BUSINESSES

"Top Billing" Businesses

... Discussed In-Depth
... Geared To Today's Opportunities

The twelve businesses discussed in the following pages, have been selected upon the basis of:

- Potential profitability
- Operational simplicity
- Operational comfortableness
- Timeliness
- Growth prospects
- Distinctiveness
- Operable with minimum capital
- Proved out by related businesses or current trends
- Year 'round profitability
- Applicability to most areas throughout the country

These businesses can, in most cases, be implemented with comparative small capital outlay, often as little as one thousand dollars. They represent the "pick" of businesses observed or gleaned as a result of extensive hard-nose experience of many years in observing the pros and cons of existing businesses, and the needs and potentials for new businesses that, in many instances, are not readily available today.

It's my opinion that this chapter in itself can well be worth many times the price of the book; properly implemented, it can be worth a FORTUNE!

Operate A Mobile "Handyman" Business

Every home, everywhere, needs a continuing flow of "odd jobs" to be done. These include: electrical repair, house appliances repairs (ranging from toaster to dishwasher to freezer), fixing water faucets, and literally hundreds of other repair needs.

Where to go to get these repairs done? The answer is not a simple one. It's as difficult to get a handyman (if you can find one) to make house calls, as it is to get a doctor to do so. Here is where your mobile handyman business cannot only provide a much-needed service, but also reap profits, week-in and week-out.

First, equip yourself with a motor van. Structure "bins" in the van to properly hold your tools and other equipment, such as:

- Masonry patching materials, wall patch materials, etc.
- Electrical repair parts and tools
- Small electrical appliance and lamp repair parts
- Chain saw and plumber's snake
- Plumber's heavy tools and repair parts
- Heavy mechanic's and carpenter's tools, masonry tools
- Hooks for rope, electrical extension cords
- Lock box for portable electrical tools
- Cabinet for small tools, repair parts, nails, fasteners, etc.
- Work bench, with vise, grinding machine
- Hand saws, long carpenter tools
- Lumber, long-handled tools
- Mitre box, clamps, drill stand, portable lights
- Caulking compounds, paints, roofing cement
- Storage area for two tool carry-trays
- Removable racks for wallboard, plywood, and for storage of folding worktable

A step ladder and an extension ladder is carried on special racks on the roof of the truck.

Included in the wide variety of services that need to be performed are those contained on the following pages. Also listed are possible prices that can be charged for these services. Naturally, this will vary from community to community based on need for this work, and "usual" fees charged by others.

Service	Possible Labor Charge
A. *Electrical:*	
Repair small appliance	$ 8.00
Replace cord on lamp	4.50
Install extension cord plug outlet	3.50
Replace light fixture	4.50
Replace light bulb in hard-to-reach place	3.50
Install new light switch	4.00
Replace switch plate	3.00
Install small window-size air conditioner (4,500 to 6,500 BTU)	12.00
B. *Plumbing*	
Hook up dishwasher where plumbing is present	32.00
Hook up dryer where plumbing and gas line are present	18.00
Replace bathroom sink	22.00
Replace faucet washer	4.00
Open clogged drain	10.00
Thaw out a frozen pipe	6.00
Flush-tank repair:	
• Adjust float rod	4.00
• Adjust linkage wire to end water loss	5.00
• Replace worn flush-ball	5.00
• Clean valve assembly	22.00
C. *Walls, Floors, Ceilings*	
Repair loose floor tiles	4.00/sq. ft.
Fill small hole in cellar floor	7.00
Pry off uneven molding at bottom of baseboard and renail close to floor	5.00
Repair moisture damage in plaster (4" x 4")	10.00
Patch up crack in wall or ceiling	8.00
Scrape loose filling around bathtub and recaulk	10.00
Replace shower curtain rod	5.00
Hang wall picture or mirror	4.00
Fasten wall cabinet or spice rack to wall	5.00
Replace hardware on kitchen cabinets (4' x 6')	12.00
Install metal towel rack	5.00

Replace:
- Toothbrush holder in ceramic tile 8.00
- Soap dish in ceramic tile 8.00
- Towel rack in ceramic tile 12.00

Install top shelf in closet 12.00
Install extra clothing pole in closet 5.00
Install hand rail for cellar steps 27.00
White wash or paint cellar (100 sq. ft.) 17.00
Build a bracket shelf (using three feet standards) 12.00
Install clothing hook 3.00

D. *Windows, Doors*

Trim off door that sticks 6.00
Silence a loose doorknob 4.00
Remove squeak from door hinge 4.00
Install a new door lock:
- Interior 9.00
- Exterior 27.00

Install door bolt 4.00
Replace door and add a finish 14.50
Replace spring door stop on storm door 4.50
Caulk around door frame 5.50
Install bi-fold doors 8.00
Loosen stuck window 4.50
Replace broken window (pre-cut to size):
- Small size 6.00
- Regular size 9.00

Caulk around window or frame 4.50
Install traverse track for drapes (eight feet) 8.00
Install bracket for window shade or venetian 4.00
Clean venetian blind 4.00
Re-string venetian blind 5.00
Patch screen on door or window 3.50
Weather-stripping doors and windows, each 4.00
Clean windows, storm windows, screens, each 6.00

E. *Other Household*

Paint radiator 7.00
Replace air valve on radiator 4.00
Change filters in furnace and oil motor 7.00
Line with contact paper:
- Closet shelf 4.00
- Kitchen cabinets (contents removed) 10.00
- Five-drawer bedroom chest (contents removed) 4.50

Reglue chair, each joint 3.00

Remove and replace drape for cleaning (eight feet)   12.00

F. *Exterior Household and Garden*
Clean out gutter system from mud and rotting leaves   42.00
Clean out gutter system and coat inside   52.00
Replace a rusted gutter hanger   7.00
Install wire strainer in top of downspout to prevent
   clogging of drainage system   7.00
Temporary repair for hole in gutter (roofing cement)   9.00
Install drain tile under downspout to divert water   14.00
Renail loose downspout hanger   4.00
Caulk around bottom of porch floor (to prevent
   rot and decay)   6.00
Replace broken or damaged porch flooring   10.00/sq. ft.
Replace a piece of damaged house siding   10.00/sq. ft.
Replace damaged window sill   14.00
Repair section of a wooden picket fence   7.00/sq. ft.
Reset fence post in concrete   14.00
Replace or install shutters   22.00/window
Grease garage doors   4.00
Install knocker on door   4.50
Install house number on door   4.00
Replace push door bell   4.50
Install outdoor mailbox:
   • Small mailbox to house   5.50
   • Roadside mailbox anchored in cement   18.00
Repair cracked mortar joint   7.00
Repair small section of cement walk   12.00
Repair loose bricks or cement step   12.00/sq. ft.
Reset loose stones on a patio   5.00/sq. ft.
Seal roof leak entering around:
   • Chimney or chimney cap   12.00
   • Soil pipe   12.00
   • Flue   12.00
Install outdoor clothes line (pole anchored in cement)   19.00
Remove storm windows and store. Clean exterior side
   of window, wash and install window screen   8.00/window
Remove screen and store. Clean exterior side of
   window, clean and install storm window   8.00/window
Remove or put up window-size awning   6.00
Set up play gym (sand box, swings, anchored in cement)   32.00
Set up steel wall pool (12 feet) set in sand, and
   install pump   78.00
Maintenance of pool (vacuum out and clean filter:
   • Steel wall portable pool (repair holes in lining) 15.00

- Built-in pool   18.00

Sharpen blades:
- Rotary blade on power mower   5.00
- Garden scissor   4.50
- Knife   4.50
- Hedge Shear   6.00

Cut down small tree (about 12 feet) and saw into
    sections   20.00

Good Earnings Potential

Earnings of twenty five thousand dollars a year and higher are possible from the operation of **each** van. In time, you may want to expand by adding expert assistants and vans . . . and to spread out to adjoining areas.

Annual contracts are also possible, particularly with large apartment houses and office buildings . . . who need both "preventive" maintenance supervision, and continuing odd-job repairs.

Become An "Odd Lots" Dealer

An odd-lots dealer can get it for *you* wholesale, but for himself he does much better. "Below cost" barely hits at the rock bottom price he pays—ten dollars for brand name copying machines, eight dollars for metal tennis rackets, electric typewriters for eighty five dollars, men's suits for twenty two dollars. These are just a few examples of possible "knockdown" prices! Over production, mistaken design, faulty manufacture, or any other miscalculation that clogs a manufacturer's warehouse and sends ordinarily self-confident vice presidents on ego-shattering martini binges, can wind up in the laps of the nation's few hundred odd-lots dealers.

It doesn't stay there long. The fast-on-his-feet dealer finds another customer. A store might be looking for merchandise to put on sale, a bank might be planning a promotional giveaway, or a jobber seeks merchandise to distribute to cut-rate stores.

Odd-lots dealers do particularly well when the general economy is particularly bad. A bad Christmas season for manufacturers is good for the odd-lots dealer who can find an outlet for anything, as long as the price is low enough.

Publicity isn't a big issue in odd-lots dealing. It's the last thing companies want, particularly large, publicly owned firms trying to dump merchandise without their shareholders or the public any the wiser. Executives want to hide their failures from the company. Whatever the reason, no manufacturer wants to live with his mistakes—nor can he afford to, for that matter. Hard-to-move stock preoccupies salesmen, fills space needed for new merchandise, and grows increasingly unsalable the longer it stands.

Odd-lots dealers must be able to look at a product, calculate its cost to the manufacturer, and negotiate the lowest price. Some manufacturers consider odd-lots merchants such "vipers" they grimly hang on to their stock at any cost short of bankruptcy. Of course, these hard-core opponents have been known to relent—sometimes in the middle of night when he will be inspired to call a dealer when no one in his office can catch on to what he's doing.

On the other hand, once the merchandise is sold, the responsibility passes completely to the dealer, who is responsible for every one of the one-hundred-thousand wigs he's bought, or the snow boots purchased in July.

Odd-lotters think fast on their feet. Though there aren't that many of them around, the competition is steep and time is essential. When a company relieves itself of unsuccessful merchandise, it wants cash. The odd-lotter should be prepared to pay (and can often get bank loans to assist him in doing so).

He also has to transport the goods to his own or rented warehouses and store them until he has a buyer.

Under optimal circumstances, he already has a buyer lined up when he buys an odd-lot. A veteran dealer knows the most hazardous part of his work isn't finding merchandise for sale, it's finding a buyer.

Dealers often employ "finders" who work on commission. The finder will work his region for manufacturers to buy from. For this he receives about a 3% to 5% commission.

There's one kind of overhead an odd-lots dealer doesn't have to worry about. He doesn't require a business office—or any office at all. He can work at home—and it can be a lavish one, furnished with odd-lot samples—when he's not traveling.

A two to three thousand dollar profit on a deal is acceptable, but it can rise much higher. Depending on the profit, a dealer usually makes five to twenty deals a year.

An odd lots dealer constantly juggles his array of golf balls, foods, stuffed toys, and salad bowls with buyers. He constantly telephones manufacturers for lots he can buy, and buyers to see what he can sell.

For an odd-lots dealer, there's never much breathing time between the two questions, "What have you got?" and "Do you have the spot cash?"

Own Your Own Children's Day Camp

It is possible to establish a profitable business of "Day Camps" for children. This can be done with minimum capital: no structural purchase is needed—no building, no land, no swimming pool, not even classroom facilities. Nevertheless, you are offering all these facilities to camp participants!

In consequence, because you have had such minimal capital outlay and minimal overhead, you are able to offer your camp facilities for an unusual low fee, as low as thirty-five dollars a week (much below that of other places) and still make substantial profits.

How is it accomplished? Similar type camps make arrangements with nearby parks to use their park and pool facilities for the children at designated rental fees—as low as twenty dollars a day. This also gives them use of indoor facilities of one of the parks nearby buildings (e.g., field house) during inclement weather. On such occasions, movies are shown or indoor games are conducted.

The profits can be significant. For example:

Possible Income:
   200 enrollees at $35 a week: $7,000 a week

Estimated Expenses:
   Assume that your weekly expenses comprise:

Advertising	$ 200
Personnel	350
Van (for pick up and delivery of children)	150
Facilities rental	150
Miscellaneous	150
TOTAL:	$1,000

Based on the above figures, you can see that earnings can be quite substantial—even with higher operating costs (provided, of course, your enrollment is one hundred or more).

Expansion is also achievable, particularly so in metropolitan areas. You can conduct multiple camps in other sections of the city or in surrounding communities. Generally, one advertisement can cover all these branch locations. In consequence, you are able to achieve significant economies in one of the foremost usual expense categories—"promotions." You are also able to achieve economies in personnel, being able to "rotate" key personnel from one camp to another.

Personnel is obtainable fairly inexpensively on a part-time basis. One constantly available source of personnel is present and former teachers. Usually they are on vacation during the summer months when these camps are operated, and are glad to earn extra money. They have unequalled qualifications for conducting such camps and working with children, since their regular teaching duties constantly involve them with children.

Personnel required, and average compensation, comprise:

- One counsellor for fifteen children, at twenty-five dollars a day
- One Registrar at twenty-five dollars a day
- Three van drivers (for morning and afternoon) at two dollars an hour (one van per each ten children)
- Leasing of van at fifty dollars a week each (normally leasable from most auto and truck leasing companies)

In entering this type of business—involving child care—it is important that you check out current city and state licenses, etc., required in your particular area ... and that you conform to health, safety, and other regulations pertinent to this business in your community.

Other Children-Oriented Businesses

Fond of children? Want to make child care your business? You may also want to consider other related businesses, involving the care, recreation or instruction of children that have been undertaken, and profitably operated, by entrepreneurs in various parts of the country. These include:

1. Operating a "Sitters" service. Accumulate a list of reliable sitters in your area (and there are usually a large number who can be recruited among retirees, grandmothers, mothers, mothers of grown children, etc.) who have

the time and seek added income. The "sitter" rate in most areas is $1.50 an hour, and your commission—in conducting this service—is usually 15% of the total amount.

2. After-School care: Working mothers in particular need this service . . . one that provides a reliable place for children to go after school hours, and where they can stay until the mother returns home and can be picked up by her. Often this type of care may commence at 3 p.m. when school is dismissed until 6 p.m. or later. If the school is located a distance from your home or facility, you may want to arrange a pick-up service.

Bicycle Sales And Repairs

Throughout most of the 20th Century, bicycles have been looked upon, primarily, as kids' toys and as the means of transportation for local deliveries and mail. However, with the tremendously increased interest since World War II in the maintenance of good physical condition (dramatized so effectively by the late heart specialist, Dr. Paul Dudley White), "bike-riding" has become the exercise of choice to millions of Americans.

In 1969, only 12% of the bicycles sold were of adult size and, no doubt, the majority of those went to teenagers. And, in that year, the number of bikes manufactured was considerably under seven million units. But, in 1971, with sales jumping from seven million units in 1970 to nine million (an increase of 22%) in 1971, the boom had begun, reaching 15.4 million units in sales for 1973. And it is forcast that, for the next few years at least, the retail bicycle shop, advantageously located and having efficient repair departments, will continue doing very well.

The average margin of profit on bicycle sales does not seem as high as it ought to be (about 35%). However, through building sales up to the more deluxe models, and through the promotion of accessories, it is often possible to raise the margin of profit to 50%.

The average bike sale runs about ninety dollars. However, in more affluent areas, a one hundred fifteen dollar price seems quite standard. Sales of accessories add an average of about eighteen dollars to these figures.

Currently, some 91% of all bikes purchased by adults are of the ten-speed type. These can be bought in some discount houses for as low as sixty dollars or, in the more exclusive sport shops and department stores, fancy European racing bikes can be bought for up to six hundred dollars.

A smart retailer who knows the bike business well will often purchase unknown European or Oriental brands, marking them up a full 100%, thereby producing an overall margin of 50%. The bike dealer who does likewise should do well, just as long as none of his competitors begin stocking the same brand and start a price-cutting spree. When stocking an unknown brand, however, one should make sure that the distributor has a large inventory of parts in his warehouse. Obtaining parts for imported bikes has been one of the dealers' greatest problems. And, often, they must wait six to eight weeks for shipment.

As a new dealer in the bicycle business, you can gain a head start, and often gain the lead over established competition, if you can set up a relationship with a reliable parts distributor. Presently, nine out of ten distributors are new, having unregulated inventories of both parts and finished bicycles. You cannot depend upon their word. Hence, it will pay you to do business, even if the prices are somewhat higher, with an established firm.

In recent surveys dealers were showing excellent sales figures, ranging from fifty- to two-hundred-fifty-thousand dollars annually. The average cash investment runs from five to ten thousand dollars with some operators having an additional ten thousand dollars in financial obligations. Some 15% of the gross of most shops come from repairs . . . another good reason for maintaining adequate service facilities.

If you are not located in one of the temperate zone areas such as Florida, Arizona, California, etc., there is a question about what you can do to keep going during the winter. It is an interesting and hopeful sign, however, that a number of dealers in northern cities report that sales for the month of December (Christmas buying, no doubt) have doubled their sales for any other month of the year.

Investigations of the bicycle shop business have indicated that the best profit potential and smallest risk factor lies in rental operations. Many such entrepreneurs operate only three months of the year, and some of these, only on weekends. Rental stock averaged sixty bikes per rental shop of which forty-five were ten-speed models, five were three-speed, seven were tandems, and three were children's single-speed bikes.

The average rental rate was $1.25 an hour with a five dollar minimum. Most shops required a ten dollar deposit, in addition to which they held a customer's driver's license or credit card as security. More than half of the successful rental shops had regular sales facilities but located elsewhere.

The best locations for bike rental shops were those close to bicycle trails or paths. Locations near or in such tourist attractions as hotels, resorts, etc., were also highly profitable. In those facilities surveyed, the average gross per day ran about three hundred dollars on weekends with a high for several operations of over six hundred fifty dollars. Locations seemed to be the most important factor in the resort areas. One rental shop, located near a very popular resort, and open seven days a week, grossed more than twenty five hundred dollars a week with ninety bicycles.

The most successful rental agencies are usually located in vacant lots, parking lots, or gas stations. Most of the bikes used for renting were purchased second hand and cost an average of about thirty dollars each.

For those who plan to enter any phase of the retail bicycle business, it would be well to procure the "Store Manual" from the National Bicycle Dealers Association (NBDA), 29025 Euclid Avenue, Wickcliffe, Ohio 44092. The manual tells how to start and to set up your store. And also, with membership in NBDA, you will be provided with a guide to bike and accessory wholesalers anywhere in the United States. Just ask for the "Source Book."

The bike boom had been so strong that most manufacturers had not been able to keep up with the demand. However, it is expected that, partly as a result of the current recession, this condition will soon be overcome.

Of course, if you have the possibility of investing twenty thousand to thirty thousand dollars in the business and the good fortune to be selected as a Schwinn bike dealer, you won't have to worry about either quality or supply. Moreover, Schwinn gives its dealers protected territories, picks the best store sites, gives thorough management and repair training, and strong sales promotion assistance. A few other manufacturers are talking about providing the sort of dealer help that is offered by Schwinn, but such help, up to now, has been slow in developing, according to a number of dealers who were questioned.

In addition, a Bicycle Repair Manual had been published by the Bicycle Guild of America, Sherman Oaks, California, priced at one hundred fifty dollars. This price had also included various tools and free consultation for one year.

It is estimated that bicycle shops can make up to fifteen dollars an hour, just through repairing bikes. Presently, a range of six to eighteen dollars an hour (average of about ten dollars an hour) is charged by dealers throughout the United States. The Guild's manual is a most worthwhile investment if you are going into the rental business exclusively since it will help you to maintain your rental fleet.

Location:

In determining the site of your rental establishment, try to locate in a market which has at least fifty thousand people living within a five-mile radius, at least one-half of whom are under forty years old. Of course, you want to be careful not to lock horns with a dealer who is already established in the community unless you can clearly see that he's doing a poor job and that you have a very good chance of forcing him out of business.

Your store should be on a main thoroughfare and you should have good parking facilities, not only for the parking benefit to your customers but, even more importantly, to provide a traffic-free area for them to test ride their purchases. Even old hands at bike riding can be clumsy when they first try to ride the new European-style ten-speed bikes.

Naturally, the amount you invest in inventory and accessories will be governed, in large measure, by the size of your building; one thousand feet should be the minimum, and the shops on our survey which grossed over two hundred thousand dollars all had over thirty five hundred square feet.

Inventory:

Most successful dealers find that, to cover the market they must stock four brands of bicycles including three different low to medium priced brands and one fancy, expensive European brand. It is suggested that one of the lower priced brands be American and one European, while the third could be Japanese, since the Japanese parts distribution is becoming more efficient than the others.

Minimum starting inventory should be about one hundred twenty five bikes, depending upon how quickly you can get delivery. About 80% of these should be adult sizes, split fifty-fifty between men's and women's models. In men's bikes, it is a good idea to stick to basic reds, greens, and blues, while all colors should be taken in women's models, but 65% of these should be in basic colors. Children's sizes should make up the balance of the inventory with the addition of three or four tandems and at least two double seat tricycles for older citizens. Many housewives nowadays take care of their own deliveries from supermarkets so it is also a good idea to have a three-wheeler with a large rear shopping basket available.

With mom and dad riding around on multi-speed units—three, five, and ten-speed—children, too, want more and more to possess multi-speed models. Kids' multi-speed units are one of the things that will keep the bicycle sales climbing for the next several years despite the recession and other factors which would contribute to a normal slump in sales.

Other sources of extra income for dealers are in the sales of "moto-cross" accessories and conversion kits which include special wheels, tires, handlebars, forks, and even frames.

Accessories:

There are about fifty six items available as accessories for cyclists. NBDA's Source Book can be consulted as a guide to the complete variety picture. It is important to carry a wide and varied stock since necessary sales can contribute from thirty five to fifty percent of your annual volume. Accessory sales are easily made with simple suggestions. And, it is a fact that people who buy their bikes in discount houses and department stores most often go to their local dealer for accessories, advice, and repair.

Trade-Ins:

Don't be afraid to take trade-ins. They can help you overcome competition from discount houses, department stores, and even from other dealers. If the trade-in happens to be multi-speed, just add it to your rental stock. You can also clean up, repaint, and sell a trade-in as a rebuilt model for about two-thirds the regular price.

Don't pay more than ten dollars for a single-speed bike as a trade-in. You can then buy a conversion kit and make it a three- or ten-speed model for use in your rental stock or for sale as a rebuilt bike. You can, obviously, make a lot of profit from such a transaction and keep your repairman busy during slow periods.

Sales Promotion:

As a bicycle retailer, rental agency, or repair service, your basic advertising medium should be the yellow pages of your telephone directory. The cost, which depends upon the number of telephones (circulation) in your area, will be charged for on a monthly basis on your telephone bill.

You should have a monthly sale, at least once a month, promoting some items at a discount. Avoid advertising in your local newspapers on days when supermarkets have their big food ads. But, you'll find it pays to advertise regularly in the womens and sports pages. Some bicycle manufacturers will share the cost of your advertising, and this is a point you should check when arranging to take on a line.

Your best advertising will come from your own sponsorship and promotion of bicycle events. For instance, buy a number of unicycles and put on a unicycle race in your own parking lot. You can get publicity from your local newspaper, which wants to induce you to advertise in it, and often from your local television station which may show the race on the news or on a sports program. Send out an advance release, suggesting that such media may wish to cover the event. And, after it's over, send out a newspaper release and photographs announcing the results.

There is also a lot of advertising value in your ownership and promotional use of old fashioned bicycles . . . the circa 1900 high-wheel bike which you can probably pick up from an antique dealer. They are great eye-catchers and publicity builders, either placed in your front window or used as equipment for a riding contest.

Among other methods of building up your sales could be your sponsorship of a bike "cross country" event or a bicycle rally. And further, if there are any bicycle clubs in your area, offer to give their members a substantial discount on all repairs. Many bike manufacturers have films of bicycle races, trips, etc., which they will be glad to make available to you for showing in your local school, meeting hall, or other public place. And, as a final idea for building sales, offer your rental customers a certain amount, possibly ten to twenty dollars credit toward the purchase of a new bike, as a result of similar amounts expended on rentals.

Operate A Tool-Rental Shop
(For Do-It-Yourselfers)

Only the most avid home handyman buys his own power saws, floor sander, blow torch, or even the various sized brushes and other equipment needed for a painting job. But he might not do these jobs at all, if the sophisticated, expensive equipment to simplify his work weren't available—possibly through you.

Tool rental is essential to the sometime-carpenter, who prefers to do his own repair and construction work. Small carpentry firms cannot afford to stock all their own equipment. What the recreational and professional carpenter requires is a rental service that has sturdy equipment at reasonable rates.

The range of equipment is so varied the first question to decide is whether your customer will primarily be the professional or non-professional. They demand every tool for painting, from protective canvases to various sized brushes, ladders, rollers, and spray equipment. For building jobs they require lathes, sanders, etc., plus machinery to smooth and polish floors, correct ceilings, repair walls.

Tool rental is not only important to the sometime-carpenter, but also to small carpentry businesses that can't afford to purchase their own equipment.

Own Your Own Framing Business

Where art flourishes, so does the framer. And art has become a billion-dollar business in America. Major exhibits at New York City's Metropolitan Museum of Art are so crowded even on weekdays, you can barely see the paintings. Investment counselors recommend paintings and sculpture as excellent long-term investments for extra cash. Since the 1950's, this country has been the vital center of the modern art world. Our well-educated, hard-working population has taken to art as a means of relaxation and self-expression, and if we're not dabbling in watercolors or oils, we're snapping pictures.

Framing no longer requires the high degree of craftsmanship it did when ornate, heavy frames often dominated large paintings of battle scenes or landscapes hung over the mantelpieces of the well-to-do. Today frames are simpler, intended only to complement a photograph or painting.

However, a skilled craftsman has many potential customers. There's always a demand for a custom-made frame for an important work of art. Sentimental mementoes—a baby's picture, a $1 bill that changed someone's life, an exquisite piece of needlework—are frequently encased in expensive custom frames often far more expensive than the monetary value of the object itself.

Frames are simpler, but they have also gotten thicker. The added width, such as a lucite frame, gives a three-dimensional appearance to a flat surface.

A popular hobby today is collecting small objects such as glass bits, wood, or seashells and arranging them in a glass-covered case as a tabletop, rather than lining them up in a cabinet. The case may be no more than two inches thick, and is essentially a frame for homemade art.

A framing business requires about five thousand dollars initial start-up capital. Most of your inventory will be stock, or ready-made frames, hand-carved, and imported. These are used for oils and photographs. You can also expect to sell a large volume of metal section frames, made of aluminum or chrome-covered steel and prepackaged in various sizes, so that the customer assembles his own frame. There are also the clear, thick, all-lucite frames that have a very contemporary look, and are also prepackaged.

You'll need nails, glue, picture or nonglare glass, acrylic (a clear plastic used instead of glass, but which scratches more easily), lengths of wood, paint, spray equipment, and a wide color selection of matboard. Among the tools a custom framemaker needs are:

1. Craftsman forty-five degree table saw with 12-inch blade for mitering complex moldings.

2. Stanley-Marsh miter set-up for cutting moldings up to six inches wide.
3. A small hand vise, with leather-covered faces that won't mar moldings.
4. Craftsman half-inch electric drill for boring holes for corner-fastening brads.
5. Portable saber saw for intricate frames.
6. A paint-spray booth with fan and compressor.
7. A glass cutter.

Many frame shops also sell prints, paintings, and well-designed posters. There's a huge variety of visual material suitable for framing today that you can use as window-displays. A passerby who hadn't given a thought to a picture frame—or for that matter, a picture—will be intrigued by the vibrant colors of a modern print, enhanced by a matting in a complementary tone and set off by a stained wood frame. The poster might have been nothing more than a large piece of paper to him without the solidity of the frame and the compelling color brought to his attention by the mat color playing off the hues of the print. A small, but choice selection of prints can increase your profits, since they take little room to store and can command a high price. People are prepared to pay more than they originally intended to for a work of art they want to live with.

In a highly mobile society, framed objects are all the more important. They are portable, unlike furniture, and can humanize a sparsely-furnished room.

They soften the impersonal feeling of hotels and waiting rooms, at a relatively low cost to owners who do not want to make a big investment in furniture.

And here is where you can seek your larger customers. Study the real estate news to learn if motels are being built, or hotels are being renovated. From the business pages you might discover corporate headquarters moving to town. Art is chic in executive offices, and an enlightened employer might consider a few paintings in his plant to maintain good relations with his employees.

Perhaps a new art gallery would make a deal with you, buying frames at a low cost in return for passing your name on to clients. Interior decorators are also excellent contacts, and through custom work for them you can broaden the variety of your work. You will certainly need sources of inexpensive paintings, prints, and color photographs you can frame and sell in large orders.

Practically every needlepoint shop also requires and seeks out expert framing in behalf of its customers, on a continuing basis. With the cost of handwork, papers, glue, rent, taxes, and the whole slew of costs, your markup should be a minimum of 50%. Estimate handwork at about ten dollars an hour—fifteen dollars if it is intricate. Framing requires an artist's hand and eye—why not yours?

Profit From Ceramics

Ceramics offers a wide range of income-earning possibilities for the skilled craftsman. He can sell his own work, teach, sell supplies to other craftsmen and rent his kiln for firing. Each function complements the other, adding up to a more secure income. If sales are down, you still can teach. Charging other ceramicists for the use of your equipment reduces your overhead. Selling supplies bought in quantity lowers the cost of materials for yourself and allows a profit on the remainder you sell.

Whatever else you do, selling your own work will be crucial to your business success. First, know your market. Scour crafts shops, department stores, housewares boutiques, interior decorators, and plant or florist shops to learn what kind of ceramics are in demand and at what prices.

A knowledge of the market will help to decide the kind of ceramics to concentrate on for business. As a hobby you may have enjoyed handmade, one-of-a-kind pieces with subtle, multi-colored glazes that took time and painstaking care for each piece. You will have to decide whether to continue investing a great deal of effort in one expensive piece that will sell in smaller numbers or to switch to producing large amounts, using molds, or even mass-producing them. You may wish to specialize in purely ornamental pieces such as figurines, or utilitarian objects, such as coffee mugs.

In the beginning your advertising will be informal. Word-of-mouth among friends, or a small ad in a local newspaper can bring the first customers. Seek publicity by entering your work in crafts shows. A list of forthcoming events, as well as other information, can be obtained from the American Crafts Council, 29 West 53rd Street, New York, New York. Read crafts publications both to keep up-to-date and for further publicity opportunities. Banks and public libraries sometimes give space to exhibits by local craftsmen. Design a striking card with your name, or have one designed for you, that can be enclosed with work you sell.

You may be new at the game, but proving your professionalism at this point is all the more important. When filling orders, send your best work—never seconds. Later, when you're established, there will be a market for imperfect pieces.

Price your work sensibly. Don't overvalue it, but make sure you get a profit. Know what each piece costs. Include materials, labor for every phase of production, packing and shipping. Average the total cost over the number of pieces made at one time. Casting, trimming, decorating, glazing, stacking and unstacking the kiln, should be timed. It will take a while before you can estimate your costs exactly. And don't forget breakage. A universal hazard in ceramics manufacture, large factories estimate a fifteen percent to twenty-five percent loss. In computing labor, multiply the number of hours by the going rate for skilled artisans. Special techniques that make your work unusual can command an extra profit.

Keep in mind the retailer's markup in pricing your work. While becoming acquainted with the market, investigate the markups different stores will add to the price they pay you. Some shops may add as little as 20%, but department stores often add 50%, for instance—worth remembering so that the retail price won't discourage buyers.

In the beginning you will probably be selling to retail outlets on consignment, getting paid on the basis of how much the retailer sells, not what they order. The remaining merchandise is returned to you. When a store has an accurate idea of how your work sells, you may no longer be required to sell on consignment.

Before sending out a single piece, set up a record-keeping system. Note on index cards, or in a ledger, the store, number of pieces, style number or description, price, date of delivery, and the commission arrangement. At least twice a month visit the stores where your work is sold to check on sales and find out which pieces sell best. Change the pieces that aren't moving, and remember to enter any change on your records immediately. Don't trust your memory, particularly when selling on consignment.

A few slow sales shouldn't be taken too much to heart. Stores have their own problems of overstock and slow sales periods.

Bill all merchandise F.O.B. so that your customers pay shipping charges. Careful, professional-looking packaging is vital to your business image and winning the loyalty of customers who expect merchandise to arrive in perfect condition. Fragile, protruding parts such as cup handles or perhaps all of delicate artwork, should be wrapped with special care. Wrapping materials which act as a cushion—corrugated paper or bubble plastic—are the best materials for packing.

It's much simpler to supply two or three large retailers on a regular basis, than have a lot of small customers. But until you know all the ropes, view this as a long-range goal. You will need experienced assistants. You can begin working toward your goal by producing two hundred to five hundred of one piece at one firing in a kiln. When you finally net the big order, you should have the capacity to produce what is asked and more. For example, if a store orders one thousand plates, you should be able to make one hundred more (and do make some to cover the possibility of breakage). Mass production means larger profits for you and concentrating salesmanship on a small number of customers, but you must be prepared to hold these customers as well. Think big from the start. Don't settle for anyone less than the head buyer in a department store, unless, of course, he sends you to his assistant.

A completely handmade, unique pottery item can be sold at a high price—six dollars for a coffee mug compared to three or three dollars and fifty cents for a mug of high-quality craftsmanship that is only partly handmade. On the other hand, using creative decorating patterns on simple basic pieces can lessen your work and increase your output without altogether losing the individuality of each piece.

Plain white plates you have cast and pressed, or even purchased, can be clear-glazed before overglaze decals and lettering for anniversaries and other special occasions are added. You can do custom lettering for individual customers, too.

Your approximate expenses for this kind of work will include plates cast in your own molds (fifty cents), and plates bought ready-glazed (seventy-five cents to two dollars and fifty cents, rising to a three to five dollar range for high-quality porcelain).

A decal costs about fifty cents, the glaze for a greeting fifteen cents, an underglaze one dollar.

If you have a studio of your own, you will need a potter's wheel, a kiln, ample shelf space for storage and for materials. Overhead expenses can be avoided initially by joining a potter's cooperative.

But you need your own studio to teach. Lessons can be offered as a series— six two-hour lessons for sixty dollars is a fair rate, including materials. Individual instructions can range from fifteen to twenty five dollars for one two-hour session.

One part of your studio can be set aside for displaying and selling your students' best work as well as your own.

There may be ceramicists in your community with limited equipment who will gladly pay for the use of your kiln. Charge about one cent a square inch for each firing.

Your students will naturally turn to you for supplies, which you can buy in bulk. But inventing your own glazes or mixing your own decorative materials rather than buying them from a supplier will add to the reputation of your studio and attract students.

A talented and efficient potter can earn a comfortable living and enjoy every minute of it.

Operate A Hobby Shop

If you're the kind of person who must enjoy his work and above all relishes being his own boss, a hobby shop presents many possibilities—too many, in fact, to be contained under one roof. The answer to "which hobby" is easy if you happen to have one and know it intimately. If not, you'll have to scout around for one you can handle.

Read newspapers and magazines with an eye to new trends and recreation. Study ads for classes in jewelry making, or book binding, or building model planes and boats. Flip through hobby magazines, and if groups meet in your community, inquire to see if attendance has grown sharply. Visit recreation areas.

Think in terms of materials. Paper, for instance, is an inexpensive, versatile material that lends itself to many intriguing uses. You can sell the basic construction materials for kites, birds, placemats, or other objects that can be made from paper and, where necessary, laminated.

Perhaps you'd like to seek out the hobbyist-gameplayer, who not only enjoys playing chess, checkers, cards, or backgammon, but wants to make his own game equipment. Sell finished sets as well.

In the hobby world, needlework over the past few years has shown that star quality you're looking for. Having made a stunning comeback after years of being considered a little-old-lady activity, it includes a former football hero among its adherents.

Strictly speaking, needlework is a kind of embroidery. But don't let that limit you. Add knitting, crocheting, and even a couple of looms for weaving classes. Knitting and crocheting use the same kind of yarns in many cases, and the only other equipment you'll need are needles. Hobbies usually require far more complicated and expensive materials.

Because the basic equipment is simple, you can sell basic inexpensive yarns and high-priced imported ones from Ireland, England, and France. There are craft cooperatives in New England and in rural areas reviving the basic craft of yarn-making we lost with our frontiers. The American Crafts Council in New York City has information on them.

Even a very small shop will have room for three or four small looms in the rear. For a three-week course, with two two-and-one-half-hour sessions a week, you can charge about seventy five dollars, allowing your students to use the looms at no cost when no classes are being given.

Wool can sell anywhere from one dollar a skein to five dollars or more for expensive yarns.

Materials for needlework will be most expensive, since imported silk thread is often used. Needlework kits, with the design already imprinted on the embroidery canvas are available, and sell for as much as thirty dollars.

But you must also be prepared to help your customers design their own needlepoint when they're advanced enough in the craft.

In publicizing your store remember that, although your customers will be mostly women, they will be diverse in their work and interests. Many a fetching needlepoint flower bouquet has been made during long community meetings, or watching television. Needlepoint may not yet be the kind of hobby a man will do in other men's company without thinking twice, but it has made some inroads as commendable therapy for high-pressured jobs, and it certainly beats drinking. In New York City, needlework classes have been held for men.

More than most businesses, a hobby shop must answer your personal needs. If you are satisfied, your customers will be, too.

Odd-Lot Plywood Merchandising

In this do-it-yourself age, providing a product or service for weekend carpenters can be very profitable even when business in general is bad. There will always be people building cabinets, tables, or sleeping lofts (and hundreds of other items) custom-tailored to their homes and incomes.

Home improvements require building materials in far smaller amounts than most lumberyards and industrial suppliers are willing to sell. Your business is "distinctive," practically non-competitive, because you can provide your customers with exactly what they seek. The exact size (no matter how odd-ball) and the exact quantity (even if only one) can be custom-cut to their specific needs. Most lumberyards are not equipped for that type of business, or discourage it.

A typical transaction—and a typical problem—might begin with a customer who wants half a regulation 4 x 8 panel of ¾ inch fir plywood. You'll gladly divide the regulation panel—that's what your business is all about—

which you have purchased at the going wholesale price, ten dollars. The retail price for the complete panel is fifteen dollars, or seven dollars and fifty cents to the customer who wants half of one. He will also pay a small charge for trimming; perhaps five cents a square foot.

The next customer may want half a 4 x 8 panel of fir birchwood, and so on.

Instead of making a large profit from a few important customers, you can do as well by running a bustling store attracting many small customers. Odd-lot plywood merchandising has many advantages industrial suppliers don't. Your profit won't be narrowed by discounts on large orders. Your sales will be strictly cash and carry.

On the other hand, supplying materials to home builders requires a large stock of varied materials. Suburbanites build fences, school children have shop projects, businessmen need signs, lawyers take courses in using a saw, women find an interesting piece of wood and want to turn it into something useful, divorced people improve their new homes to save money.

Your customers expect a choice between plywood or hardwoods; black or yellow plastic. Part of your business is keeping an eye on interior decorating trends. But much of your attention will be devoted to personal service. Amateur carpenters are often inexperienced. You will not only cut panels to order, but be called on for advice in finishing them. In a busy shop this requires at least one other employee, and perhaps as many as five.

Aside from the building materials that are basic to your business, an odd-lots merchandiser can profit from others' mistakes: a contractor who has cut one thousand pieces of Formica too short, a woodworker who has cut pine doors with the grain horizontal rather than vertical, fifteen hundred plywood remnants left over from a custom-trimmed large order, legs for a table design that was never put into production.

You can pass on the bargain from acquiring large lots of surplus at a low price to your own customers. Some of these lots won't move, and you, in turn, will have to seek a buyer for them rather than take up space that could be filled with profitable merchandise.

Unlike construction contractors, however, your customers don't have to stick to their original plans to the last detail. They won't lose a customer by buying metal handles for cabinets because the price is low.

Your publicity doesn't have to be slick, but it should be constant. One way to move those odd-lots of surplus is advertising them where potential customers congregate. Special materials for boats can be advertised on a flyer hung at a local yacht club. A builders' association or hobbyists' newsletter makes an excellent advertising outlet.

Your most popular materials will be plywood and Formica, together possibly coming to 60% of your gross sales. Other materials that can make a significant profit are hardwoods (10%), specialty plywoods (10%), and hardware (15%). Trimming fees can come to another 10%. You might also charge for a delivery service. Put aside a corner for carpentry literature. There's a lot of it around, and it can save you time in answering questions, and it takes little space.

Odd-lots merchandising is a demanding business. But in time you'll have the satisfaction of knowing you've made so many homes and businesses pleasanter places to be.

Marketing Specialty Foods

Americans are better known for the enormity of their appetite than for the quality of the food they eat. But our national craving for dried-out burgers on soggy buns coexists with new tastes we've acquired as inquisitive travelers and health-conscious weight-watchers. Furthermore, processed foods have so permeated our lives that truly farm-fresh produce has been raised to gourmet status.

Roadside Vegetable Stands

A vast market for special foods exists throughout the nation—in rural areas, in cities, in suburbs. A food specialty is almost anything not generally available in supermarkets or food stores by the standards of quality, uniqueness, and price. The best-known example is fresh produce sold from roadside stands. Fresh tomatoes, corn, squash, and apple juice have always been among the trophies vacationing city dwellers have brought home. Formerly, price was an all-important factor—with no middlemen, price was expected to be considerably lower. Today, city residents will often pay city prices for ripeness, freshness, and taste. Tanned from the sun, windburned from skiing, they look for eggs that have not been injected with antibiotics, tomatoes that have not been ripened with gas, fruit that hasn't been months in storage.

A roadside stand can be profitable along highways en route to tourist areas, entertainment or sports centers. This can be a weekend or daily business, established on a cooperative basis with other food growers.

Home-Baked Delicacies

Going one step further, those fresh, delicious foods can become ingredients for a home-cooked specialty, a pie, a soup, a cake, candy. Find a wholesaler for plastic or strong, tight waxed cardboard containers, and cook away. As the raw materials for your own magical recipes and home-grown produce can triple in price because of the added labor and ingredients, you might sell bundles of wood, too.

If you make an ambrosial chocolate cake, pecan pie, and Viennese torte, but don't want to open your own shop, explore local restaurants that are looking for home-baked products they cannot make in their own kitchens— new restaurants, perhaps, or established ones seeking to improve or change their menus.

Have business cards or hand bills made and distribute them to the big hotels in town, the chamber of commerce, and restaurants. If they don't sell your products directly, they can give invaluable word-of-mouth publicity. Someone owns a vacation retreat in your community, and plans to celebrate a big occasion—an anniversary. He might know local stores.

Through baking industry magazines, you can obtain the names of suppliers for special decorations, such as figures for wedding cakes, bells, and arches.

After your pies have become part of the biggest events in town, the next step might be an enlarged catering business. If you're a versatile soup-to-nuts gourmet cook in a moderately well-to-do area, there's a demand for excellent meals that need only heating by the host. Again, weekend home owners who have come to relax, not cook, are promising customers. Though French cooking is as natural to you as walking, don't neglect any ethnic cooking skills, whether your background is Norwegian, Chinese, Italian, or Hungarian. Publicize your goulash, torte, or cabbage soup as specialties.

An increasingly popular and profitable variant of this direct relationship between grower and consumer goes one step further. People yearning for a day in the country frequently enjoy spending it picking fruit. It's a fine labor-saving device for the grower, too, who supplies boxes, ladders to reach tree branches, and transports people to and from the groves. Your harvesters buy whatever they've picked at a checkout point, where their crates are weighed. Again, the grower charges less per pound of strawberries, apples, or peaches than retail, his price need be only slightly less—what would go to the middlemen he keeps, not to mention the pickers he hasn't had to hire.

Your Own "Home Foods" Restaurant

Homemade delicacies can be the basis of your own restaurant, a small one along a well-traveled road. But if you go to the expense of a restaurant, be sure its appearance quickly appeals to the eye of drivers riding past. The air of a country inn, with a cheerful, immaculate interior and checkered curtains will attract tired, hungry riders dreading yet another meal at usual, unimaginative roadside chains.

If you're an inveterate fisherman, the same can be done with seafood—fresh clams on the half shell along a road can be a most refreshing break from driving on a hot summer's day. Packaging seafood, of course, is a more difficult undertaking.

Some of the finest native American cooking is now being done in the name of health foods. Those strong, honest fruit breads, sweets made with honey or molasses rather than refined sugar or nuts, coconuts, sesame seeds, rich yogurts sweetened with homemade jams. You don't have to be a vitamin fetishist to love every invigorating, wholesome biteful. If you don't know how to make food that makes people feel as if they're solving their own personal environmental problems, buy one of the many cookbooks on natural foods and learn. Again, in a rural area, you're more likely to get the organic, unpreserved raw foods you need to begin with. Natural foods on sale a few feet from the big country kitchen where they were made will lure health-conscious travelers.

Explore possible outlets—restaurants, and retail shops (don't forget department store food sections) in nearby convenient delivery areas.

Health food restaurants and stores are a variant of the small, unpretentious "home cooking" type of restaurant. They specialize in hearty soups, salads, and, in general, feature non-meat menus (although fish frequently is served). Rather than serve a wide variety of food each day, they will stretch the variety over a week, featuring two or three different soups a day; ten or more during a week. In one such restaurant specializing in soups, chili is a staple, for customers who want solid food. The menu fits the size of the kitchen and the shoestring budget of the owners, assures customers the fare is always fresh, and combines low prices with a pleasant environment. To attract customers on weekend nights, many of these new-style home cooking eateries have jazz groups and good, local singers and musicians who want an audience and will either forgo a fee entirely or will settle for a small payment. You can add a $1 cover charge or encourage a tip for the musicians. A sampling of prices you'd charge: a cup of soup, 75¢; a bowl, $1.25-$1.75; chili, $1.50; dessert, $1.00-$1.50.

High quality can make the difference between success and failure; between the same old thing and an eatery that catches on.

Ice Cream Store

Yours may not be the only ice cream or pizza parlor in town, but you can lure hordes of people with rich, homemade ice cream (don't hide the machine you make it with and keep the cream, milk, and ingredients in a glass refrigerator case) in many exotic flavors. A tiny ice cream store in New York City attracted long lines of ice cream lovers—twenty five people waiting isn't unusual. The recipe for their homemade ice cream was actually a franchise bought from a popular hole-in-the-wall ice cream specialist in San Francisco.

Pizza

No food has proven as versatile as the basic pizza. And few pizzas have proven as popular as the Hawaiian pizza invented in California. Lured by the unexpected which has become a kind of American version of a tarte—a dough shell containing almost anything edible. A California variation that at first attracted tasters with an attention-getting combination is a Hawaiian pizza, made with pineapple and ham. But a catchy idea must be followed up with good taste and value, in order to beat the competition. If you put more and better cheese, tomato sauce, sausages, or pineapple on your dough, depend on the pizza grapevine (and some advertising) to lure customers, in spite of the presence of four other pizza parlors within half-a-mile of yours.

If you enjoy food and are experienced in preparing it, don't hesitate to start a business of your own. But *do* pause to learn the pitfalls ahead. They will be much less so if you can foresee problems and know what you are doing.

And remember the legendary success story of Mrs. Rudkin, who began by grinding wheat in a coffee mill to make her own homemade bread for a sickly child. When her family lost their source of income during the Depression, her fresh, wholesome, rich bread which she kneaded by hand became their livelihood. The cost per loaf was high for those days, but twenty five cents a loaf didn't phase customers who wanted pure butter, whole milk, natural vitamins, and texture in their bread. Today, Mrs. Rudkin's business still thrives as Pepperidge Farm Bread, one of the largest mass-producing quality bread-making firms.

And there's always room for another success story.

Operate An Advertising Specialty Sales Business

The basic importance of advertising specialties is that there is no "waste readership" problem (as, for example, in publication advertising). The advertising specialty is "appreciated" . . . it reaches exactly whom you want it to reach . . . and it flashes your name to your customer constantly, over a period of time.

The successful advertising specialty salesman sells "ideas" not a specific item. Hence, in seeing the prospective customer, he endeavors to understand his business problem and to solve it, by showing him the exact type of advertising specialties that can fit his specific need.

Distribution

Even more important, the successful advertising specialty salesman will also point out methods for "distribution"—specific ways the prospect can send out or "distribute" the specialty items to his trade to obtain maximum benefits from them.

In a previous issue of *Successful Selling,* we discussed the general aspects of Advertising Specialty Selling, including types of advertising specialties available, and recommended selling methods.

We subsequently received numerous requests from salesmen asking, "Can you supply us with specific examples of how advertising specialties have been sold to various types of businesses? This will aid us greatly in applying these methods to our own sales approaches."

Actual Examples Listed

Therefore, we have compiled a list of actual successful case histories—listed below. They will help to "nudge" your own ideas for your own advertising specialty prospects.

Problem #1: A fishing lure manufacturer had a problem of how to focus his trade name in the customer's mind. Normally, the customer buys the lure—not the name.

Salesman's Recommendation: Supply stores with Advertising Rulers "to measure fish for legal size and limit" (copy to be changed according to states) imprinted with firm's lure name.

Distribution: Given free to sporting goods stores for free customer distribution.

Problem #2: How to encourage return patronage business for a grocery store?

Salesman's Recommendation: Since it was nearing the first of the year, supply each customer with a desk calendar. This conveys a constant reminder of the store's name and phone number.

Distribution: Calendar was placed in customers' shopping bags for a period of two weeks.

Problem #3: Newly-opened shoe store desired to dramatize its grand opening . . . also to provide an ever-handy name reminder.

Salesman's Recommendation: Since customers were "adult" . . . give free nail files in attractive leather cases (imprinted with firm's name and address).

Distribution: These were distributed to those making purchases in store during opening day.

Problem #4: A clothing store sought methods for building good-will and obtaining continued patronage.

Salesman's Recommendation: Give free billfolds to customers. The bill-folds to be embossed with store's name. Inside (in money flap) is inserted message reading: "Our clothing values put extra money in your pocket."

Distribution: Inserted in pockets of suits. Customer was grateful for this unexpected "bonus"; also received "impact" store's name whenever he used the wallet.

Problem #5: A wholesaler wanted to stimulate his salesmen to sell more.

Salesman's Recommendation: Conduct a contest, with winner getting a two-week vacation in Las Vegas. To "spur on" salesmen's efforts, send them regular mailings—each to contain a reminder of Las Vegas. For example: Letter #1 to contain a miniature roulette wheel; Letter #2, a combination lighter-roulette wheel; Letter #3, a gambling table "odds" sheet; Letter #4, a pair of dice, etc.

Distribution: Six different advertising specialty items were purchased, sent to the salesmen once a week, creating appropriate contest "atmosphere."

Problem #6: A farm co-op wanted to "remind" farmers about his services and to encourage their phoning.

Salesman's Recommendation: Supply customers with a scenic twelve-sheet wall calendar, with room in each daily block for farmer to inscribe his milk and egg production.

Distribution: Supplied to each of their member stores. Given free to each farmer visiting the store.

Problem #7: A manufacturer sought a "door-opener" to help their sales-men get in to see department store buyers . . . to win their good-will and preferential treatment.

Salesman's Recommendation: Supply buyers with a ballpoint pen, imprinted with buyer's name (also store's name).

Distribution: A card was first sent to the buyer advising him that an attractive pen was being imprinted with his name—and asking him to verify correct spelling of his name. This "focussed" buyer's attention on the gift ... incurred his good-will ... helped salesman get in to see him.

Problem #8: A wholesaler needed some method for getting salesmen past secretaries who "blocked" his path toward seeing her boss.

Salesman's Recommendation: Give secretaries a small vial of perfume (pinned on a card with a message thanking the secretary for her cooperation).

Distribution: This was handed to secretary by the salesman as he visited the various offices.

Problem #9: A restaurant (just starting business) sought an opening-day promotion to help cultivate "family" trade.

Salesman's Recommendation: "Orchids from Hawaii" should be given to each woman patronizing the restaurant during opening day (note attached to orchid contained restaurant advertisement).

Distribution: This give-away was advertised in newspapers, also in the restaurant window, also via direct mail.

Problem #10: A liquor dealer was losing his customers to a shopping center, and was hard-pressed to cope with this competition.

Salesman's Recommendation: Supply customers with coasters (imprinted with liquor store's name, address, and phone number)—for easy ordering.

Distribution: A mailing was sent out containing a "gift card." Customer, on presenting gift card in store, received coasters.

Problem #11: A magazine wanted to pinpoint its various "closing dates" to advertisers and advertising agencies.

Salesman's Recommendation: Supply advertisers with wall calendar that had closing dates printed in the various date boxes. Hence, they would always have it available for quick, easy reference.

Distribution: Mailed to prospects, with accompanying letter that explained how to best use the calendar for "closing date" reference.

Problem #12: A bank desired to cultivate the trade of children, reasoning that "if you develop the child, you develop the adult."

Salesman's Recommendation: Piggy banks were given to the child with each new account opened by child or parent.

Distribution: Mailings were sent announcing these give-away piggy banks. These were also publicized by newspaper ads and bank window signs.

Problem #13: A manufacturer wanted to get across the "oldness" and reliability of its organization.

Salesman's Recommendation: Use facsimile Confederate bills to dramatize "oldness" of the firm.

Distribution: A letter was sent to depositors and prospects (accompanied by Confederate bill). Letter stated: "When the original of this bill was first distributed, our firm was already five years old . . .," etc.

A baseball catcher must be "alert" to catch the pitcher's signals. Similarly, the Successful Advertising Specialty Salesman is always alert to catch "signals" about prospect's business problems—enabling him to recommend the most effective specialties for his needs.

5.

421 DIFFERENT MAIL ORDER BUSINESSES

The mail order business offers opportunities provided by few other types of businesses, because:

- It can be operated from practically any place and at any pace.
- It can be implemented with minimum capital.
- It offers growth potential—it's the type of business that can pay "annuities."
- It can be operated by practically anyone—spare time or full time.
- You can operate a mail order business to realize a full-time income or as a means of supplementing income.
- You can obtain customers nationally, even internationally.
- Little experience is required.
- It's the type of business that can remove you from the eternal "rat race."
- Personalities are not a factor in this business.
- Collection problems are minimized, in view of the impersonalness of this type of business.
- Can be handled by a husband and wife team.
- Appeals to diverse income groups, life styles, and age segments.
- Greater demands on available time, more working wives, create a need for convenience buying.
- Appetites to buy always exceed time and money allocated to conventional shopping. Mail order brings the store to the prospect.

According to a study reported in a mail-trade magazine, 30% of all mail order persons began with a capital of less than five hundred dollars, while another 30% commenced with five hundred to three thousand dollars.

There is a fascination and mystique to the mail order business. I recollect that on leaving college, I obtained my first job with Sears and Roebuck Company in Chicago, a company that had built its wealth from mail order. The first day of my employment, I and several other neophyte employees were summoned to the president's office. He discussed what he considered to be the Sears Roebuck philosophy, saying: "You should know that the entire edifice of the multi-billion dollar mail order business of Sears and Roebuck is built on one human factor—'mystique.' The 'mystique' of the package that was coming to them in the mail. What was it going to look like? This 'anticipation' is what builds the thrill, drama, and excitement. From the moment the package is opened, the mystique is gone . . . ."

Selecting the Idea

There are mail order ideas all around you—it's a matter of looking. You'll find them in your local newspaper, in your corner store merchandise display, in your local department store, in your classified telephone book.

Criteria for selecting a mail order item includes:

- Is it distinctive? Does it provide something that is normally difficult to obtain?
- If not unusual, does it provide a sought-after service. For example: A New Jersey company, Habands, has built a flourishing business in the mail order of wearing apparel. Their secret of success is the "convenience of service" that they offer to their customers, at a budget price.
- Regional Identification Products, for example: cheeses and salamis from Wisconsin, Indian craftsmanship from New Mexico, steaks from Chicago stockyards, fish products from Boston.
- Specialties. These comprise products that are exclusive with you, or non-merchandised previously on a national basis.
- Novelty items—for example: personalized records and story books (generally designed for children), etc.
- Instruction courses. These comprise courses on a variety of subjects that teach the reader "how to do it." It is advisable that prior to selling instruction courses via mail you check pertinent legalities in various communities.
- Home products. These comprise products that are home-prepared, nostalgic. For example: cookies, jellies, candies, pies.
- Personal products. Examples of these are photo blowups, orthopedic products, skin preparations, marriage manuals, etc.

- Products derived from your own experience. For example: the electronics-oriented person who offered do-it-yourself electronic kits. Or the successful builder who mail ordered his "success secrets" to other builders.
- Does it fill a need? For example: During recession periods, people seek new careers or ways to supplement their earnings. There is consequently an increased responsiveness to money-making or vocational instruction courses that can help attain these objectives.
- It is timely? Does it conform to important current needs? For example: During the recent gas shortage period, gas was often siphoned from the tanks of parked cars. John Talbot devised a simple wire tool which prevented this siphoning. The product filled an immediate current need and over one hundred fifty thousand were sold in a comparatively short time. The Bi-Centennial celebration, also being timely, has enabled mail order tie-ins. For example: Mort Sobel sold nearly twenty thousand electric wall clocks that depicted the Boston Tea Party. And, conformant to the "natural living" rage, a flood of nature books, products, and services were marketed via mail order.
- Is it distinctive? For example: Huge profits were achieved mail ordering children's books personalized with "your own child's" name (plus the names of brothers, sisters, and even family pets). These were imprinted in the text as part of the story. It was a "distinctive" product that appealed to both parents and children. Another distinctive mail order venture: Intelligence Quotient (I.Q.) Tests. A questionnaire was submitted that enabled the self-checking of one's own I.Q. Distinctiveness is also achieved through "personalization." For example: Two successful mail order programs comprised; (1) personalized photo lampshades (with any person's photo reproduced on the shades), and (2) personalized photos on faces of clocks, and even pillows.
- Does it offer a convenience? For example, a kitchen device that grates, mashes, chops, etc., in one operation; or wearing apparel that can be ordered through the mail, saving time visiting stores.

How To Figure Costs

Normally costs are figured on a three-to-one or a five-to-one basis. This means that if a product cost you one dollar, it should be sold for at least three dollars and, hopefully, five dollars. This will normally cover product costs, mailing, etc., and give you an adequate profit.

Need To "Sample"

It is important, prior to plunging into your mail order program, that you should conduct prior tests. Do not, for example, mail fifty thousand at one time; the costs would be prohibitive and your product may have an inherent flaw. An initial mailing of, say, two to five thousand may give you a successful indication. If this proves profitable, you may want to mail ten thousand as the next step. And if this is profitable, you would then be justified in mailing fifty thousand or possibly even one hundred thousand.

In the following pages, a number of "tips" on mail-ordering are provided based on my own experiences . . . and the experiences of others. This section is not expected to be complete, nor intended to. To provide all the facts about mail-ordering, a complete course of instruction, in effect, would cover more pages than this book will permit.

In providing these pointers on mail-ordering, I'd like to acknowledge certain individuals whom I consider "par excellence" in this highly special-ized field. Their experience in mail-ordering has been nurtured over many years—twenty years and more—and has been proven by outstanding ac-complishments.

I refer, first, to my good friend Nat Sherman, the renowned tobacconist. He operates a retail tobacco shop in New York—yet is internationally famous, and his products sell throughout the world. He has achieved this through ingenious mail-ordering . . . sending out millions of catalogs each year. Mr. Sherman's salient advice is: "Offer a product that has quality, and is different, then let everyone, everywhere know about it!"

I refer, second, to another friend, Hubert Simon, considered one of the fore-most mail order authorities in this country. If ever the title "precisionist" in mail-ordering evaluation and implementation can be conferred, Hubert should be first to receive it, in my opinion.

Three other Sherman credos that have been proved effective: (1) Be liberal in offering free samples, etc., (2) Don't begrudge credit card costs—the added orders will more than offset this cost, and (3) Assess results of your first mailing—if good, double and triple the next mailing (after eliminating indicated flaws).

Promotions:

Mail order projects can be promoted through various media. For example:

1. Direct mail (sent to selected prospect lists).

2. Publication ads:
   • newspapers, magazines, and other media that reach your average prospect.

3. Radio and television:
   • usually seek to get quick phone responses.

4. Telephone contacts:
- where great numbers of such phone calls are made, it is often economical to install a Wats line (payment of flat monthly rate permits unlimited calls).

Media Selection

Select Advertising media that reaches the maximum number of readers pinpointed to the types of products or services that you offer. For example, you'd select a women's readership magazine (or a women's page in a newspaper) to promote feminine products (cosmetics, etc). Similarly, you'd select a men's magazine (True, Argosy, Popular Mechanics, etc.) to promote such items as body-building equipment, and other male-oriented products.

Ad Size

In determining the best ad size, you are usually governed by the size of your budget: How much can you afford to spend? As a rule of thumb, don't "plunge in"; it is often preferable to use smaller space, particularly at the outset (while you are undergoing the "trial and error" stage).

Also take into consideration this rule of thumb: If yours is a popular, "known" product (one that requires minimal explanation) you need less descriptive space than for an "unknown" product that requires more detailed explanatory data.

Sectional and Split Run Advertising

Both terms described below are important in mail order advertising:

1. Split Run Advertising: whereby your ad appears in "every other" paper rather than in all papers. This plan is often used for response testing, since you can thus test several ads under identical conditions; ads that move different copy, headlines, prices, art, etc.

2. Sectional Advertising: whereby your ad appears only is designated cities or regions, rather than throughout the total circulation areas of the media. Resultantly, you can direct your message to a specific city or region containing the specific marketing criteria and demographics that you seek.

Both of the above types of advertising enable you to conduct tests and, at the same time, achieve greatly reduced advertising rates.

Ad Position

Right hand page position, and right column top-of-page position attract maximum readership and thus constitute "preferred" position. You should also note these terms in designating the positioning of your ad:

1. R.O.P. means *Run of Paper*. The ad can be placed on any page of the paper at the discretion of the media.

2. "Requested" position: This terminology indicates that you have a "preference" for a designated place in the paper (at no added cost). However, there is no assurance that this position is available and that you will obtain it.

3. "Required" position: This mandates a required position on the page, and the media cannot publish your ad in any other position. (You often pay a premium of approximately 50% over the regular rate for such mandated position.)

4. "Reader"-Type ad: This is an ad that resembles a news-write-up rather than an advertisement. The only differentiating factor is the word "Advertisement" at the top of the ad. This often attracts readership in excess of the usual type ad. A premium rate of approximately 50% above usual advertising rates is charged.

5. Order fulfillment: Strive to fill orders within twenty to forty eight hours of receipt. Lengthy delays often cause rancor and cancellations.

6. Special inducements. It often helps to close your ad with a "final inducement" offer. For example:

   • Try it five days free.
   • Send no money.
   • Order on approval.
   • Risk nothing.
   • Purchase price refunded if not satisfied.

7. Testimonials: These are always effective. They convey credibility. The reader can identify with those who have already purchased the product.

8. Ad "eye-catchers": It is always helpful to include a decorative device as part of your ad design, that gets attention. For example:

   • small cartoonized illustrations;
   • interspersed spot illustrations;
   • boxed copy.

9. Basic ad appeals: The things that prompt most people to read your ad and buy your product include:

- Health—how will it make them feel better?

- Self-improvement—how will it help them achieve increased earnings, or be a happier person?

- Vanity—how will it help them look younger? Slimmer? Or more popular? (Remember the famous phrase, "They all laughed when he sat down to play the piano.")

- Profit appeal—e.g., "buy direct and save."

Direct Mail

Direct mail advertising usually comprises these basic elements:

- Outer envelope.
- Letter.
- Business reply envelope (or card).
- Order blank (this can either be part of the brochure—to be cut off—or a separate item).
- Testimonials (if available).
- Last minute discount offer (or discount slips).
- Warranties.

Where To Obtain Mailing Lists

There are many sources for obtaining mailing lists, inclusive of:

- Rental of customer letters (from other sources reaching some other prospects).
- Vital statistics (births, marriages, etc.).
- Newspaper write-ups.
- Phone books (both alphabetical and classified).
- Industrial and professional listings (the various associations usually have directories containing membership lists).
- Religious and fraternal memberships.
- Other mail order firms (rental or purchased lists).
- State industrial directories (generally available from each state).

National List Brokers

In most metropolitan areas there are list brokers who provide catalogs of available name lists. It is to your advantage to become acquainted with those in your area. Make sure that you affiliate with a reliable organization.

Below is contained a list of brokers in the New York City area who have been members of the National Council of Mailing List Brokers:

George Bryant & Staff
71 Grand Avenue
Englewood, New Jersey 07631
122 East 7 Street
Los Angeles, California 90014

Dependable Lists, Inc.
257 Park Avenue South
New York, New York 10017

Alan Drey, Inc.
600 Third Avenue
New York, New York 10016
333 N. Michigan Avenue
Chicago, Illinois 60601

Guild Company
171 Terrace
Haworth, New Jersey 07641

Walter Karl, Inc.
33 Maple Avenue
Armonk, New York 10504

Moseley Mail Order List Svce., Inc.
38 Newbury Street
Boston, Massachusetts 02116

Names Unlimited, Inc.
40 East 34 Street
New York, New York 10016

The Roskam Company
Box 855
Kansas City, Missouri 64141

Locating Product Sources

Product sources can be located in various ways. For example, your local classified telephone directory (which is probably your best, quickest, and most accessible source, particularly if you are located in or near a metropolitan area). In addition, most states provide state-wide industrial directories (often available at no charge or for a minimal price). Thomas Register publishes a directory that lists product sources on a nationwide basis. A catalog on "sources that will drop ship merchandise to you" is published by a company called Rutwards in Norwalk, Connecticut.

Permits to Obtain

There are various mailing formats that you should learn about. Unfamiliarity can cost you a lot of money and may mean the difference between profit and loss. For example:

1. Bulk mailing permit. This gives you a lower rate for mailing at least two hundred letters at one time, arranged and tied by zone, Procedural details are available from the post office.

2. Decide on how you want the mailing "stamped." For example: pre-cancelled stamps, metered mail, or envelopes with prefixed stamps, printed permit indices.

3. Open flap envelopes and self-mailers also help achieve savings when printed matter is mailed.

File Maintenance

1. Keying of ads: Ads are "keyed" to inform you of the source of a reply and which media "pulls" most. Thus you can compute cost per customer, per inquiry, or per dollar sales . . . which is vital in mail order advertising. You can't afford to continue to advertise in ineffectual media.

2. Methods of keying include:

   • Variation in name or initials; e.g., John A. Jones, John B. Jones, etc.
   • Variation in address; e.g., 30a Ridge Road, 30b Ridge Road, etc.
   • Use of Department number; e.g., Department 5, Department 6, etc.
   • Use of booklet symbol; e.g., "ask for Booklet B, Booklet C, etc."

3. Advertising Record Sheets: Example of Record Sheet for direct mail advertising:

Date	Name of Mailer	Title or No. of Circular	Number of Circulars	Price Paid	Key

4. Example of Record Sheet for magazine advertising:

Date of Issue	Name of Magazine	Amount of Space	Number of Insertions	Total Cost	Key

Front of Prospect File Card

Harry Porter **810 Temkin St.** **St. Paul 7, Minn.**	**Key 14**

            9/6/45   9/12/45   12/15/45
               1●   3●   2●

Back of Prospect File Card

States he is a mechanic   9/20/45   Book A $2.50 $2.50
interested in books on
small power machinery

What Price To Pay

There must be sufficient margin between cost and selling price to cover operating expenses and net profit. This spread between the cost of goods and selling price is called the gross profit margin. Here is an example of how costs and profits are figured, the standard "merchandising equation":

	Percent
Sales price	100
Cost of goods sold	- 60
Gross margin	40
Operating expenses	- 30
Net profit	10

Cost of goods means not only the prime cost but also freight or other transportation charges against each incoming shipment. The expense of doing business, including salary or wages to the proprietor, must come out of the gross margin. What is left is the net profit.

Assume you buy one thousand units at one dollar ($1,000 cost) and wish to mark-up cost price sufficiently to arrive at a selling price to cover expenses and net profit:

Estimated Expenses:

Advertising expense	$ 200
Proprietor's wages	100
Outside wages	50
Printing	50
Postage and wrapping	200
Total estimated expense	600
Estimated profit	400
Estimated expense and profit (amount to be added to cost)	1,000
Cost of goods sold	1,000
Estimated gross sales required	2,000

A selling price would be set in this calculation of $2 per unit. The mark-up would be 50% of the selling price. Percentagewise, the operation would appear as follows:

Sales ($2,000)	100%
Cost of goods sold	50%

Expenses:
Advertising	5.0	
Proprietor's wages	10.0	
Outside wages	2.5	
Printing	2.5	
Postage, etc.	10.0	
Total expenses		30%
Net profit		20%

Figuring Mark-Up

Mark-up should be based on sales and not on cost price. A glance at the mark-up conversion table which follows shows that a 100% mark-up on cost is a 50% mark-up on sales; also, a 200% mark-up on cost is a 66.6% mark-up on sales. A 100% mark-up on sales is possible only when the goods have been secured free, without any cost, and then sold at a price.

To show why and how a percentage mark-up over cost is different from a percentage mark-up on selling price, the following example is used:

Cost price	$1.00
Mark-up	+.50
Selling price	$1.50

Example: Desired mark-up on sales, 50%:

$$\frac{50}{100-50} = \frac{50}{50} = 1 = 100\% \text{ added to cost}$$

Example: Desired mark-up on sales, 75%:

$$\frac{75}{100-75} = \frac{75}{25} = \frac{1}{3} = 300\% \text{ added to cost}$$

300 "PLUS" MAIL ORDER PRODUCTS AND SERVICES

Following are a few typical lines and articles:

1. Devices and gadgets—Candid cameras, photo enlargements or enlargers, luminous materials.
2. Jewelry—Bracelets, rings (often of unusual design or materials).

3. Textiles—Remnants, quilt pieces; also wearing apparel, such as shirts, ties, raincoats, etc. (often there is an inducement).
4. Health and comfort—Arch supporters, exercising equipment.
5. Agricultural—Nursery stock, plants, shrubs, seeds; garden equipment and small tools.
6. Furniture—Fancy woods, items easy-to-assemble, light weight outdoor articles.
7. Machinery and tools—Small lathes, drilling and sawing equipment for the hobbyist and home craftsman.
8. Entertainment—Musical instruments, toys, games, puzzles, and novelties.
9. Collectors' items—Postage stamps, scarce items, such as early book editions.

Sale Of Supplies And Equipment

The small industrial producer, the small craftsman, and the home worker, all purchase materials and supplies to facilitate the making of articles for resale or providing services.

Sale Of Office Supplies

Begun in a very limited way, some projects of this kind have climbed into the big business classification. A ready market exists for small-quantity sales of stationery, printing, postal scales, filing and indexing equipment.

Subjects in the information-selling field, e.g., making money, increasing knowledge for pleasure or profit, how to gain prestige by being able to speak in public, how to play a musical instrument, how to learn speed typing and shorthand at home, etc.

Selling Services

Persons qualified in a trade or profession are often able to market their services by mail. For example:

1. Stenographic and clerical:
   • addressing and circular mailing
   • typing of manuscripts (sometimes with revision and editing)

2. Assistance in publication work:
   • writing of sales literature and information folios
   • editorial aid to authors, photoplay writers, and businessmen
   • printing, mimeographing, multigraphing, planographing

3. Skilled trade and professional services:
   - photographic work (as development of films)
   - commercial art work
   - patent attorneys (assistance in securing a patent and rendering of advice in the marketing of a new invention)
   - analytical chemistry (consultant chemists specialize in analyzing products and suggesting improvements, including better marketing policies)
   - economic advisers, as in the line of tax relief, especially helpful to smaller industrial corporations
   - advertising writers, who help business concerns with advertising problems
   - mail order counselors, catering to beginners, also small mail dealers who wish to perfect their methods and expand

4. News and information services:
   - current information bulletins and special releases, put out by specialized reporters situated in a strategic center
   - market analysis reports in investment and commodity fields
   - syndicated materials, as a column for newspapers

Self-Help Programs

Formulas are being successfully sold by mail. Many of them can be built around simple household preparations.

Help To The Handyman

This strikes a chord for those who are interested in making money or saving it. For example, anyone familiar with work in various trades—radio, electrical, carpentry, painting, and miscellaneous mechanical jobs—has a fund of information which might well be worked up into an inexpensive mimeographed treatise or series of them, including drawings and diagrams.

Writing For Profit

A large proportion of the adult population has the urge to write. These would-be authors range all the way from those merely seeking the "pride of authorship," to those who have the desire to earn a living at it. Also, to supplement earnings from their full-time job.

Application Of Chemistry

This offers a wide choice. For example, in the field of cements and glues, caulking compounds, liquid coating solutions and solvents. Not only is there opportunity in selling information in this field, but also in merchandising useful preparations of your own.

Hobbies

Hobbies range all the way from playthings to highly technical pastimes. Many people have hobbies which follow definitive patterns. Hobbies can become part-time income sources, and finally full-time occupations.

Health And Exercise

This is a subject in which a large percentage of the population is interested.

Mail Order Ideas

The following "ideas" comprise actual mail order programs gleaned from current mail order publications:

- Reading improvement
- Writing feature articles
- Writing short articles
- Needlepoint
- Cooking
- Catering
- Shoe bronzing
- Recipes
- Gourmet foods
- Exercise equipment
- Wine-making equipment
- Income opportunities
- Career opportunities
- Winning at cards
- Stamps
- Coins
- Second-hand equipment
- Exporting
- Save on taxes
- How to relax
- Ornamental iron designs
- Typewriter ribbons
- Carbon paper
- Office supplies
- Office equipment
- Typing instructions
- Toys
- Loans
- Telephone message transcriber
- Hypnosis
- Astrology
- Palmistry
- "Re-mailing" address
- Hydraulic jack repair
- Information research
- Pimples removal
- Reducing
- Figure improvement
- Neck massage
- Mimeograph
- Self-adhesive labels
- Quick copy offset printing
- Name and address labels
- Personalized pencils
- Rubber stamp presses
- Embossed business cards
- Typewriters
- Adding machines
- Calculators
- "Cartoon" instructions
- Sign painting
- Sign painting instructions
- Polished gem stones
- Treasure finding equipment

- Sporting goods
- Embossing
- Printed stationery
- Imprinted apparel (T-shirts, etc.)
- Sleep techniques
- Hearing aid batteries
- Shoes
- Wearing apparel
- Social Security numbers (on metal plates)
- I.Q. Tests
- Snow removal
- Window cleaning
- Cheeses
- Sausages
- Steaks
- Fruits
- Cakes
- Fire alarms
- Locksmith supplies
- Will forms
- Products from Japan
- Drafting equipment
- "Buy wholesale" products for cats and dogs
- Digital watches
- Directory of corporations selling new products
- Inventions wanted
- Invention protection
- Invention ideas
- Patent drafting, blueprints
- Inventions "Search"
- Home physical checkup method
- Self-improvement books
- Construction techniques
- New Testament home study
- Self-mastery
- Veterinary instruction
- Guide to medical schools
- Shortcuts to success practice guide
- Degree program in electronics engineering
- Piano instruction
- Auctioneering

- Plastic molds equipment
- Formulas
- Laboratory chemicals
- Chemistry and biology catalog
- T.V. screen enlarger
- Tobacco
- Cigarettes
- Pipes
- Hearing aids
- Recycled work clothes
- Watch and clock repairing
- Offer to buy gold, silver, platinum, jewelry, rings, diamonds, etc.
- Imported poster from Spain
- Gift catalog
- Home addressing
- Envelope stuffing
- Newspaper clippings
- Flower arranging
- Oil painting
- Swiss music boxes
- Poems, songs wanted
- Musical instruments "kits"
- Guitar playing
- Player piano rebuilding
- Accordian rebuilding
- Stereo tapes
- Hard-to-find records
- Shortwave
- Motion picture and sound equipment
- Color slides
- Photo finishing
- Camera equipment
- Binoculars, telescopes, microscopes, magnifiers
- Portrait painting instruction
- Glass blowing kit and supplies
- Make Tiffany-type lamps
- Make figurines, plaques, etc.
- How to sculpture molds
- Stained glass instruction
- Exotic lumber
- Making rubber molds
- Learning arts and crafts

- Watch repairing
- Bartending
- Collection agency operation
- Camera repair
- College degree
- High school degree
- Locksmith instruction
- Piano tuning
- Typewriter repair
- Extension and post-graduate awards
- Smoking equipment
- Sewing machine repairs
- Improve personality
- Aviation jobs
- Printing instruction
- Finger painting
- Electronics degree
- Diesel truck driving instructions
- Harpsichord playing
- Harmonica playing
- Build your own banjo
- Fishing lures
- Camping "trips" equipment
- Trampoline kit
- Cultivating powerful muscles
- Karate
- Barbell courses
- Marine engines
- Boat kits
- Canoe kits
- Fiberglassing
- Hang gliders
- Jet engine planes
- Motorcycles, bicycles
- Dune buggy
- Gas-saving invention
- Auto supplies
- Radar detector
- Auto theft protection
- Ring valve job
- Antique auto parts
- Automotive tune-up checks
- Auto polisher
- Increasing gas mileage
- Wheel alignment method

- Making gas caps tarnish-proof
- Lawn mower repairs
- Bicycle repairs
- Electric car building
- Fly traps
- Discount appliance parts catalog
- Windmill power plant
- Waterless land details
- Wind generators
- Swimming pool seals
- Unit for economizing on heating fuel
- Steam engines
- Home remodeling
- Solar heating for home
- Brass hardware
- Portable drill press
- Building a barn
- Picture framing
- Cabinet making
- Combating termites
- Clock kits, movements, dials
- Build log cabins
- House expansion plans
- Hydraulic gas device
- Learn landscaping
- Insect-eating plants
- Real estate and farms
- Overseas employment
- Creative job campaigning
- Civil Service careers
- Used clothing
- Become a mortgage broker
- Learn advertising business
- Make money with your camera
- Advertisement distribution to homes
- Raising earth worms
- Ginseng seeds for planting
- Suede, leather cleaning
- Magic tricks, jokes, ventriloquism
- Games, toys, puzzles, novelties
- Ship model kits
- Model airplanes
- Steam powered backyard railroads
- Antiques, relics
- Indian goods and curios

- Flap sanding wheel
- Carpet and upholstery cleaning
- Optical tape measure
- Lubricant, rust preventer
- Woodworking bench
- Collection Agency
- Sales letters
- Neckties
- Fruit preserves
- Sewing instructions (on records)
- Book exchange
- Learn foreign languages (on records and cassettes)
- Sailing instructions
- Invisible reweaving
- Venetian blinds cleaning equipment
- Restringing tennis rackets
- Sell to Uncle Sam
- Automatic needle threader
- Making costume jewelry
- Selling home products
- Aluminum awnings
- Plastic laminating
- Water softener dealerships
- Auto rust-proofing
- Decals, emblems, patches
- Automatic garage door opener
- Antique telephones
- Autographs
- Military medals
- Dolls of many lands
- Nazi war souvenirs
- Surplus property list
- Electric plating equipment
- Machinery, tools, supplies
- Machine shop projects
- Sand blaster
- Metal cutting lathes
- Engines, motors
- Live seahorses
- Pets
- Make money raising rabbits
- Raise chinchillas
- Poultry, game birds
- Frogs, fish, reptiles
- Earthworms, live baits
- Fishing secrets revealed
- Fishing tackles
- Leather, vinyl restoring
- Electrical appliance repairing

6.

74 BUSINESSES YOU CAN OPERATE FROM YOUR HOME... SPARE-TIME!

IF YOU CAN WRITE WELL ... MONEYMAKING IDEAS FOR ASPIRING WRITERS

Fiction Writing

The Plan:

Given fertile imagination, a knack for storytelling, and an ability to write, you are equipped to enter the profitable field of fiction writing. Some two thousand different publications are constantly in the market for this type of material.

How It Works:

Study the various writers' trade magazines on the market and familiarize yourself with the magazine markets and the type of stories desired. Then read several issues of the magazine that most fits your writing style and analyze the characteristics of the fiction stories it has accepted. Once you have absorbed the magazine style and requirements, you will be ready to prepare and submit a "flow" of stories conformant to their needs.

Possible Profits:

Payment for fiction stories varies according to the type of magazine. Pulps pay five cents a word and up, confession magazines three cents a word and up, and some first-class slick-paper magazines start their rates at ten cents a word.

Literary Broker

The Plan:

An enterprising housewife equipped with a typewriter and writing talent, converted her spare time into cash by criticizing, revising, retyping, and marketing manuscripts for writers.

How It Works:

Consulting writers' trade magazines, she familiarized herself with current manuscript needs of different magazines and book publishers and the material and style required. She then placed a small advertisement in her local newspaper, and later in several of the writers' magazines, advertising her complete writers' service. Manuscripts deemed unsalable were returned for correction, accompanied by her typed critical notes. However, if she deemed the article satisfactory in its submitted form, or after minor corrections, she would then retype and submit it to the magazine for which she considered it most appropriate.

Possible Profits:

Rates were twenty dollars per thousand words for criticism and revision, five dollars per thousand words for retyping, and 10% commission on all manuscripts successfully marketed.

Inventors' Bureau

The Plan:

Every city and hamlet in the country has its local inventors—and each is interested in marketing his invention. Enterprising individuals can earn lucrative income through representing these inventors in this marketing quest.

How It Works:

Establish an inventors' bureau; publicize the inventions and aid in marketing. Inserting a small advertisement in your local paper announcing your services will secure you a list of inventors. They generally seek such assistance. You can also be of invaluable marketing assistance by studying the invention, determining who would most likely desire to buy it, and then contacting these sources, either by mail or in person.

Possible Profits:

Similar services normally charge one hundred dollars and up for invention "evaluation" plus 10% to 15% of all proceeds that result from your marketing contacts.

Article Writing

The Plan:

Earn extra dollars by writing non-fiction articles for trade and business magazines. Interview enterprising merchants in your locality, make notes about their merchandising methods or interesting personal facts, and sell the articles to appropriate trade magazines.

How It Works:

Does your corner ice cream parlor have a clever window display? Does your neighborhood grocery use clever signs? Have you remarked on the pleasing service of your community bakery, or the unusual premiums given by your neighborhood drug store? All these make interesting stories for the hundreds of trade magazines adapted to almost every type of business. Study the various writers' magazines and acquaint yourself with current markets and the individual requirements of the various publications. Type the article neatly on standard size paper, double space, and include a front sheet which contains your name, the title, a resume of the article, and the number of words. Also enclose snapshots wherever possible.

Possible Profits:

Trade magazines pay from five cents to ten cents a word for desirable articles and from five to twenty five dollars for accompanying photos.

Ghost-Writers' Bureau

The Plan:

Become the person "behind the scenes" who writes a great variety of articles which are published under the names of others. Many people with writing talent discover that such a bureau provides them with an excellent means for earning money in their spare time.

How It Works:

Your prospective customers are legion, and include students, politicians, scientists, trade associations, and businesses of various types who must prepare articles and reports but who often need help in getting these written. Contact them personally, through letters or through a local advertisement. Offer to write anything desired; for example, speeches, letters, biographies, scientific reports, research topics, and publicity articles.

Possible Profits:

Charges vary with the time and effort required. Some average rates are twenty five dollars for a letter, fifty dollars for a speech, and one hundred dollars for a technical report.

Job Letters

The Plan:

"A friend, an unemployed engineer, asked me to compose a letter for him in application for a job. He got the job—and I got the idea that has enabled me to turn my letter-writing ability to good profit. I organized an 'Employment Letter Service Bureau.'

How It Works:

"Your prospective customers are unemployed people seeking jobs, and employed people seeking better employment. I reached these prospects by placing an advertisement within the Business Services column of my local newspaper, offering to compose forceful persuasive letters to be sent to prospective employers. After securing the customer, I studied his or her qualifications and listed experience, education, personality, etc. I then prepared my letter to present qualifications as strikingly and sincerely as possible, keeping in mind the specific requirements of the prospective employer.

Possible Profits:

"Payment is ten dollars and up for custom-prepared job solicitation letters."

Sales Letters

The Plan:

"Almost every business concern has occasion to send out regular sales letters to their customers. I solicited a number of concerns in my town and offered to compose their sales letters on a part-time basis. Within a month I represented ten different firms, with a good regular income resulting.

How It Works:

"To write a strong, persuasive sales letter, first study the concern and the product, and then picture in your mind a typical prospective customer for whom this product is intended. Write the letter briefly, but tell the whole story. Be conversational and sincere, appealing to the 'typical' customer you have visualized. With this plan in mind you should produce a splendid sales letter with forceful appeal. Of course, all letters should be typewritten—modern business requires it.

Possible Profits:

"I get a standard rate of fifteen dollars for each letter and, in several cases, performed my services on a monthly retainer basis, such as two hundred dollars a month (average of eight letters a month)."

Collection Letters

The Plan:

A young store clerk has boosted his income by selling to merchants and professional people a "collection system" consisting of a series of letters which aid them in collecting their delinquent accounts.

How It Works:

He composed a series of six letters which were briefly but forcefully written. They graduated in tone from a polite reminder to a stern letter threatening legal recourse. He adapted the contents of the letter to the class of business or profession to which it applied. He then sent a typewritten form letter to merchants informing them of his service. Since most business people have delinquent accounts which they are anxious to liquidate, he secured a good percentage of responses.

Possible Profits:

He received twenty five dollars from each customer for a series of six collection letters. In several instances he cooperated with his customers by selling his service on a percentage-of-returns basis, earning 10% of all money collected.

Amusement Directory

The Plan:

A Detroit housewife earns part-time money by reporting "what's happening" by way of entertainment in her town, through the medium of a weekly mimeographed amusement directory.

How It Works:

"Everyone's interested in entertainment and such a regular magazine struck me as appropriate. I sent letters to local theaters, night clubs, and similar places of entertainment, and they were glad to supply me regularly with information concerning their current programs. I then edited this material, classifying it according to the type of place and the entertainment offered. Thus, a person who was interested in movies could consult the movie section; others could turn to the section on night clubs, and so on.

"The entertainment places also placed advertisements in the magazine, since it reached a concentrated class of prospects. I typed and mimeographed the magazine and distributed copies in hotels, railroad depots, bus stations, and similar spots most likely to be frequented by visitors from out of town.

Possible Profits:

"The publication comprises twenty-five pages, with eight pages of advertising (at two hundred dollars a page). I net two hundred fifty dollars weekly from this part-time project."

Epicurean Journal

The Plan:

Everyone likes food, and almost every person likes to eat something "different" at a novel dining place. With this thought in mind, an enterprising Missouri housewife compiled an Epicurean Journal, listing interesting eating places about town.

How It Works:

She wrote up the outstanding restaurants in town, classified them according to their cuisine and location, and described any unusual history, decorations, or service that they offered. Editorial material told about the quaint Italian restaurant with its excellent spaghetti, the lively Russian Cafe and its heady vodka, the unique Swedish restaurant specializing in Smorgasbord. She profits in two ways: first, by selling listings of the places mentioned, at varied prices, depending upon the size and patronage of the restaurant seeking the listing; secondly, by selling the book itself, since it contains useful, interesting reading matter.

Possible Profits:

The books sell for seventy five cents each, and she disposed of some three thousand copies to the restaurants and to the public. Each descriptive listing sells for about twenty dollars, with one hundred restaurants buying listings in the book. She earns approximately twenty five hundred dollars for each edition—and publishes a new one annually.

Newspaper Correspondent

The Plan:

Writing up and submitting stories on local events to neighboring newspapers constitutes a profitable part-time source of income to one young man in Macon, Pennsylvania.

How It Works:

It occurred to him that newspapers in nearby cities would be interested in news from his locality. He wrote inquiring whether they could use a regular correspondent, and was told to submit his articles. He secured news on local events, including meetings, parties, accidents, etc. He also interviewed local hobbyists and interesting people for feature articles. Gradually the metropolitan newspapers regarded him as their regular correspondent for his locality and began to send him actual assignments.

Possible Profits:

He was compensated on "space rates," which often start at three dollars a column inch. In his spare time, he was able to earn from thirty to sixty dollars a week, and indulge in the thrilling work of a newspaperman.

Shoppers' Paper

The Plan:

A Chicago housewife, talented in writing and research, has augmented her household budget by writing up material for a shoppers' paper, distributed through several department stores in her town.

How It Works:

She wrote information of universal interest to women, including subjects such as household and beauty advice, dressmaking hints, garden and home information, latest dress styles. Supplied with this material, she then visited four department stores (noncompetitive) located in various sections of the city. She sold them the idea of publishing this information under their own names as a monthly Shoppers' Paper, to be distributed within their respective localities. Since the material was read by housewives, the department stores received effective advertising. Printing and distribution expenses were shared by the department stores on a cooperative basis. Such a project is also salable to laundries, dairies, and other concerns selling to women.

Possible Profits:

She secured one hundred dollars a month from each department store for each issue of the paper. Her earnings thus netted four to five hundred dollars a month.

Women's Club Magazine

The Plan:

One young housewife in Arkansas, a member of several women's clubs, felt that a regular magazine would provide interesting reading matter for the various club members. As a result she conceived the plan of publishing a women's club magazine.

How It Works:

She reports news of current and future activities for her club, mentioning as many names as possible. She also reports social items about the members and their families. In this way the magazine contains interesting reading matter and is eagerly sought by the club members. She has worked up similar publications for other women's clubs in her town, securing items of interest from their secretaries, or through personal interviews. Now local merchants advertise in the publication, since it reaches a comparatively wealthy class of women who, of course, are valuable shoppers.

Possible Profits:

The magazine sells for twenty five cents. Since it is mimeographed, it costs only five cents to produce, netting her a twenty cent profit on each copy, or twenty dollars for a hundred magazines. In addition, she receives as high as one hundred dollars for each page of advertising. She makes some three to four hundred dollars on each issue.

Apartment House Periodical

The Plan:

Writes an enterprising young man:

"I reside in a large apartment building within a metropolitan area. The building covers a complete block, and some five hundred families live here. The very size of this building inspired me with the idea of working up an apartment house periodical. I felt that the tenants would like to know about each other and would be deeply interested in such a publication.

How It Works:

"I canvassed the tenants and obtained news to be used as editorial matter in my proposed publication. I also contacted the building manager for news concerning the building itself, such as improvements, removals, etc. I then typed up this matter in magazine form and had it mimeographed. Realizing that local merchants were eager to contact the many tenants of the building, I secured their advertisements for the publication. Thus I established a thriving newspaper.

Possible Profits:

"The magazine sells for twenty cents, while each advertising page secures one hundred fifty dollars. As a result, putting out the publication bi-weekly, I realize profits of about three hundred dollars a month."

Convention Publicity

One young man in New York observed that many conventions met in the hotels of his city, comprised of business associations, trade unions, and similar groups. He reasoned that they would welcome local publicity, both in advance of, and during, their convention. He wrote to the secretaries offering to prepare such publicity writeups to be submitted to both local newspapers and trade publications pertinent to their field. In a great many instances they agreed to use his services. They would furnish him with advance copies of speeches and other data to use as reference material in preparing his publicity in their behalf.

How It Works:

It was fairly easy to obtain publicity in local and other media since in most instances prominent authorities in each field of endeavor attended their respective conventions (medical, business, trade, etc.) and the things they had to say was usually dramatic, "newsworthy."

Possible Profits:

He charged a flat retainer fee of five hundred dollars (paid in advance) plus one hundred dollars for each accepted write-up.

Local Odd Spots

The Plan:

Every town has its "odd spots"—a quaint lecture hall, an unusual night club, a unique opera house. Listing these places in book form has been the means of making a nice livelihood for one New York woman.

How It Works:

"The idea of such a book occurred to me when friends, visiting my town, always inquired concerning unusual places to visit. I reasoned that other visitors—and even local residents—would be interested in such information. I secured the editorial material through personal observation, newspaper contact, and library research. After working it up in attractive form, I made the rounds of prospective advertisers such as hotels, movies, night clubs, etc., since the books would usually be read by people visiting the town, in the market for entertainment. When I had secured a substantial amount of advertising, a printer agreed to finance the printing of the book. Distribution was made through hotels, bus depots, railroad stations, and newsstands.

Possible Profits:

"The booklets sold for thirty five cents each, and the advertising rates were two hundred dollars a page. I have cleaned up a lump sum of twelve hundred dollars on each issue."

Short Paragraphs

The Plan:

Are you the "fifty-yard dasher" as a writer, rather than "cross-country"? In other words, are you more skilled at writing short essays rather than long articles? Then a lucrative income awaits you in writing and selling short paragraphs to many newspapers and magazines throughout the country.

How It Works:

This material comprises a medley of subjects, such as science, literature, sports, history, art, and almost all other topics. The information is written up tersely and interestingly—about eight lines for each paragraph to be used by publications as "fillers," that is, to "fill in" small spaces between the longer articles when making up the paper or magazine. Most of the information for these paragraph fillers may be derived through research in encyclopedias, science books, and other volumes. After you have written up a number, classify according to topics, type them up neatly, and submit them to a selected list of publications. You will find a list of these magazines in any of the writers' market magazines.

Possible Profits:

Payment for these paragraph fillers averages about twenty dollars and since volume sales may be achieved, a good income is assured for consistent production.

Juvenile Stories

The Plan:

"My children and their young friends always listened to my stories eagerly, and I was told that I could improvise interesting and exciting juvenile stories. This started me on the plan of writing juvenile stories for magazines in this market, and I have augmented the family income considerably.

How It Works:

"It is really simple, if you find the knack, to write this type of story. The principal rule to remember is that it must be simple and natural and sound as if you were talking to the child before you. Create interesting juvenile characters, suspense, and a moral ending, and you will find that words just flow. As my experience grew, I worked up a series of stories based upon real characters which has been running for over a year in a well-known magazine. I would suggest that you first study the juvenile magazine for which you intend to write, to familiarize yourself with its editorial requirements.

Possible Profits:

"Juvenile stories sell at regular magazine rates of about five cents a word. With fair production, writing about six hours a day, I have been able to earn about fifty dollars a week consistently—and that money certainly comes in handy."

Columnist

The Plan:

There is always a market for interesting news and feature columns in many newspapers, and this can form the basis for lucrative part-time work.

How It Works:

If you have a knack for writing and a nose for news, it should not be difficult to create a novel column idea. Subjects may be theatrical news, local news notes, scientific oddities, food news, political analysis, and other subjects. Write up several specimens of the column you contemplate doing and submit them to your local newspapers. The more local color that you can inject into your column, the more salable it becomes. Each column should run approximately one thousand words.

Possible Profits:

These columns usually run each day in daily newspapers. The weekly payment is about fifty dollars—and you will find this work interesting and enjoyable.

Real Estate Magazine

The Plan:

Almost any real estate concern would jump at the chance to get an attractive sixteen-page magazine printed for them (under their own name) for distribution to their prospects. Yes, they'd be delighted to get this service, especially if it were free! . . . . You can furnish this, and also earn a splendid income for yourself. An ambitious young man tells how he successfully carries out the project.

How It Works:

"First, I compile the editorial matter for the proposed magazine. This comprises articles of interest to the home owner and prospective buyer, such as building maintenance, interior decoration, architectural modes, gardening, etc. I then contact my local real estate concern and offer to make up some three thousand of these magazines for them, imprinted with their own name —without any charge to them. All they must do in return is to give me a list of business firms they patronize, and a letter authorizing me to contact these concerns in their behalf, soliciting advertising for the magazine. A great number of concerns depend upon the consistent patronage of realtors. These include plumbers, carpenters, architects, masons, painters, decorators, and numerous others. They appreciate this important patronage and are willing to reciprocate with an advertisement in the magazine. I, therefore, found little resistance in securing enough ads to fill the magazine. Later I increased the profits of this publication by contacting real estate concerns in nearby towns on the same plan.

Possible Profits:

"The approximate cost of printing an issue of the sixteen-page magazine, using an inexpensive duplicating process, comes to two hundred dollars. The ads sell for one hundred dollars a page, so that two pages pay the cost of the magazine and eight pages of ads yield a profit of six hundred dollars a month."

LIKE RESEARCH?

If you like statistics . . . if you love rummaging through books . . . if you have a methodical mind, and a knack for sifting facts . . . then there are numerous ways to achieve extra earnings. In all fields of manufacture and industry information is required on innumerable subjects. *You* can gather that information. In some instances your assignments will mean delving into library volumes, in other cases personal interviews are required.

Profitable Hobbies

The Plan:

Almost everyone has a hobby, and almost everyone is eager to make money. Inspired by these two truisms, an enterprising young Chicago woman is augmenting her income in her spare time by publishing a pamphlet listing profitable part-time hobbies, and explaining how they may be converted into cash.

How It Works:

She analyzed the kinds of hobbies that are most likely to find a commercial market, such as woodworking, photography, writing, needlecraft, metalcraft, marionettes, etc. She then included brief "how to do" facts about each of these hobbies, and suggested where and how the products of this handicraft could be sold. The material for this booklet was, in the main, derived through research on the various subjects in her local library. Contacts of local dealers and manufacturers yielded much information as to prospective salability of the products. She first typed the booklet, then had it mimeographed, and eventually it was placed on sale through local newsstands.

Possible Profits:

It cost her about eight cents each to produce the booklet, which sold for fifty cents each. Deducting expenses of advertising, she was able to net fifteen hundred dollars during the first six months of sale of this booklet, and it is still attracting a large number of customers.

Genealogical Research

The Plan:

"Delving into the 'family trees' of townspeople—and supplying them with information concerning their remote ancestry—has given me a splendid part-time occupation to increase my income.

How It Works:

"We all want to know about ourselves and our ancestral origins. Whether your name is 'Tyrell,' 'Brown,' 'Henderson,' or any one of thousands of names, a complete sketch of your family history is available in the Genealogical department of your local library (if you reside in a metropolitan area). If you live in a rural community with limited library facilities, you may secure this information through the Congressional Library in Washington. After gathering the information, I prepared my paper for presentation to my customers. Another source of revenue also presented itself. My local newspaper, recognizing the 'reader interest' in this data, purchased my material for a series of articles regarding the derivation of townspeople.

Possible Profits:

"People are glad to pay five dollars for each report in this service, and I have been earning forty dollars weekly in my spare time through the enterprise."

Name Lists

The Plan:

"Gathering names has brought me big spare-time dividends," states an enterprising Nebraska teacher. She is one of a number of women engaged in this profitable, fascinating work.

How It Works:

"I classify the names according to 'buying habit' and type them up neatly. They are then ready for sale to merchants, industrial concerns, and professional people who use them for mailing lists. The names should consist of people or firms who are prospective buyers of the customer's products or services. The name lists are compiled through references in newspapers, in city hall, courthouse and Federal records, income tax reports, trade directories, and related sources. For example, names of newlyweds will sell to furniture concerns, insurance houses, clothing stores, and other businesses appealing to those about to establish a new household. Birth lists are salable to those who market juvenile merchandise.

Possible Profits:

"Name lists sell from twenty to thirty five dollars a thousand names depending on the value of the names and the difficulty in obtaining them. The same list may be sold to many concerns."

Odd Facts

The Plan:

Gathering odd facts enables one Indiana housewife to earn substantial spare time income.

How It Works:

She studies newspapers, magazines, books, encyclopedias, etc., and copies all items that contain unusual information, whether they pertain to people, plants, animals, trades, science, sports, or a variety of other subjects. She then transcribes this data into neat short-paragraph form and then sells it to popular-type magazines for use as space "fillers" and, in addition, to appropriate trade magazines. For example, an item about a plant family that eats beefsteak will sell to a nature study or a scientific magazine; an item about some unusual method for detecting criminals will sell to a detective story magazine, and so on. There is an extensive and consistent market for such oddities. Another approach is also possible. After you have compiled a list of these oddities, classify them according to subject matter, and sell these lists to writers for use as story plot ideas.

Possible Profits:

Payment for these oddities is usually a minimum of ten dollars each, but as high as twenty five dollars each when they are exceptionally interesting.

Advertising Research Work

The Plan:

By day he was a store clerk in a small Pennsylvania town. In the evening, however, his methodical mind and his typewriter became the tools which enabled him to make a good spare-time income as an advertising research man. If you like meeting people, asking questions, and finding out the "why" of things, here is a lucrative occupation which may be pursued almost everywhere.

How It Works:

The large advertising agencies and industrial research organizations are constantly investigating some phase of merchandising. This alert young man secured a list of their names from the library, and sent a letter to each of them inquiring for research assignments based on interviews. He explained that his business experience made him competent to ask desired questions, and to ask them intelligently. He offered to interview farmers, businessmen, housewives, professional workers—practically anyone, anywhere. Once he was accepted by an advertising agency or other concern as research worker, his services were solicited on a score of subjects. He was asked to ascertain the kind of breakfast food his neighbors used, on what day they generally shopped, whether they liked conservative or brightly-designed packages. This information enabled the advertising agency to form conclusions regarding the most suitable advertising campaign for that community.

Possible Profits:

He charged a minimum fee of six dollars an hour, or fifty cents an interview, whichever was the greater.

Questions And Answers Bureau

The Plan:

"The spirit of inquiry hits all of us . . . . Questions are always popping up in our minds and we'd like them answered. Many of these questions are statistical, requiring research. This inspired me with the idea of conducting a questions-and-answers bureau which has since brought me splendid financial returns.

How It Works:

"I began by inserting an advertisement in my local newspaper, offering to answer all research questions for a fee of one dollar and up. As I got into the swing of this work, I became more and more adept. I visited my local newspaper editor and offered to conduct a column answering all the various questions sent in by his readers. The charge would be fifty cents for each answer, which would pay me for my research. The editor agreed to the plan, since it featured a column composed of the most interesting items, at no cost to him.

Possible Profits:

"Inquiries sent to us are accompanied by self-addressed envelopes and average about two hundred per day. I have been averaging two hundred dollars a week, and enjoy my work very much."

Handwriting Analysis

The Plan:

By learning to analyze handwriting and thus give personality and vocational counsel, an enterprising Detroit clerk has activated a profitable part-time business.

How It Works:

He studied several books on the subject of handwriting analysis, until he became familiar with the subject. When he felt thoroughly competent, he inserted a small advertisement in his local newspaper, and in several magazines of general appeal, offering to analyze character and vocational possibilities based on handwriting. The applicant would submit a specimen of his handwriting along with information concerning himself, such as age, place of birth, and present occupation. A five hundred word typewritten report would then be prepared, giving him full analysis of his handwriting with suggestions on basic aptitudes and self-improvement. Since most people are interested in improving themselves, the response was widespread. Later, a local daily asked the man to conduct a column analyzing the handwriting of local notables.

Possible Profits:

Each handwriting analysis secures a price of five dollars. The main expense is advertising for customers and it is possible to earn in excess of one hundred dollars weekly doing this part-time work. Newspapers paid regular column rates.

Employee Letters

The Plan:

As secretary to the head of a large industrial concern, a young Chicagoan aided his employer in the writing of weekly "pep" letters to the several hundred factory employees within the concern. These letters were inspirational and instructive, intended to increase the employee's efficiency and enjoyment of his work. An Idea! Why not represent other concerns, and write "Employee Letters" for them?

How It Works:

These bulletin letters covered a variety of subjects of interest to the employee, such as factory safety, production efficiency, personal improvement, news notes, and similar subjects. He compiled a series of these letters and visited a number of large concerns, explaining the advantages of supplying these bulletins regularly to their employees. Information to be placed within the letters was secured through individual study of the organizations subscribing to the service, and also through library research in books on sales management, factory production, marketing, etc. The letters were written up in chatty, intimate, readable style, just as if the employer were talking to the employee personally.

Possible Profits:

The service is sold on a subscription basis, twenty five dollars a month for one letter each week. With ten different organizations as his clients, he nets a substantial amount for part-time work.

Research Agency

The Plan:

Operating a general research bureau to supply facts on many different subjects has brought a good part-time income to a librarian in Michigan.

How It Works:

"As librarian, people asked me thousands of different questions on all kinds of topics—and that's what started me in this work. I realized that many people, including writers, scientists, students, etc., would be in frequent need of such information. I announced my services through an advertisement in my local paper, and the inquiries came in at the rate of ten a day. Library research provided me with data covering all these inquiries. It's surprising how much information one can obtain through proper use of library facilities.

Possible Profits:

"Rates for my services depend on the length and difficulty of the topic. Minimum is one dollar, while intricate questions bring a price as high as fifty dollars each. Since most of my customers would submit their questions to me regularly, I built a splendid year 'round business."

Library Cataloguing

The Plan:

Many people have a great number of books which they have accumulated over a period of years. Frequently they want to refer to a particular volume for some specific passage, but become discouraged after going through several books. This fact formed the nucleus of a profitable part-time business of library cataloguing for one Minnesota librarian.

How It Works:

First starting out with her friends, and doing all their cataloguing, she then secured additional customers through an advertisement in her local newspaper. She cross-indexed the books on neat 3 x 5 index cards, according to author, title, and topic. This compares with the system employed by most libraries.

Possible Profits:

Her charges vary from fifty dollars to one hundred dollars for each cataloguing job, depending on the quantity of books. She is earning three hundred dollars a month from part-time work, and has secured consistent patronage.

BUILD YOUR OWN BUSINESS

". . . What you can do or dream you can do, begin it. Courage has genius, power, and magic in it. Only engage and then the mind grows heated. Begin it and the work is completed."

—Goethe

Regardless of your talents, and whether you live in a small rural hamlet or a widespread metropolitan area, there are dozens of pleasant, profitable occupations awaiting your performance. Some of them may be worked exclusively at home, while others require some supplementary outside contact. Some are more adaptable to smaller towns, while others may be performed best in larger towns. That little idea which adds a few extra dollars a month to your income, and eventually earns you a few extra dollars a week, may gradually expand and become the basis for a profitable full-time occupation.

Cartooning Course

The Plan:

She had a friend who was a talented cartoonist—she was skilled at writing. Together they organized a cartooning course which is reaping rich dividends.

How It Works:

Many people aspire to become cartoonists, because of the profit and glamour attached to this field. In addition, it is a form of art easily mastered by neophyte artists. The plan involved a series of twenty lessons written in so simple a style that a person with any talent at all could grasp the rudiments of cartooning. The explanatory material was first typed, then mimeographed. Specimen illustrations were drawn in pen and ink, or in wash. In this way the material for the course was assembled in attractive form for mailing to prospective students. Customers were secured by placing a short advertisement in the local papers and, eventually, by advertising in the classified columns of several national magazines.

Possible Profits:

The course of twenty lessons brought a fee of thirty dollars from each student, which yielded a net profit of twenty dollars after advertising and production expenses were deducted. This, then, left a substantial profit, especially since the pair now has about one hundred twenty students enrolled in the course, and new students enrolling regularly.

Correspondence Course Exchange

The Plan:

Thousands of persons throughout the country are prospects for correspondence courses. An aggressive young stenographer has boosted her regular income by organizing a correspondence course exchange during free hours.

How It Works:

She placed small advertisements in her local newspapers offering to purchase old correspondence courses on all subjects, e.g., engineering, radio, art, salesmanship, etc. She then placed a separate advertisement offering to re-sell these courses at greatly reduced prices. Replies to both these ads were many, and she was soon busy buying, selling, or exchanging these courses among her many applicants.

Possible Profits:

She assesses a 20% brokerage commission for the sale or exchange of these courses and as the volume of her business steadily increases, so do her profits. Today her side line surpasses her full-time occupation.

Co-Operative Mailing

The Plan:

An alert Michigan housewife added to the family income by organizing a Co-Operative Mailing Bureau at which she worked during evening hours. She provided a service which enabled three or more non-competitive merchants to group their advertisement mailings within the same envelope—to be sent to the same prospects—and thus greatly reduce their postage expenses.

How It Works:

"I first contacted five merchants in my community whose products didn't compete and who tried to reach the same prospect—the home owner. These included a real estate firm, an oil dealer, an insurance company, a furniture house, and a building modernization firm. I explained how, by grouping their mailing, they could reduce postage cost by one fourth without reducing the effectiveness of their literature. They were all enthusiastic about the plan, since postage comprises a major expense of direct mail advertising. I soon had fifteen of such co-operative groups as my customers, and an average of ten thousand letters every month. Eventually, many of them gave me their mailing lists and I did all the work.

Possible Profits:

"I receive five cents for each co-operative letter sent out and am paid extra for the typing and the stuffing of envelopes. I am now earning one hundred sixty five dollars weekly, spare-time."

Vocational Guidance

The Plan:

"Have I chosen the right vocation?" This problem confronts many people and has, as a result, become the means of a lucrative part-time income to an ambitious Chicago schoolteacher.

How It Works:

She first performed this service among her friends, and subsequently advertised in publications of general appeal. She offered to give complete vocational analysis for a stipulated fee. Upon receiving the application, she would submit a questionnaire, requesting data on the applicant's age, schooling, present job, etc. This data enabled her to gauge the qualifications of the writer, and to offer suitable vocational advice. Consultation of various psychology books yielded much information concerning questionnaires, vocational adaptability, and other necessary subjects aiding her in the work.

Possible Profits:

She charged ten dollars for each analysis. Receiving some thirty applications a week, she netted about two hundred dollars a week after deducting costs for advertising and miscellaneous expenses.

Important Dates

The Plan:

An enterprising student earns a substantial part of his tuition and expenses by maintaining an "important dates" file.

How It Works:

Hundreds of persons with poor memories have important dates that they wish to remember, including birthdays of relatives, anniversaries, distant engagements, etc. The young man advertised in his local paper, stating that he would send a reminder postcard several days in advance to anyone who would list these dates with him. The responses were very satisfactory. Remembering important dates is usually a "thorn in the flesh" to most people. His own memory was kept refreshed by an efficient index card system.

Possible Profits:

He charged a three dollar "enrollment" fee, and one dollar for each reminder mailed, and is earning three hundred fifty dollars a month for part-time work through this fascinating service.

Advertisement Clippings

The Plan:

"While in idle conversation with my local furniture dealer, he complained that he constantly 'ran dry' of good advertising and merchandising ideas for his store, and said it would benefit him to know what others engaged in the same line of business were doing to stimulate trade. Presto! An idea arose in my mind about organizing an Advertising Clipping Bureau, furnishing retailers with advertisements used by other merchants in similar trades. The project has been earning me a nice income.

How It Works:

"I consulted as many newspapers as I could get my hands on, both local and out-of-town, and clipped out all the outstanding advertisements. Then I classified them according to trades, e.g., shoes, furniture, jewelry, etc. These advertisements were then sold as a monthly service to the respective business concerns, and they thus had latest, up-to-the-minute references as to what others in their line were doing to stimulate business. I now have many types of merchants subscribing to my service, and am starting to advertise for out-of-town concerns.

Possible Profits:

"The service sells for fifteen dollars a month, or one hundred fifty dollars for a full year. My only expense consists of subscribing to many newspapers, of clipping and pasting, and of mailing. I net an average of one hundred thirty five dollars weekly."

Re-Forwarding Letters

The Plan:

"Fool Your Friends. Send Them Letters Postmarked *New York.*" This is the basis of a novel idea which earns profits for an alert young woman in New York. The project is workable in most communities.

How It Works:

She placed a short classified advertisement in one or two national magazines offering this service; as her responses increased, she placed the advertisements in additional magazines. The advertisement explained how applicants could "fool" their friends and derive much fun through sending letters to their friends postmarked with the name of her city. The idea appealed to many people as an opportunity for a "good joke" on their friends, and the response was gratifying.

Possible Profits:

She charged one dollar each for re-forwarding a single letter, and fifty cents each in quantities of five letters or more. She has been able to net five hundred twenty five dollars a month for a few hours' evening work each month.

"Native" Recipes

The Plan:

If you are a good cook, earn extra money by typing out your recipes of culinary treats that are indigenous to your region and selling them. An easy way is through church guilds, charity bazaars, women's exchanges, etc.

How It Works:

The recipes may be sold through the local guilds as a fund-raising enterprise, since they share in the proceeds. In organizing your recipe file, write up as many as possible—one hundred or more. They can be reproduced on a duplicating machine from typewritten stencils on 3 x 5 cards, and then arranged in recipe boxes. In addition to churches and charitable organizations, these recipe files, which make excellent gifts, can be sold through gift shops, etc.

Possible Profits:

Such files easily bring five dollars each on the basis of one hundred or more recipes attractively classified in a beautiful file box. Church guilds can sell the recipes for five cents to ten cents each, retaining 20% for themselves.

College Blue Book

The Plan:

Residing in Ann Arbor, Michigan, a town which contains the state university, a young woman, employed as a typist during the day, is earning a substantial part-time income through issuance of a "College Blue Book."

How It Works:

This book is based upon data concerning sororities and fraternities and their various members. It lists names and locations of their houses, and includes historical data, names and biographies of members, their scholastic activities, etc. This information is easily received through contact with the various fraternities and sororities. The book is then sold throughout the university area. Merchants are glad to advertise in it since the type of student who belongs to a fraternity or sorority is usually well-to-do and, therefore, a good prospective customer.

Possible Profits:

The books sell for one dollar each and are eagerly purchased by most fraternity and sorority members, comprising about 60% of the student body. Advertisements secure a price of one hundred fifty dollars a page, since the book has year 'round readability and is, therefore, valuable to the merchant. She earns about twenty five hundred dollars for each issue—once a year.

Entertainment Bureau

The Plan:

Residing in a town of some fifty thousand population, a young woman with musical ability and a flair for promotion has established a lucrative business through organizing and selling the services of a local entertainment group.

How It Works:

She got in touch with local people talented in various forms of entertainment, such as musicians playing orchestra and band instruments, ventrilo-quists, dancers, etc. Organizing a group of these entertainers and identifying them with a snappy name, she had letterheads printed and sent typewritten letters to prospects offering the services of this group for various social affairs. She specializes in cooperating with clubs, churches, and charitable organizations, and offers them a share in the proceeds of the entertainment in connection with their fund-raising programs. As a result, every club member becomes a salesman in her behalf, seeking to sell the ticket around town.

Possible Profits:

She receives a commission of 15% for her services in securing engagements, and has been netting some one hundred twenty five dollars weekly, part-time.

Laundry-Card Advertising

The Plan:

While unpacking a freshly-laundered shirt and removing the buffer card that laundries insert to retain the shirt's shape, a young Chicago bachelor conceived a brilliant idea for earning extra money.

How It Works:

"It occurred to me that, since these shirts were received by men, the space on these buffer cards would have advertising value to concerns selling men's products, for example, clothing concerns, liquor and cigarette companies, radio firms, and many, many others. I typed explanatory letters to a list of laundries offering to supply them with free buffer cards provided they allowed advertising matter to be placed upon them. Some twelve different laundries readily agreed—it saves them much money. I then typed letters to a list of prospective advertisers, outlining the benefits of their ads upon these cards and secured advertisers for each side of the buffer card."

Possible Profits:

The advertising space was sold upon the basis of "circulation." For example, he charged ten dollars per month for each one thousand "circulation." He netted six hundred dollars a month after deducting expenses.

Telephone Advertising Card

The Plan:

"I was irritated . . . and lo! I earned eight hundred dollars in three months as a result. The thing that irritated me was thumbing through a bulky telephone directory whenever I desired to phone my local merchants, public institutions, etc. For my personal convenience, I made up a list of telephone numbers most frequently consulted. And then came a thought—why not compile a quantity of cards with popular telephone listings for distribution to the public?

How It Works:

"On a cardboard about 6 x 9 inches, I listed some sixty names and telephone numbers of business concerns and public institutions such as police and fire departments, railroad and bus depots, post office, library. The card is slit on the top, enabling its suspension over the telephone for 'handy shopper's reference.' Merchants paid for having their concern's name printed upon the card, and only non-competitive concerns were included. I contacted them through typed explanatory letters. As the final step, I had some ten thousand of these cards printed and distributed to householders throughout the city.

Possible Profits:

"Each merchant paid thirty dollars for his firm's listing, so that the gross profits were eleven hundred dollars, of which I netted eight hundred after printing expenses were paid. This work requires only a small amount of time, and is repeated each year."

Who's Who Directory

The Plan:

Every person is interested in news about himself, and that formed the basis for a novel "Who's Who" Directory compiled by a clerk's wife in Seattle, Washington. She publishes one of these directories each season and enjoys a large subscription list.

How It Works:

She secured biographical data concerning the various personages in town, such as their antecedents, their business and social activities, etc. She then arranged this information along with photographs in a "Who's Who," which she offered for sale. The book was attractively printed with the name of the buyer stamped on each cover in gold. A local printer agreed to finance the printing of the publication on the basis of future proceeds.

Possible Profits:

She sold these books for five dollars each, while they only cost her one dollar seventy five cents each to print. She also received a "fee" of one hundred dollars for each biographical write up. Her profits, then, were substantial.

Wholesale Prices

The Plan:

"The pained ego of my small daughter inspired me to find the means of augmenting my income. She complained that her friend wore much prettier dresses than she. Upon questioning the friend's mother, I found out that she bought her daughter's dresses wholesale. She said it enabled her to manage nicely on a small income. Lo! An idea for making money.

How It Works:

"By adroit questioning, and canvassing of directories of various trades by mail, I managed to secure a comprehensive list of manufacturing and whole-sale companies who were glad to accept business direct from consumers. I subsequently listed their names, addresses, and products sold in classified form within this 'directory' which, when completed, consisted of forty pages. I then had this mimeographed. When it was ready for sale, I secured many customers through a short advertisement in my local papers.

Possible Profits:

"The companies participating pay a fee of fifty dollars each for having their names listed, while interested buyers pay one dollar each for the directory."

Hobby Collections

The Plan:

An enterprising clerk in Arkansas bolstered his regular income through the publishing of a "State Hobbyist" booklet twice a year, listing the names of hobbyists and their hobbies in his state.

How It Works:

He reasoned that most people have hobbies and are interested in knowing about others with similar hobbies. He secured the names of hobbyists by consulting local hobby clubs and through newspaper research. He then typed up this information, and persuaded a local printer to publish the booklet on a share-of-the-profits basis. Distribution of the booklet was made through local newsstands and by an advertisement in the local paper. The booklet was received enthusiastically because of its local interest and is now being issued regularly.

Possible Profits:

Sale price of the booklet is one dollar. He nets five hundred dollars from each issue of the booklet.

Names Of High School Students

The Plan:

Collecting and selling names of recent high school graduates has provided a means of livelihood for one invalid woman residing in Cleveland.

How It Works:

"I recognized the value of such names to certain concerns and advanced schools. I realized that trade schools would be interested in contacting these graduates so as to secure their enrollment. Various merchants, such as clothing concerns and jewelry stores, would also be interested in selling their products to these young people, since they have reached that age when they are interested in securing clothes, automobiles, and similar items. There are some twenty high schools situated in my town, and I secured the names of coming graduates by contacting these high schools. I then typed these names neatly upon individual lists, and sold them by typing letters to prospective purchasers outlining the value of these lists.

Possible Profits:

"Charges were two dollars fifty cents for a hundred names, and fifteen dollars a thousand. Since there are a substantial number of buyers, the profits are gratifying. In addition, several purchasers also requested that I do envelope typing and stuffing for them, bringing me an extra fee. I secure and sell new lists with a new graduation class each semester."

Intelligence Tests

The Plan:

"As psychology teacher in a large high school, I realized that most people are interested in learning about themselves, especially about their 'I.Q.' or intelligence quotient. This provided me with the idea of selling individual intelligence tests through the mail.

How It Works:

"I worked up detailed questionnaires, obtaining personal information from applicants. These facts included age, sex, biographical data, and reactions to various situations. Also included were questions testing their general fund of knowledge. Data for such tests was secured through studying various psychology books. I then inserted an advertisement in suitable newspapers and magazines, offering to supply such intelligence tests and thus provide the person with useful information concerning his abilities, his problems, and his work. Many people replied because of the interest and usefulness of such tests. If you lack experience, you may consider collaborating with a professional psychologist in your area to help prepare the tests and answers.

Possible Profits:

"My price for each of these tests was fixed at five dollars. My largest expense was advertising, about 50% of my returns. I was able to net an income of three hundred fifty dollars monthly, for pleasant work in my spare time."

Birth Lists

The Plan:

Collecting lists of local birth dates and selling them to concerns interested in using this information for advertising purposes, proves a splendid part-time means of livelihood for one housewife in Oklahoma.

How It Works:

Business concerns find such birth lists valuable. They can thus circularize these individuals with a congratulatory message on the occasion of their birthday, offer a "birthday gift," and tactfully include a sales talk concerning their products or services. This constitutes an intimate, personalized advertising appeal that proves very effective. The enterprising housewife consulted the birth records of her city hall for the data concerning local birthdays, and then typed letters to business firms explaining the lists, and the advantages of purchasing them. The response was immediate and enthusiastic.

Possible Profits:

She sold the names for thirty dollars a thousand, and issued a new and revised list each year. Her side line is bringing her a steady income of sixty five dollars weekly.

Translating Bureau

The Plan:

Versed in several languages, one alert, young New York woman organized a translating bureau which is bringing her nice financial returns. Her work consists of translating letters for the foreign-born citizens of the city, and also extending translating services to business and industrial concerns.

How It Works:

She placed a sign in the window of her home announcing this service; in addition she got in touch with persons influential in the foreign neighborhoods to advertise her work. Gradually she has added translating work from business and industrial firms receiving orders from foreign countries. She has made arrangements with a part-time staff of workers for translation of languages not familiar to her.

Possible Profits:

Rates vary with the type and length of the translation, ranging from three to ten dollars each. She works on a monthly retainer fee basis with several of the industrial concerns. Her net earnings are one hundred sixty five dollars weekly.

CAN YOU PROMOTE THINGS?

Do you have a pleasing personality? Do you like to meet the public? Are you a good organizer, and persuasive? If so, there are many, many ways for you to make extra money. You can sell yourself and your ideas to people. Personal contact is usually required—it is necessary that you get around to see people frequently.

Party Stunts

The Plan:

She was the life of the party, and adept at planning clever stunts that would guarantee the enjoyment and success of all affairs. This talent led to the profitable money-earning side line of selling party stunts.

How It Works:

The party stunts she created were novel and called for the participation of all present. For example, one such "stunt" consisted of a "Newspaper Party" complete with twelve invitations, four novel games and stunts, and unusual place cards—all prepared in journalistic style. Another party plan was entitled "Ye Merrie Olde England," and the invitations were illuminated scrolls, conveyed by a boy dressed as an English page. She secured customers by sending letters to a select list of prospects, and subsequently by placing an advertisement in her local papers. She also contacted organizations, clubs, churches, etc., to help plan the many events they hold.

Possible Profits:

She sold each of these party stunts for fifty dollars for the complete set. After deducting printing and other expenses, she netted thirty five dollars on each, and since she now has about fifty steady customers, is earning a sizable income. Occasionally she is asked by her customers to work up individual ideas, adapted to their particular parties, which she does for proportionately higher rates, depending on the amount of work required.

Barter And Exchange Circular

The Plan:

"It is human to swap things," states an enterprising young Texas housewife. "Then again, practically all of us would like to dispose of 'white elephants.' With these thoughts in mind, I organized a 'Barter and Exchange Bureau,' and issued a weekly circular describing the many articles that people in and around my town wanted to exchange, and for what.

How It Works:

"I secured my first listings through personal contact among my friends. One man wanted to trade a banjo for a rug; a woman offered twenty jars of homemade jam—for what?—and so on. I then sent sample copies of the circular to a general list of prospective customers, and it wasn't long before I had many subscribers and listings. Everyone seems to be fascinated by the opportunity of bartering things. My expense consisted of paper and postage only, since my typewriter produced the circular.

Possible Profits:

"The circular sold on a subscription basis of five dollars a year. A fee, based on the value of articles, was set on all sales and exchanges made through its columns. I thus profited in two ways. It is also possible, as your circular grows, to charge nominal rates for each listing."

Church News Pamphlet

The Plan:

"There were always many events and activities taking place in my church, and I felt that church-goers would like to be kept posted on them. This inspired the idea of a weekly church magazine which has increased my regular income, and requires only a few hours work each week.

How It Works:

"I approached the minister of my church with this plan and he shared my enthusiasm. He agreed that the magazine would weld the interests of his congregation. He also offered me the use of the church mimeograph machine. I then secured from him a report of future activities and news of past events, including a description of these affairs and the names of the persons in charge of them. I typed up this material preparatory to the mimeographing, and subsequently issued an eight-page magazine. It was distributed free to the church members each Sunday, as they left the church. I then proceeded to interest several local merchants in advertising opportunities of the magazine. These efforts were rewarded by two full pages of advertisements.

Possible Profits:

"My advertising rates were fifty dollars a full page, thirty dollars a half page, and twenty dollars a quarter page for each issue. Where they contracted for several successive issues, the rates were proportionately reduced. I averaged four hundred fifty dollars an issue above the cost of materials."

Travel Bureau

The Plan:

An enterprising stenographer is enjoying a nice supplementary income by bringing together prospective travelers and car owners who travel. They share expenses, and thus reduce traveling expenses by half.

How It Works:

Many car owners—such as salesmen—are constantly traveling along specific itineraries. She secured their names, and the approximate dates and routes of their travels, by explaining her service in a newspaper advertisement. Another advertisement in the "travel opportunities" column of her local paper brought her in contact with prospective travelers desiring rides on a share-the-expense basis. Gradually, as she became well-known, she was constantly phoned by car owners or travelers for arrangements, and has thus built up a flourishing business.

Possible Profits:

She charges a "flat" brokerage fee of fifteen dollars for each referral, and earns in excess of sixty dollars weekly.

Children's Library

The Plan:

She loves children, is fond of books, and is a good organizer. These constituted the personal ingredients that add up to substantial part-time profits for one small town woman in Indiana. She has organized a juvenile library and playroom in her home for local children.

How It Works:

By consulting her local librarians, she was informed as to what books were most favored by children, and then equipped herself with a supply of books at a small cost from a local book store. She also equipped this "library" with children's games, such as erector sets, sculpturing materials, chemical sets, jigsaw puzzles, and similar games so endearing to a child. The place has become an ideal rendezvous for the tots when their mothers attend their bridge clubs and is a social meeting place for all the local children.

Possible Profits:

She charges eight dollars a week for each child, and with fifteen members, nets about one hundred twenty dollars for pleasant, interesting, part-time work.

Good At Organizing?

The Plan:

A New Jersey housewife noted the paper disarray and clutter that characterized the desks (and general office surroundings) of most business executives and professional people whom she had occasion to visit. An idea! Why not enter the business of "organizing" them!

How It Works:

She placed small ads, wrote letters, and made personal phone contacts to prospective clients offering to "tidy up desks and files." The volume of responses she receive surprised her and she has helped to "tidy up" the heaped-up desks and cluttered-up files of over three hundred clients representing professions and businesses of all types. She organizes a simple filing system that enables quick placement or disposal of all letters and other papers that normally clutter a desk. The very simplicity of her system is highly appealing to her customers, who often are top executives of multi-million dollar corporations.

Possible Profits:

She charges one hundred dollars "per diem" per visit (some visits take several days and she charges multiples of one hundred dollars). She now averages twenty five thousand dollars a year . . . and has hired an assistant to take care of the growing number of her clients.

Town Directory

The Plan:

One young man, residing in a city of two hundred fifty thousand population has established a splendid part-time business publishing a regular "town directory," giving names and addresses of important institutions, locations of various streets, description of transportation facilities, and other important facts.

How It Works:

The book lists all public institutions, such as police and fire departments, hospitals, railroad and bus stations, etc. It includes, in addition, names of streets and their location; further information describes local transportation facilities and how they may be used most efficiently. After compiling and classifying this information, he then got in touch with merchants with the plan of selling them advertising within the proposed book. Such advertising has definite value, since the reader interest is constant, and the directory is thumbed regularly. A local printer agreed to finance the printing, pending receipt of proceeds through sale of the booklet and payment for the ads.

Possible Profits:

The books sell for twenty five cents each, and cost only five cents each to print up in large quantities. In addition, advertising yields a substantial revenue, selling for one hundred dollars a page because of its year 'round value. His proceeds amount to twenty five hundred dollars a year on the book, which is revised regularly.

Community Showroom

The Plan:

A farmer's wife is contributing to the household income by reserving a portion of her home as showroom, exhibiting and selling homemade produce, such as canned and baked goods, prepared by her neighbors.

How It Works:

She reached prospective exhibitors by personal visits and letters. Upon receiving products offered for sale, she arranged them attractively in a well-lit space in her home, usually the parlor. Subsequently, she sent out sales letters to a prospect list, describing the products purchasable within her home exhibit. Townspeople became accustomed to bringing their commodities to her home for sale, and she has established a permanent business.

Possible Profits:

She secures a commission of 15% of the proceeds on all articles sold through her home, and is netting thirty five dollars weekly in her spare time.

Newlyweds Journal

The Plan:

Over twenty five hundred dollars in two months! That's what an enterprising Washington housewife earned through writing up a premium booklet of interest to "just married" people, and selling advertising space to various concerns.

How It Works:

"First I wrote up my editorial matter. This consisted of recipes, household hints, notes on home decorating, etc., which would interest such newlyweds Armed with a 'dummy copy' showing this material in an attractive book layout, I visited prospective advertisers, such as dairy companies, furniture concerns, laundries, real estate firms, etc., and secured ads. My next step was to get names of newlyweds by searching court records and checking newspaper columns. Over a period of two months, I compiled a list of fifteen hundred such names. Upon the printing of this book, it was sent free to all these newlyweds. A printer agreed to finance the printing, because of my advertising contracts. Some twenty thousand of these books were printed and distributed during the next two years.

Possible Profits:

"The advertisements sold for one hundred dollars each page. Merchants were glad to pay this amount because it reached prospects who would need their products or services; in addition, the book had permanent readability. I netted some three thousand dollars after paying the printer."

Local Handicraft Exchange

The Plan:

Observing that many local hobbyists in her town produced a variety of fascinating items in weaving, sewing, sculpture, ceramics, etc., a college girl in Madison, Wisconsin, organized a local handicraft exchange and sales bureau, which yielded her exceptionally good returns.

How It Works:

She got in touch with all those who made such objects, obtaining full information concerning the items they made. She then listed descriptions of the various handicraft products and sent these bulletins to townspeople whom she believed would be interested in the purchase of these items. The handicraft objects were all fascinating and useful, and constituted a valuable asset to the home or person—either as wearing apparel or home furnishings. She sent out a new, currently revised handicraft bulletin each month.

Possible Profits:

She receives her profits in the capacity of broker, collecting 15% profits on the proceeds from all sales. Her earnings reach as high as four hundred dollars monthly.

7.

400 FRANCHISED BUSINESS OPPORTUNITIES

IF YOU ARE CONSIDERING ENTERING A FRANCHISED BUSINESS
. . . HERE ARE THE THINGS YOU SHOULD CHECK OUT

What is franchising? One good explanation is: "A system used by a company (franchisor) which grants to others (franchisees) the right and license (franchise) to market a product or service and engage in a business developed by it under franchisor's trade names.

Franchising has been a part of the legitimate American economy for years, and recently has experienced enormous growth, accounting for annual sales of nearly one hundred billion dollars.

One reason for this growth is that franchising has caught the imagination of the small investor and provides him the opportunity to become self-employed. The risk of failure is reduced when the franchisee starts in business under a successful corporate name and receives helpful training and management assistance from experienced personnel of the franchisor.

However, all franchising arrangements do not produce good results. The rapid growth of franchising has attracted a number of unprincipled operators who often take your money and give little or nothing in return.

To evaluate a franchise opportunity, it is suggested that you view the proposal in the light of the following points:

Who Is The Franchisor:

If the franchisor is well-known, has a good reputation, and has a successful franchising operation, you can naturally proceed with confidence.

You should find out everything you can about the operation including:

1. number of years it has existed;

2. whether the franchisor has the successful franchisees he claims;

3. whether he has a reputation for honesty and fair dealing with his franchisees.

A personal contact with franchisees is an excellent way to learn about the franchisor. Obtain the names and addresses of a representative number of franchisees in the particular area in which you are interested, travel to see them, and learn all aspects of their operation.

Take the opportunity to view samples of the franchise products or services, equipment, advertising materials, etc., and to obtain profit data and other pertinent information about the operation.

Beware of a franchisor who will not freely give you the names and addresses of his franchisees!

Consult Dun and Bradstreet, and the Better Business Bureau to find out the financial standing and business reputation of the franchisor.

Sometimes, a dishonest promoter will deceptively use a franchise name and trademark that is similar to a well-known franchisor. Be certain you deal with the particular franchise organization you are interested in and that the individual representing this franchise has authority to act in its behalf.

Be skeptical of franchisors whose major activity is the sales of franchises and whose profit is primarily derived from these sales or from the sale of franchise equipment or services. This may be the tip-off to an unscrupulous operator.

The Franchise Commodity:

You should determine the length of time the commodity or service has been marketed and if it is a successful promotion. Is it a proven product or service, and not a gimmick?

Decide whether you are genuinely interested in selling the commodity or service. Be skeptical of items which are untested in the market place. For future market potential decide whether the commodity or service is a staple, luxury, or fad item.

If a product or service is involved, be certain it is safe, that it meets existing quality standards, and there are no restrictions upon its use. Is the product or service protected by a patent or has it liability insurance? Will the same protection be afforded to you as the franchisee?

If the product is to be manufactured by someone other than yourself, identify the manufacturer and learn how your cost for the item will be established. If a guarantee is involved, determine your responsibilities and obligations as the franchisee.

Under the franchise agreement, will you be compelled to sell any new products or services which may be introduced by the franchisor after you have opened the business? Will you be permitted to sell products and services other than the franchise commodities, at a future date?

The Franchise Cost:

Find out the total cost of the franchise. The franchise promotion may only refer to the cash outlay needed to purchase the franchise with no mention made that it is only a down payment and other charges and assessments may be levied against you to operate the franchise.

If other monies are involved, how is the balance to be financed? How much will the interest be? Establish what the down payment is purchasing. Is it a franchise fee? Or does it purchase any other equity such as the building, etc.?

Where do you purchase equipment and fixtures necessary for opening the business?

Franchisors often attempt to secure income on a continuing basis through the sale of supplies to their franchisees. If this is part of the proposed agreement, how will the price of these supplies be established? What assurance do you have that the prices will be reasonable or competitive? Does the franchise agreement prohibit you from purchasing these supplies from a source at a lower price?

Another method franchisors use is to charge franchisees an assessment of royalties based upon a percentage of gross sales on a continuing basis, and franchisors often assess franchisees an additional percentage of gross sales to cover advertising costs.

Think of franchise costs in the light of your financial position. Consider the operating capital you will need to get the business going and to sustain it during the months when profits are small and expenses high.

What Profits Can Be Expected?

Many franchise arrangements provide excellent income-producing opportunities, but not all yield the fantastic profits promised. Many produce less profits than represented.

Since "profits" are the overriding motive for entering a franchise business, don't accept the promoter's word. Verify the profits for accuracy. Ask to see certified profit figures of franchisees who operate on a level of activity on which you expect to operate. Use personal contact with franchisees, quiz them regarding their financial rewards and evaluate their profit figures in the light of the territory and size of operation you have under consideration.

Training And Management Assistance:

Most franchisors promise to train their franchisees. The type and extent of training varies.

Inexperience and lack of training can produce disappointing results. Clearly understand the specific nature of the training.

1. Will the training include more than a manual of instructions, or of hearing lectures?

2. What is the length of the training and where do you go to receive it?

3. Who will pay your expenses for the training?

4. Will the training include an opportunity to observe and work with a successful franchisee for a period of time?

5. Do you believe that after taking the training you will be capable of operating the franchise successfully?

6. Will the franchisor furnish management assistance after the business is established?

Spell this out specifically in your contract. If advertising aid is promised, will it be in the form of handbills, brochures, signs, radio, TV, or newspaper advertising, etc.?

If you are required to furnish money for a franchisor-sponsored advertising program, what advertising benefits can you anticipate and at what dollar cost?

Some franchisors promise management assistance with periodic visits by the supervisory personnel of the franchisor. Find out the specific nature of assistance, the frequency of visits, and whether they will be available in time of crisis or when unusual problems arise.

The Franchise Territory:

This is a critical factor to consider in evaluating a prospective venture. Here are some good questions to ask.

1. Do you have a choice of territories?
2. What specific territory is being offered?
3. Is it clearly defined?
4. What is its potential?
5. What competition will you meet in marketing the commodity today? Five years from now?
6. Has a market survey been made of the area?
7. Who prepared it? Ask for a copy and read it carefully.
8. What assurance is given that your territory is an exclusive one?
9. Are you protected from the franchisor selling additional franchises in your territory at a later date?
10. Does the contract allow you to open other outlets in your territory, or another territory, at a future date?
11. Has the business site in the territory been selected? If not, how will this be decided?

Termination, Transfer Or Renewal Of Franchise Agreement:

Some termination provisions can cause unexpected and sometimes severe financial loss to a franchisee.

Franchise agreements may provide that at the end of or during the contract term if, in the opinion of the franchisor, certain conditions have not been met, the franchisor has the right to terminate the agreement.

The contract generally provides the franchisor with an option to repurchase the franchise. Under these circumstances, if the contract does not provide a means whereby a fair market price for the franchise can be established, the franchisor could repurchase the business at a low and unfair price.

On occasion, franchisors include a provision in the agreement that the repurchase price will not exceed the original franchise fee. This means that a franchisee who spends considerable effort and money building the business could be faced with selling it back at the price he paid for it.

Does the contract give the franchisor the right of cancellation for almost any reason or must there be a "good cause"? Beware of contracts which, under the threat of cancellation, impose unreasonable obligations such as a minimum monthly purchase of goods or services from the franchisor or unrealistic sales quotas.

Understand the conditions under which the agreement could be terminated and your rights in the event of termination.

Keep these points in mind:

1. How will the value of the franchise be determined in the event of termination?

2. How can you terminate the agreement and what would it cost you?

3. Does the contract contain a provision that would prohibit you from engaging in a competitive business in the franchise territory in the event termination occurs?

Have a clear understanding of contract provisions dealing with your ability to transfer, sell, or renew the franchise.

What would happen to the franchise in the event of your death?

Some reputable franchisors provide for an arbitration clause which allows for a fair evaluation of the franchisee's contribution in the event of termination. Under this agreement, the franchisee would recoup his initial investment or make a profit.

Franchise And A Personality Name:

When a "name" personality is connected with a franchise consider his participation in the business. Is he a figurehead with no capital investment? Will he make contributions of time and effort to promote the business? What guarantees do you have that he will make appearances at your business? Does he have a name of lasting value in identifying your franchise with the public? How sound is the franchise operation without the prominent name?

Promoter Selling Distributorships:

Be wary of promoters who primarily sell distributorships for some "new wonder product.'' Exaggerated promises are common in these promotions. In this promotional plan, the distributors solicit sub-distributors and salesmen to sell the product from door-to-door. The idea is that a large portion of the distributor's profits will come from a percentage of his sub-distributor's sales. Unfortunately, some distributors and sub-distributors find that after making sizable investments of money, time, and effort, there is little profit and they hold a large stock of unsalable products.

FRANCHISED BUSINESS OPPORTUNITIES

The following franchised business opportunities comprise selections annotated from the ''Franchise Opportunities Handbook'' of the U.S. Department of Commerce and International Business Administration, plus other sources. They are classified according to ''General Business Categories,'' so that you may select the type of category that best suits your desires and individual suitability.

Bear in mind that, in addition to any franchise investment stated herein, the franchisee in most instances should also have ''reserve funds'' to cover unexpected expenses and contingencies, and to support himself for at least the first six months until adequate cash flow is generated from the business itself. Remember, too, that the amount of investment is continually subject to change.

In all instances, ''investigate before you invest.'' Conform to the franchise selection criteria contained in preceding pages.

Automotive Products and Services

A-1 TUNE UP COMPANY, INC.
19200 Greenfield, Detroit, Michigan 48235
Dennis E. Sante, President

Provides diagnostic machines and a supply to tune up tools, along with in-house training of qualified mechanics and office personnel. Investment: $12,000 to $15,000.

AAMCO AUTOMATIC TRANSMISSIONS, INC.
408 East Fourth Street
Bridgeport, Pennsylvania 19405
Chris Romeis, National Sales Manager

AAMCO distributors repair, recondition, and rebuild automatic transmissions for all cars. A total investment of $39,379 is required to open an

AAMCO center in a major market. A total of $23,295 is required in a secondary market.

ABC MOBILE SYSTEMS
9420 Telstar Avenue
South El Monte, California 91731
Stanley J. Carter, President

ABC Mobile Brake is a wholesale brake supplier specializing in on-location service and machining of brake drums, rotors, etc. Investment $13,000.

AMERICAN FLEETCARE SYSTEMS CORPORATION
6709 Convoy Court
San Diego, California 92111
Keith Roper, Vice President

American Fleetcare businessmen provide on-location preventive maintenance including lubrications, oil changes, filter changes, and a preventive maintenance inspection to truck fleet owners via a specially equipped van. This service eliminates the normal trips required to take trucks out to service stations or garages for preventive maintenance and the down time or shift differential cost of providing preventive maintenance in a company-owned garage. Investment: $10,000.

ASTRO PROGRAMS, INC.
17534 West McNichols Road
Detroit, Michigan 48235
R.V. Michael

Astro Tune Up Centers are a unique system of stationary and/or mobile auto/truck repair service designed for commercial fleets, as well as general customers. Astro auto parts are available to provide competitive pricing, and building and/or mobile van leasing is arranged. Total investment ranges from $10,000 to $23,000 for local franchise, and $25,000 to $40,000 for regional franchise.

AUTOMATION EQUIPMENT, INC.
P.O. Box 3208
Tulsa, Oklahoma 74101
Orville Strout, President

Conveyorized automatic car washers, self-service car washers, and automatic and manual truck washers. Investment: $1,000 to $5,000 lease plan. $10,000 to $20,000 purchase plan. 100% leasing plan—80% franchising of purchase plan.

BERNARDI BROS., INC.
101 South 38th Street
Harrisburg, Pennsylvania 17111
C.W. McKee, Manager of Marketing Services

Manufacturing of automatic conveyorized Turbo-Tunnel car wash, Turbo-Brush automatic brush car wash, and Turbo-Spray automatic and self-service car washes. Customer remains in car while it is automatically washed, or customer may use the equipment to wash his car. May be operated by coin meter. Investment: $8,000 to $20,000.

BOU-FARO COMPANY
274 Broadway
Pawtucket, Rhode Island 02861
Carmine DeCristoforo, Vice President

Stop and Go transmissions—a transmission auto repair center. Investment $15,000.

CAR-MATIC SYSTEM
Division of Vail Spring Works, Inc.
P.O. Box 12466
Norfolk, Virginia 23502
W.W. Vail, President

Car-Matic System operates a two-level merchandising program. A distributor covers an entire marketing area. Retail profit centers handle the direct to consumer sales. A Car-Matic distributor supplies the retail profit centers in his marketing area with rebuilt automatic transmissions, engines, and other parts. He also operates a retail transmission and engine exchange center at the same location. Investment: Distributor - $29,974; Retail outlet - $13,200

CHRYSLER MOTORS CORPORATION
Parts Division
P.O. Box 337
Center Line, Michigan 48015
E.W. Howenstein, Manager, Business Management

The MOPAR jobber sells automotive parts for all popular makes of cars and trucks under the MOPAR label, at wholesale, to service stations, garages automobile dealers, fleets, farm equipment dealers, etc. To implement the program, the Parts Division of Chrysler Motors Corporation has appointed a network of strategically located independently owned warehouse distributors. These warehouse distributors have been authorized to franchise MOPAR jobbers who meet Chrysler's standards. Investment: Depends on location and number of other factors. However, less than $40,000 is rarely recommended

COLLEX, INC.
Limekiln Pike at Haines Street
Philadelphia, Pennsylvania 19138
Kenneth Magistrate

Collex Centers are a unique concept in collision service. The system is based upon customer service and sophisticated work methods of auto body repair. Each Collex Center is fully staffed, completely equipped, and already doing business before it is turned over to the licensee. No start up is involved and operations generally run five to five and one half days a week. Area franchises are also available for investors, individuals, and/or groups interested in developing a chain of Collex Centers. Investment: Minimum total investment of $75,000 is needed for one Collex Center. This includes a license and service fee of $15,000.

COLORBACK, a division of
MOTOR VALET INDUSTRIES, INC.
2250 East Devon Avenue
Des Plaines, Illinois 60018
Eugene W. Hubert, Vice President Sales

Colorback provides franchisees with a mobile van truck equipped to renew or change the colors of leather, nylon, or vinyl. This service is offered to car dealership branches. Investment: A total investment of $14,800 is necessary.

COOK MACHINERY COMPANY, INC.
4301 South Fitzhugh Avenue
Dallas, Texas 75226
Doug Garber, General Sales Manager

Sofspra carwash locations. Investment: $10,000 to $20,000.

COTTMAN TRANSMISSIONS, INC.
575 Virginia Drive
Fort Washington, Pennsylvania 19034
Richard O. Silva, President

Cottman Transmission Centers repair, service and remanufacture automatic transmissions for wholesale and retail trade. Investment: $18,500 to $26,200.

DELKO TRANSMISSIONS TRUCKS, INC.
270 Fourth Avenue
Brooklyn, New York 11215

Install and service automatic transmissions. Investment: $18,000.

DIAMOND QUALITY TRANSMISSIONS CENTERS OF
AMERICA, INC.
7935 Dorcas Street
Philadelphia, Pennsylvania 19111
Alfred Gold, President

Diamond Quality Transmissions Centers adjust, repair, service, recondition,
and remanufacture automatic transmissions and three or four speed "stick"
transmissions for cars and light trucks. Investment: $10,000 cash down,
balance financed.

ENDRUST MARKETING CORPORATION
1725 Washington Road
Pittsburgh, Pennsylvania 15241
M. Harrison, President

Automotive rustproofing; franchisees being owners and operators of body
shops or automobile sales companies. Investment: Minimum of $996.

FIREHOUSE 5
Challenger Division, Hanna Industries
P.O. Box 3736
Portland, Oregon 97208
Eugene A. Harfst, President

Automatic carwash system contained in a special image building with
descriptive signs and other special fixtures. Operating with or without gas
retailing equipment, Firehouse 5, though unique, is not wholly a franchise.
Equipment and building are investor purchased. Investment: $33,500.

THE FIRESTONE TIRE & RUBBER COMPANY
1200 Firestone Parkway
Akron, Ohio 44317
W. F. Tierney, Wholesale Sales Manager

Complete business franchise includes all phases for selling tires, auto and
home supplies, and automotive services. Investment: $50,000.

WW FLEET LUBRICATION FRANCHISES
316 State Street
Hackensack, New Jersey 07601
Irv David

WW Fleet Lubrication provides truck preventive maintenance service to
truck fleet operators at their truck terminals thereby eliminating down time

and loss of income. The franchisee uses specially-designed equipment which is installed within the truck so that it is mobile. Some of the services are: lubrication, oil change, and tires/batteries/accessories. WW also has available power wash and steam cleaning equipment as an additional investment for the franchisee. Investment: $16,000.

B.F. GOODRICH TIRE COMPANY
500 South Main Street
Akron, Ohio 44318
W.W. Morris, Dept. 0657, Bldg. 25-d, Manager
Dealer Development

Establishes franchised dealers on a protected basis to sell and service B.F. Goodrich tires and related service merchandise. B.F. Goodrich provides real estate assistance in procuring leases of suitable locations, either existing or new facilities. Investment: Varies as to market.

THE GOODYEAR TIRE CENTERS DIVISION
1144 East Market Street
Akron, Ohio 44316
J.W. Barnett, Manager, Tire Centers Division

Retail and wholesale sale of tires and automotive service and other car and home-related merchandise. Investment: $35,000.

HYDRO-SONIC SYSTEMS, INC.
16360 Broadway
Maple Heights, Ohio 44137
Joseph Neidus, Vice President

Mobile washing of trucks, trailers, and other fleets of vehicles. Investment: Total cost of franchise is $15,950.

KAR-KARE CORPORATION
P.O. Box 36
Charlotte (Pineville), North Carolina 28134
Earl T. Garrick, President

Complete tire, battery, and auto service including shocks, brakes, electronic tune-ups, alignment. Investment: Varied amounts.

KWIK KAR WASH
11351 Anaheim Drive
Dallas, Texas 75229
Ray Ellis

Kwik Kar Wash offers a complete self-service car wash ranging from one bay to ten bays. Open for public use twenty-four hours a day. Kwik Kar Wash provides building, equipment, and self-service operation for either twenty-five cents or thirty-five cents per cycle. Investment: A typical four-stall installation requires an investment of approximately $35,000 excluding land.

LEE MYLES ASSOCIATES CORPORATION
325 Sylvan Avenue
Englewood Cliffs, New Jersey 07632

One-stop transmission service. These centers perform complete automatic transmission service, from minor adjustments through and including major repairs and reconditioning. Investment: $28,500.

MAACO ENTERPRISES, INC.
381 Brooks Road
King of Prussia, Pennsylvania 19406
Daniel I. Rhode, Executive Vice President

Franchise sales for MAACO Auto Painting Centers. Service includes both auto painting and body work. Investment: $99,500.

MACCLEEN'S, INC.
1717 Brittain Road
Akron, Ohio 44310
L.B. Holmes, Executive Vice President

Automatic car wash, two bay operation—each having five brushes with individual blower dry systems and wash dispenser. Investment: $20,000.

MALCO PRODUCTS, INC.
361 Fairview Avenue, P.O. Box 892
Barberton, Ohio 44203
Lionel Glauberman

Distributor sells complete line of automotive chemical specialties including cleaners, oil additives, brake fluid, etc., to service stations, garages, new and used car dealers, and industrial outlets. He is assigned a territory that can support him. The distributor and his men travel the area using small trucks and step vans, selling to the above accounts. Investment: $2,500-$3,000.

MEINEKE DISCOUNT MUFFLER SHOPS, INC.
6300 West Loop
South Bellaire, Texas 77401
Harold Nedell, Executive Vice President

Merchandising of automotive exhaust systems and shock absorbers. Investment: $36,345 for inventory, equipment, signs, furniture, fixtures, estimated lease, and utility deposits.

MIDAS INTERNATIONAL CORP.
222 South Riverside Plaza
Chicago, Illinois 60606
William Strahan

Automotive exhaust systems, shock absorbers, and front end alignment. Investment: $113,000 plus working capital.

MILEX, INC.
One Plymouth Meeting
Plymouth Meeting, Pennsylvania 19462

Milex Precision Engine and Brake Tune-Up Centers diagnose and repair the ignition, carburetor, and braking problems of passenger vehicles with the use of sophisticated electronic equipment. Investment: $45,000.

MITON CAR WASH EQUIPMENT, INC.
P.O. Box 58
Buffalo, New York 14150
Lawrence Scaletta, President

Manufacturer of car wash equipment for sale to distributors. Distributor is franchised to sell complete line of the company's car wash equipment and is assigned an exclusive territory. Investment: $15,000 to $50,000.

NATIONAL AUTO GLASS COMPANY, INC.
3434 West Sixth Street
Los Angeles, California 90020
M. Mark Turner, Manager, Marketing Services

Retail auto glass installation centers. Investment $10,000 to $15.000.

NATIONAL AUTO SERVICE CENTERS, INC.
1751 Ensley Avenue
Clearwater Florida, 33516
Leonard D. Levin, Secretary

Eight bay automotive service centers. Full service repair, including air conditioning, tune-up, brakes, alignment, tires, electronic analysis, etc. Also, charging system, shock absorbers, and mufflers. Investment: $40,000.

OTASCO
11333 East Pine, P.O. Box 885
Tulsa, Oklahoma 74102
Robert E. Shireman

Retailing of home and auto supplies, sporting goods, major appliances, private label and major brands. Investment: $40,000 minimum.

PAINTMASTER AUTO/TRUCK PAINT CENTERS
1110 Highland Building
Pittsburgh, Pennsylvania 15206
Alfred H. Wagman, President

A high speed, production line method of repainting automobiles and trucks. Features a color-mixing paint unit which makes more than five thousand colors available in just minutes. Production system can deliver one car each half hour. A big percentage of business is done with car dealers. Franchise "package" includes all machinery, tools, painting booth, baking and drying oven, automatic paint mixers, accounting system. It also includes the assistance of licensed electrical contractors and other personnel to erect the equipment. It includes an inventory of paints for two hundred cars. Services are limited to repainting, derusting, rust-proofing, and minor body repairs. Paintmaster Auto Paint Centers are known for their low prices. Standard repaints are only $39.95. Investment: Varies with type of equipment ordered. The minimum cash required is $45,000.

PARTS, INC.
Sub. of PARTS INDUSTRIES CORPORATION
601 South Dudley Street
Memphis, Tennessee 38104
John J. Tucker, Vice President Sales

Jobber operation wholesaling automotive parts, supplies, equipment, and accessories. Investment: Varies on basis of inventory investment but generally speaking, about $5,000 to $10,000.

PENN JERSEY AUTO STORES, INC.
9901 Blue Grass Road
Philadelphia, Pennsylvania 19114
J.L. Rounds, Director of Franchising

Home and auto store. Investment: $53,450 complete.

POLY-OLEUM CORPORATION
16135 Harper Avenue
Detroit, Michigan 48224
Clair Mohr, President

Poly-Oleum Corporation offers dealerships in the expanding auto-truck rust-proofing market. Tooling materials, compounds are provided by Poly-Oleum. Investment: $8,500.

PORTA SERVICE, INC.
1734 Main Street
Lafayette, Indiana 57904

Mr. Porta is a registered trademark and is engaged in portable washing and lubrication services using unique truck-mounted equipment (patented) and going to the customer's location to perform these services.

POWER MIST
Jaymar Corporation
435 Cherry Avenue, P.O. Box 790
Charlottesville, Virginia 22901
Henry W. Jackson, President

A broad spectrum coin-operated, self-service industry program focusing upon coin-operated car washes and self-service discount gas to provide nucleus for optional "Country-Kleen" laundromat, "Country-Fresh" dairy store, "Klean and Steam" coin-op dry cleaning, and "Photo-Key" hut. Car wash systems include 25 cent self-service, two-minute automatic spray, "Carvenience" drive-through, and standard tunnel wash. All developed by the Power Mist which originated the 25 cent self-service car wash franchise.

Self-service gas system with remote control is marketed under exclusive arrangements with Pace Oil Company and Refinery. Where discount gas installation is included, complete gas equipment financing can be provided including gasoline products. Franchisee may select any portion of program meeting financial or site location dictates. Program includes equipment, pre-fab buildings, construction, installation. Investment: $1,000 to $60,000.

POWER VAC, INC.
500 Graves Blvd., P.O. Box 771
Salina, Kansas 67401

Professional power wash business engaged in the cleaning of truck fleets, buildings, boats, heavy equipment, service stations, etc. Investment: $5,000 to $12,500, plus operating capital.

POWER WASH, INC.
47 Lincoln Highway
South Kearny, New Jersey 07032
Archie B. Joyner, President

Franchisee washes trucks, trailers, cars, etc., with mobile equipment at customers' locations. Investment: $2,000. Financing of equipment up to $12,000 and account financing.

RAYCO CAR SERVICE
3250 West Market Street
Akron, Ohio 44313
Gordon F. Gustafson, President

Installation and repair service including these categories: tires, exhaust systems, shock absorbers, seat covers, convertible tops, upholstery, brakes, front end, audio equipment, and accessories. Investment: $50,000 to $100,000.

ROBO-WASH, INC.
2330 Burlington
N. Kansas City, Missouri 64116
James E. Widner, President

A two minute, fully automatic, high pressure car wash unit. A license is granted the franchisee in exchange for a nominal license fee and percentage charged for each car wash. License runs for ten years. Investment: Minimum of $15,500 and up, depending upon building, location, and equipment requirements.

SERVICE CENTER
High Performance Auto Parts
11034 South LaCienega Blvd.
Los Angeles, California 90403
Sheldon Konblett

A complete "turn-key" retail store specializing in high performance auto parts, etc. Investment: $30,000.

TRUCKOMAT
Div. of Truck-O-Matic, Inc.
P.O. Box 37
Walcott, Iowa 52773
William I. Moon, President

Fully enclosed automatic truck, trailor-trailer, and bus truck wash with fuel stop facilities. Investment: With an adequate financial statement a prospective franchisee will need approximately $80,000 cash.

TUFF-KOTE DINOL, INC.
3650 East Ten Mile Road
Warren, Michigan 48089
Victor Shanley, Vice President Sales

Manufacture and sell to our franchised outlets, rust-proofing compounds, which they use to rust-proof cars and trucks for both individual owners and fleet operators. Investment: $8,500 to $12,500.

VALLEY FORGE PRODUCTS COMPANY
150 Roger Avenue
Inwood, New York 11796
H.E. Fisher, President

As manufacturers of auto replacement parts, they are establishing mobile distributorships to sell to service stations, repair shops, garages, and fleets. Investment: $20,000.

WASHMOBILE CORPORATION OF NEW JERSEY
1010 Hudson Street
Union, New Jersey 07083
W.C. Koppel, President

Manufacture of car wash equipment. Washmobile "Countdown" has a functional stainless steel housing, completely automatic, and consists of motors, gear boxes, air cylinders, industrial brushes, electric controls to run machine automatically, all copper piping, with automatic detergent system and detergent and wax tanks and gauges. Investment: $19,750.

WESTERN AUTO SUPPLY COMPANY
2107 Grand Avenue
Kansas City, Missouri 64108

Retailing of hard lines—principal lines are automotive, sporting goods, tools and wheel goods, appliances, televisions, radios and other electronics, housewares, and paint. Investment: $12,000 to $35,000.

WHITE STORES, INC.
3910 Call Field Road
Wichita Falls, Texas 76308
Weldon Herring, New Store Sales Manager

Franchisee retails hard lines, major lines, including tires, batteries, automotive parts and accessories, television, stereo and other electronics, housewares, sporting goods, tools, and summer goods. Furniture available. Investment: $20,000 to $35,000.

ZIEBART AUTO-TRUCK RUSTPROOFING
1290 East Maple Road
Troy, Michigan 48084
A.W. Stoddard, Vice President New Dealer

Rustproofing auto and truck bodies via special tooling and sealant. A building with 2,400 square feet and 14-foot ceiling and door heights is desirable. Some two- or three-bay abandoned gas stations are used primarily for pleasure car rustproofing. Investment: $15,000.

Auto/Trailer Rentals

ADAM LEASING
Philadelphia, Pennsylvania

Adam Leasing offers a "turn-key" automobile leasing franchise. Franchisees can lease to the public any type of car working with local inventories and using Adam's non-recourse credit line. Investment: $10,000 minimum.

AIRWAYS RENT-A-CAR SYSTEM, INC.
Playa del Rey, California

International company engaged in rental of cars, trucks, and recreational vehicles in 52 countries around the world. Investment: $35,000 and good credit rating.

BUDGET RENT-A-CAR CORPORATION OF AMERICA
Chicago, Illinois

Daily rental of new automobiles to the public. Investment: $30,000 with $100,000 balance sheet.

DOLLAR-A-DAY RENT-A-CAR SYSTEMS, INC.
Los Angeles, California

Automobile and truck rental. Investment: Approximately $50,000.

ECONO-CAR INTERNATIONAL, INC.
Daytona Beach, Florida

Worldwide vehicle rental system utilizing cash or major credit cards for rental of current models, standard and compact, fully equipped vehicles at economy rates. Investment: Depends on size of franchised area. Financing of automobiles.

HERTZ CORPORATION
New York, New York

Hertz System, Inc., offers franchises for the conduct of car and truck rental and leasing businesses in the United States under the "Hertz" name. Investment: Varies according to franchise-operating capital as required by location.

LASCAR LEASING SYSTEMS, INC.
Pennsauken, New Jersey

The Company establishes a franchisee as an authorized Lascar Leasing Broker. The Lascar Dealer then shares in the profits of his leasing of automobiles and trucks. Investment: $4,500.

NATIONAL CAR RENTAL SYSTEM, INC.
Minneapolis, Minnesota

Local and one-way truck and trailer rental business. Investment: $150 minimum.

THRIFTY RENT-A-CAR SYSTEM
Tulsa, Oklahoma

Daily car rental business. Thrifty rents new, top of the line, intermediate, and compact automobiles to the general public at Thrifty rates. Investment: $25,000 to $50,000.

Beauty Salons/Supplies

EDIE ADAMS CUT & CURL
Great Neck, New York

Operating beauty salons with twelve to twenty stations under the Edie Adams name. Investment: $15,000.

THE BARBERS, HAIRSTYLING FOR MEN, INC.
Minneapolis, Minnesota

A completely systemized men's hairstyling shop. Investment: $15,000 to $25,000.

MAGIC MIRROR BEAUTY SALONS, INC.
Beverly Hills, California

Beauty Salon cosmetics sold at retail (private brand). Investment: $10,000 to $15,000.

WINSLOW MANUFACTURING
Division of Watsco, Inc.
Hialeah, Florida

Distributors either sell or lease the patented Winslow Hair Spray System to beauty salons located in their assigned areas. The system consists of a hide-away central power unit connected to convenient spray units for each beauty operator which dispenses hair sprays, setting lotions, and shampoos. Distributors earn monies on the sale or lease of the system and on the repeat business of the liquid products. Investment: $6,000 for inventory. No fees or royalties.

Business Aids/Service

AMERICAN DYNAMICS CORPORATION
New York, New York

Franchised financial counsellors educate their clients on how to use mutual funds, stocks, bonds, savings and loans, insurance, and tax shelters to achieve financial independence, Investment: $45.

AMERICAN HOME ASSOCIATES, INC.
Sherman Oaks, California

Franchising of real estate office as American Home, Realtors' also providing mortgage, escrow, and insurance services. Investment: Existing office, $2,500; new office, $12,500 minimum.

AMRICO BUSINESS SERVICES
San Francisco, California

Amrico mobile and stationary units provide complete computerized accounting systems and management guidance to small and medium sized businesses to $15,000,000 annual volume. Services rendered include computerized preparation of general ledgers, monthly profit and loss statements, job cost and payroll records, accounts receivable and payable, inventory control procedures, taxes (personal and business), cost controls with variances. A franchisee will also perform systems analyses and internal auditing services. Investment: $5,000 to $15,000

AUDIT CONTROLS, INC.
45 Emerson Plaza East
Emerson, New Jersey 07630

Series of collection letters registered by the U.S. Patent Office. Franchisee is supplied with 1,000 mailers (a direct advertising brochure) and a list of 1,000 prospective clients for $150. Investment: $150 plus postage.

BINEX-AUTOMATED BUSINESS SYSTEMS, INC.
Sacramento, California

Financial services and computer services for small businesses. Standard and customized management reporting available through a unique system of programming. Investment: $5,000 plus expenses.

H. & R. BLOCK, INC.
4410 Main Street
Kansas City, Missouri 64111

Prepares individual income tax returns. The franchise is operated in a city by an individual or partnership. The only warranty made by the franchisee is to respect and uphold a specific code of ethics. Refundable franchise deposit: $300 to $500.

BUSINESS EXCHANGE, INC.
4716 Vineland Avenue
North Hollywood, California 91062

Business offers a barter system plan for business owners that allows the business owner to trade his products (at retail) for the things he needs from the other participating dealers rather than paying cash. Company provides a computerized accounting system that allows one member to make purchases and pay for his purchases with offsetting sales to other members. Investment: $19,000.

BUSINESS GUIDANCE, INC.
359 South Country Road
Palm Beach, Florida 33480

Offers business management and service to small businesses and professional people. They include financial controls, tax preparation, and corporate advisory service with procedure and documentation of activities, stock control, and corporate benefits. Investment: $5,000 to $9,000.

COMPUTER KNOWLEDGE CORPORATION
San Antonio, Texas

Offers hospitals a total responsibility patient accounting system (called "Datatronics Costcare"), utilizing the principal of network computing via the franchising company's software, maintenance and, optionally, its equipment. Investment: $35,000, minimum.

CONTENTIAL TAX SERVICE
14507 W. Warren
Dearborn, Michigan 48126

Preparation of State and Federal income tax returns for individuals. Investment: Depends upon number of offices to be opened.

CREATIVE PROSPECTS, INC.
Rochester, New York

Advertising system to bring together students, both high school and college, with retailers who prefer to honor discount coupons as a form of advertising rather than use other media less productive. Investment: $7,500.

CREDIT SERVICE COMPANY
New Orleans, Louisiana

Credit Service Company offers a unique medical-dental-hospital collection service. The methods used insure the collection of more than twice the number of accounts that can be currently achieved through other such services, 73% as against the national average of 34%. The franchise can be operated full or part-time, and can be started in the home. Investment: $1,800.

G.S.C. ASSOCIATES, INC.
Jericho, New York

Collection of delinquent accounts, credit investigation, financial planning, computerized accounting services, and management controls. They are also involved in the factoring of certain types of accounts. Investment: $15,000.

GENERAL BUSINESS SERVICES, INC.
Washington, D.C.

Business counselling, financial management, and tax services for the small independent business. Investment: $10,500 for Area Directors; $5,250 for Associate Directors.

GETTING TO KNOW YOU INTERNATIONAL, LTD.
Great Neck, New York

A newcomer welcoming service for retail merchants and homeowner services. The franchisee sends a personal phone book and collateral materials to new families and invites them to patronize the recommended merchants. The franchisee contracts with sponsoring merchants to distribute the books. The home office prepares all standardized materials to franchisee's local specifications. Investment: $10,000 minimum.

J.D. GRAMM, INC.
Hialeah, Florida

Operates a business dealing solely with the preparation of income tax returns and related services. All stores are open from early January through April 15. Investment: none.

INCOTAX SYSTEMS, INC.
223 Datura Street
West Palm Beach, Florida 33401

Incotax Systems is a volume tax service and bookkeeping system. Investment: $15,000.

INDEPENDENT POSTAL SYSTEM OF AMERICA, INC.
Tampa, Florida

Private postal delivery and related services, primarily delivery second, third, and fourth class mail as provided for under the Private Express Statutes. Investment: $50,000 minimum.

MARCOIN, INC.
1924 Cliff Valley Way, N.E.
Atlanta, Georgia 30329

A broad based service company with direct company branch offices and franchised licenses rendering business counseling and other services primarily to small businesses. Investment: $10,000 to $40,000.

NATIONAL MERCANTILE CLEARING HOUSE
3200 Ponce de Leon Blvd.
Coral Gables, Florida 33134

Publishes manual and automated collection systems using Univac equipment and operates collection agencies, which consist of two different programs: The manual system is directly operated by the business and professional man, and the automated system by National Mercantile Clearing House on Univac equipment for the client. All processing is performed at the home office with I.B.M. and Univac equipment. Investment: $10,000.

NEW PRODUCT DEVELOPMENT SERVICES, INC.
Kansas City, Missouri

Consulting and representation service in new product development, marketing, licensing, or outright sale. Product evaluations, written presentations, negotiations, and aid and assistance to the inventor and patent holder. Investment: Dependent upon demographic population of area involved, ranging from $2,500 to $25,000.

RELIABLE BUSINESS SYSTEMS, INC.
550 Commonwealth Avenue
Newton, Massachusetts 02159

Publishes the Reliable Business and Tax Service System. Offers a bookkeeping system together with an advisory service and end of year Federal and State tax return preparation. Investment: $8,950.

SAFEGUARD BUSINESS SYSTEMS
470 Maryland Drive
Fort Washington, Pennsylvania 19030

Offers a complete basic accounting function including many special systems designed for specific industries and data processing services for the accounting profession. Distributor is under contract and operates in an exclusive territory. Investment: no franchise fee required.

SCHWELLING MARKETING CORPORATION
Milwaukee, Wisconsin

Contracts with various companies to assist them in setting up and marketing their franchises. Investment: Modest.

SCOUT-AID
Billings, Montana

Scout-Aid franchises contract with high schools and colleges to scout their future opponents in football. A franchisee sets up a network of scouts in his territory who do the actual scouting. In addition, he operates a local computer center which processes the scouting information gathered during the games. The analyzed scouting report is then sent to the coach so that he can construct his game plan for the upcoming game. If a coach wishes, he can scout the game himself and the franchisee will process his data. Investment: $6,000 to $10,000.

SIMPLIFIED BUSINESS SERVICES, INC.
215 East 68 Street
New York, New York 10021

Bookkeeping, data processing, income tax, and small business management. Investment: under $10,000.

SUCCESS MOTIVATION INSTITUTE, INC.
Waco, Texas

Markets specialized management, sales, and personal development programs to individuals, companies, governments, and other organizations. Materials are printed and recorded using modern learning methods, personal goal setting, and management by objective techniques. Investment: $10,950.

SYSTEMEDICS, INC.
Box 2000
Princeton, New Jersey 08540

Computerized accounts receivable management system and related systems for the medical and health care fields. Investment: $10,000 to $15,000.

TAX MAN, INC.
639 Massachusetts Avenue
Cambridge, Massachusetts 02139

Preparation of individual income tax returns. Investment: $2,500 minimum.

WESTERN UNION COMPUTER UTILITIES, INC.
Western Union Corporation
Fort Lauderdale, Florida

A network of computer service bureaus licensed to use the company's library of standardized computer programs, marketing, and other supporting services, enabling the licensees to offer a wide range of data processing services without maintaining a staff of programmers. Each licensee offers to small and medium size businesses a selection of data processing serivices including, among others, the processing payroll, accounts payable and accounts receivable, inventory control, and general ledger accounting. Investment: Initial license fee varies from $5,000 to $50,000 plus, for major metropolitan markets plus the net cost of operations prior to reaching the break-even point estimated to be between $25,000 to $40,000.

WHITEHILL SERVICES, INC.
New York, New York

A business management and tax service, computerized, consisting of a one-price package of five distinct services on a yearly subscription basis. Investment: $8,950.

EDWIN K. WILLIAMS & COMPANY
Santa Barbara, California.

Bookkeeping services and financial consulting to the oil industry. Investment: $10,000 to $25,000.

Campgrounds

CAMPER VILLAGES OF AMERICA, INC.
Ocala, Florida

Chain of nationally franchised campgrounds for tents, tent trailers, travel trailers, pick-up campers, and motor homes providing primarily overnight or longer accommodations for the traveling tourist. Investment: $40,000, land purchased or leased.

CAMP'N AIRE, INC.
Seymour, Tennessee

A family-oriented system of camping grounds strategically located for the recreation vehicle market. Investment: $50,000 to $80,000.

CRAZY HORSE, INC.
Newport Beach, California

Franchising existing campgrounds known as Crazy Horse Outside Inns. Franchising new campgrounds known as Crazy Horse Campgrounds. Investment: $50,000.

HOLIDAY INN TRAV-L-PARKS
Memphis, Tennessee

Resort camping accommodations for recreational vehicles offering complete full service facilities. Investment: $100,000 minimum.

JELLYSTONE CAMPGROUNDS, LTD.
Sturgeon Bay, Wisconsin

Operation and sale of Yogi Bear Jellystone Park campgrounds. Investment: $50,000 to $75,000.

KAMP DAKOTA, INC.
Brookings, South Dakota

Franchising of campgrounds to be used by camping and trailering tourists. Investment: $35,000 and up.

KAMPGROUNDS OF AMERICA, INC.
Billings, Montana

Kampgrounds of America, Inc. (KOA) is America's largest system of campgrounds for recreational vehicles. Investment: $35,000 minimum.

PONDEROSA INTERNATIONAL, INC.
Atlanta, Georgia

Ponderosa Parks are designed to accommodate the entire spectrum of campers, from tents to the largest recreational vehicles. Investment: $50,000.

UNITED CAMPGROUNDS USA
Salt Lake City, Utah

United Campgrounds USA offers a "Standard of Excellence" in the overnight and destination campground business. Investment: $20,000 for rough-out ranch; $30,000 to $50,000 for United Campgrounds USA park.

Children's Stores/Furniture/Products

ABC KIDDIE SHOPS OF AMERICA, INC.
Billings, Montana

Own and operate a quality children's ready-to-wear store. Investment: $45,000 to $75,000.

BABY MATE, INC.
Kansas City, Missouri

The direct sale of safety baby equipment. Through advertising, the prospective customer writes in for more information on their products and then the franchisee or his salesman shows a color and sound movie on their items. Investment: $800 to $3,500.

BABY-TENDA CORPORATION
Kansas City, Missouri

Baby-Tenda manufactures a line of safety equipment for infants and children. It is sold direct to the customer either in a franchised Baby-Tenda store or in the customer's home. The average sale nationally is $250 per customer. Investment: $1,300 to $3,000.

GUILD INDUSTRIES CORPORATION
St. Petersburg, Florida

Manufacturer of juvenile safety furniture sold by franchised dealers and distributors. Home demonstrations are made by audio-visual presentation provided by the company. Investment: $1,500 to $10,000, depending upon population of franchised area.

Clothing/Shoes

GINGISS INTERNATIONAL, INC.
180 N. La Salle Street
Chicago, Illinois 60601

Sale and rental of men's formal clothes. Investment $45,000 to $55,000.

HEEL 'N TOE, INC.
5225 Monroe Place
Hyattsville, Maryland 20781

Retail shoe chain which specializes in famous brand women's shoes at discount prices. The stores are semi-self service. Investment: $12,000.

JILENE, INC.
808 State Street
Santa Barbara, California 93101

Jilene offers a choice of four different women's wear stores. Investment: $30,000 and up depending on size of store.

MODE O'DAY COMPANY
2130 N. Hollywood Way
Burbank, California 91505

Ladies' apparel specialty stores. Merchandise is placed in franchise stores on a consignment basis. Investment: Capital is required for store fixtures and leasehold improvements. Average store ranges from $8,000 to $12,000.

MODERN BRIDAL AND FORMAL SHOPS
600 Route 130 N.
Cinnaminson, New Jersey 08077

Retail sales of bridal apparel and cocktail formal wear. Can be operated from the home. Investment: $12,000 to $35,000.

PAULINE'S SPORTSWEAR, INC.
3525 Eastham Drive
Culver City, California 90230

Pauline's Sportswear, Inc., franchises ladies' stores featuring inexpensive sportswear. Franchisees lease their own location (approximately 1,000 square feet) and install their own fixtures. Investment: $10,000.

RED WING SHOE COMPANY
Red Wing, Minnesota

Quality men's shoe stores, specializing in sport and work shoes in large selection of styles. Investment: $34,000.

SELF-SERVICE SUIT CENTER, INC.
(Miracle "88")
Baltimore, Maryland

Men's and students' retail clothing store set up on a self-service basis, reducing all possible overhead and striving for volume sales. Investment: $9,000 to $12,000 depending upon size of store and location.

TERRI-ANN DRESS STORES, INC.
New York, New York

Retail ladies' dresses, sportswear, and accessories. Investment: $25,000.

Construction/Remodeling Materials/Services

ALLIED BUILDERS SYSTEM
Los Angeles, California

Home remodeling. Investment: $15,000.

AMERICAN HOMEOWNERS ASSOCIATION, INC.
Milwaukee, Wisconsin

AHA offers two separate franchise programs. One consists of the operation of a homeowners membership service organization, and the other as individuals who administer the Palace Guard Home Service Contract which originates through real estate brokers. Investment: $13,000.

CENTURY BUILDING SYSTEM, INC.
Salt Lake City, Utah

Prefabricated building panels constructed of reinforced fiberglass and urethane foam, providing quality, yet economical construction for homes, schools, commercial buildings, and cabins. Buildings are erected quickly and easily using the Century system. Many different floor plans and designs are available. Investment: $12,950 for package model home and start up costs; $10,000 to $12,000 additional for property and construction.

CUSTOMFLO, INC.
Addison, Illinois

Job site (mobile) construction. This is a factory on wheels which travels to job site, having the capability of fabricating seamless aluminum or galvanized lengths of gutters and installing at the job site. Business is usually run from an individual house and the truck unit acts as both manufacturing plant and warehouse. Investment: $7,900 plus $3,000 working capital.

DICKER STACK-SACK INTERNATIONAL
Dallas, Texas

Process for construction. Investment: $13,000 for equipment. Franchisee fee based on population of area desired.

HOMEWOOD INDUSTRIES, INC.
Homewood, Illinois

Retailing of patented system of renovating existing kitchen cabinets. Investment: $5,000.

LECTROVEL
Division of Resin Systems, Inc.
Woodside, New York

Parent company manufactures resin coating systems. Sells and installs a system for the electrostatic application of a seamless nylon velvet (flocking) finish on walls and ceilings. Sales are both residential and commercial, renovation and new construction. Investment: $3,500 which is returned in both inventory and rebates.

MARBLE-CRETE PRODUCTS, INC.
Buffalo, New York

Manufacturing of man-made marble, for bathroom surrounds, integral shell bowls, coffee tables, end tables, etc. They can marbleize and duplicate highly buffed and polished marble from Italy, Germany, Portugal, and many other countries. This product is manufactured in moulds as a casting process. Approximately 2,000 square feet needed to start operation. Investment: $15,000.

MULTI-SURFACES, INC.
Scranton, Pennsylvania

Pavement maintenance-Multi-Surfaces dealers use a specialized applicator to supply protective coatings to driveways, parking areas, tennis courts. Investment: $15,000.

MUNFORD DO-IT-YOURSELF STORES
P.O. Box 98
Conley, Georgia 30027

The Munford Do-It-Yourself Stores sell building materials to homeowners and small contractors. The associate store owner is an independent businessman. Investment: $20,000.

PAVEMENT-MARKING CONTRACTORS OF AMERICA
Waterville, Connecticut

Engaged in painting traffic lines on air fields, highways, streets, parking lots, and sports fields. Investment: Approximately $5,000.

THE PERMENTRY COMPANY
37 Water Street
West Haven, Connecticut 06515

Lease steel molds which will precast in one piece outside basement stairwell entrances. Investment: $2,950.

PLY-GEMS HOME CENTERS, INC.
Jamaica, New York

Retail sales of wall paneling, kitchen cabinets, floor products, ceiling products, and all other products used to renovate and improve the interior of a home. Investment: $20,000.

PORAFLOR, INC.
65 Davids Drive
Hauppague, New York 11785

Manufactures resin coating systems. Sells and installs seamless flooring via franchised dealers. Investment: $2,950 and up depending on territory, most of which is returned in inventory and rebates.

PORCELAIN PATCH & GLAZE COMPANY OF AMERICA
140 Watertown Street
Watertown, Massachusetts 02172

Refinishing, spraying, glazing, spot-blending, and patching of porcelain and enamel finishes of all kinds, spray painting of lacquer and lacquer blending work of all kinds. Performed for appliance stores, homeowners, movers, apartment house owners, plumbers, distributors of major appliances, dentists. A shop is not necessary, Investment: $2,000.

PORCELITE ENTERPRISES, INC.
Rockville, Maryland

The Porcelite franchise offers a process to repair and refinish porcelain plumbing fixtures such as bathtubs, kitchen sinks, wash basins, and appliances. Chips are repaired and complete fixtures restored. 123 colors are available. Investment: $7,500.

SHAWNEE STEPS OF AMERICA, INC.
East Hartford, Connecticut

Shawnee franchisee's manufacture, sell, and install concrete precast steps for the homeowner and building trades. Investment: $15,000 to $25,000.

STEPS & RAILS, INC.
Syracuse, New York

Manufacturing and distribution of patented monolithic precast concrete steps and porches. Products are produced from ready-mix concrete poured into patented adjustable steel molds and are delivered completely pre-finished in stucco, stone, or brick, using a simple A-frame truck rig. Distribution in exclusive territory, wholesale to home builders and dealers; retail direct to homeowners. Investment: $5,500.

TENSION STRUCTURES, INC.
Plymouth, Michigan

A distributor of the O'Dome, a 25-foot diameter dome shaped fiberglass structure used primarily as a vacation or second home. Other applications include offices, rental units, and exhibition structures. O'Domes are sold through exclusive local dealers. Investment: $4,000 to $9,000.

TIMBERLODGE, INC.
North Kansas City, Missouri

Designing, manufacturing, and selling pre-cut redwood homes and commercial buildings. Company sells its home packages to its distributors who in turn quote and sell "turn-key" homes to their customers. Investment: $20,000.

TOP TILE BUILDING SUPPLY CORPORATION
White Plains, New York

Retail-decorative building materials. Investment: $25,000.

ZELL-AIRE CORPORATION
401 Orrton Avenue
Reading, Pennsylvania 19603

Introduce-promote Electric Heating into newly built and existing buildings. May be residential, such as single residence or apartments, commercial and professional constructions. Investment: $10,000 with $5,000 prompt payment.

Cosmetics/Toiletries

C & C DISTRIBUTING COMPANY, INC.
Terrell, Texas

Merchandising $2 and $4.50 bottles of ladies' colognes in popular brand frangrances. Investment: $3,495 to $10,245.

REXALL DRUG COMPANY
St. Louis, Missouri

Retail sales of pharmaceuticals, medicines, cosmetics, and vitamins. Investment: No franchise fee.

SENTRY DRUG CENTERS, INC.
Washington, D.C.

Full line retail drugstore, offering professional pharmacy service, health care products and selective sundries. Investment: $30,000.

Educational Products/Services

BARKLEY WYCKOFF READING SCHOOL, INC.
Bethlehem, Pennsylvania

Franchisee recruits students, responsible for teaching classes and the overall management. Investment: $3,000.

EVELYN WOOD READING DYNAMICS
555 Fifth Avenue
New York, New York 10017

Offers a rapid reading course designed to teach students to substantially increase their reading rate. Investment: Dependent on area available for franchising.

JOHN ROBERT POWERS SCHOOL SYSTEM
9 Newbury Street
Boston, Massachusetts 02116

Finishing, self-improvement, and modeling courses. Day and evening classes year 'round. Investment: $20,000.

LEARNING FOUNDATIONS INTERNATIONAL, INC.
Atlanta, Georgia

Tutorial service in seventeen basic learning skills areas as an adjunct to the standard school system. Investment: $35,000.

PATRICIA STEVENS INTERNATIONAL, INC.
P.O. Box 31818
Omaha, Nebraska 68131

Educational residence schools. Subjects taught are merchandising, public relations, executive secretarial, professional modeling, and finishing. Investment: $25,000.

Employment Services

ACME PERSONNEL SERVICE
P.O. Box 14466
Opportunity, Washington 99214

Serves both applicant and employer clients in the placement of permanent personnel in all fields. Investment: $9,500 to $19,500.

ALLIED PERSONNEL CORPORATION
Jacksonville, Florida

National employment agency offering a complete range of personnel placement services to individuals and employers. Investment: $6,000 to $10,000.

BAILEY EMPLOYMENT SYSTEM, INC.
51 Shelton Road
Monroe, Connecticut 06468

National chain of cooperating employment service offices. Investment $27,000.

BAKER & BAKER EMPLOYMENT SERVICE, INC.
114½ Washington Avenue
Athens, Tennessee 37303

Employment service agencies for small towns of 20,000 population and city suburbs. Investment: up to $8,000.

BUSINESSMEN'S CLEARING HOUSE, INC.
150 S. Wacker Drive, Chicago, Illinois 60606

Employment agency, specializing in the placement of salaries and professional employees. Investment: $15,000.

C/M WORLDWIDE PERSONNEL CONSULTANTS
Mobile, Alabama

C/M franchises ethical and professional personnel placement agencies, assisting job seekers in the clerical, administrative, sales, and technical fields. Investment: $10,000 to $25,000.

CORPORATE PERSONNEL SERVICE
Atlanta, Georgia

A unique placement and recruitment service formulated and founded by six successful independent leaders of the industry. Investment: $10,000 to $15,000 depending on size and location.

DUNHILL PERSONNEL SYSTEM, INC.
One Old Country Road, Carle Place, New York 11514

A national personnel service with offices in nearly 100 cities. Investment: $25,000.

FANNING ENTERPRISES, INC.
New York, New York

A complete range of personnel services including permanent placement in commercial, secretarial, professional, executive, and technical positions. Investment: $12,000 to $14,000.

HOMEMAKERS HOME & HEALTH CARE SERVICES, INC.
Kalamazoo, Michigan

Delivery of para-medical personnel for health care in the home and medical institutions. Investment: Minimum of $10,000.

MANAGEMENT RECRUITERS INTERNATIONAL, INC.
1015 Euclid Avenue, Cleveland, Ohio 44115

Personnel placement service business under the names of "Management Recruiters," "Sales Consultants," "Office Mates/5," and "CompuSearch." Investment: Minimum $20,000 to $25,000.

MANPOWER, INC.
5301 N. Ironwood Road, Milwaukee, Wisconsin 53201

Temporary help services including office, industrial, technical, marketing, inventory and data processing, maintenance, guard service, medical, dental, service station business, plus many more. Investment: Initial fees vary from $500 to $4,500.

PARTIME, INC.
Paoli, Pennsylvania

Furnishing skilled office, technical, sales, and marketing personnel and industrial workers to clients on temporary, as needed, basis. Investment: $15,000 to $35,000.

PERSONNEL POOL OF AMERICA, INC.
521 S. Andrews Avenue, Fort Lauderdale, Florida 33301

Temporary personnel service furnishing medical-clerical for assignments in homes, hospitals, and nursing homes. Investment $50,000 to $75,000 depending on market size.

RICHARD P. RITA PERSONNEL SYSTEM
1 Weybosset Hill, Providence, Rhode Island 02903

Executive search/placement agencies, temporary placement agencies, Investment: $15,000 to $25,000.

SNELLING AND SNELLING, INC.
4000 S. Tamiami Trail, Sarasota, Florida 33581

Employment service offering full range of employment activity in both blue-collar and white-collar fields. Investment: $20,000 to $40,000.

Equipment/Rentals

APPARELMASTER, INC.
Lawrenceburg, Indiana

A unique business service for laundry and drycleaning establishments. Includes uniform and career apparel, dust control and miscellaneous rental systems, data processing invoicing and inventory control, etc. Investment: $8,900, if paid in lump sum.

TAYLOR RENTAL CORPORATION
570 Cottage Street,
Springfield, Massachusetts 01104

A complete selection of rental items including commercial and industrial equipment as well as homeowner items. Investment: $20,000 to $30,000.

UNITED RENT-ALL, INC.
10131 National Blvd.
Los Angeles, California 90034

Rental stores with full line of inventory. Investment: $30,000.

Food/Donuts

DUNKIN' DONUTS OF AMERICA, INC.
P.O. Box 317
Randolph, Massachusetts 02368

Coffee and donut shops. Manufacture and sale of donuts at retail. Over 52 varieties of handcut donuts. Investment: $22,000 or $27,000, depending on area.

MISTER DONUT OF AMERICA, INC.
1200 Multifoods Bldg.
Minneapolis, Minnesota 55402

Franchised donut and coffee shops, drive-in and walk-in units. Retail selling of more than 44 varieties of donuts. Investment: $41,000 land and building.

SPUDNUTS, INC.
450 West 1700 South
Salt Lake City, Utah 84115

Retail, retail-wholesale, and drive-in/drive-up locations manufacturing and selling raised and cake donuts know as Spudnuts. Investment: $30,000 to $35,000.

Food—Grocery/Specialty Stores

CHEESE SHOP INTERNATIONAL, INC.
25 Amogerone Crossway
Greenwich, Connecticut 06803

Retail sale of fine cheese, gourmet foods, related gift items and wines where permissible. Investment: $40,000 to $70,000.

CONVENIENT FOOD MART, INC.
875 N. Michigan Avenue, Chicago, Illinois 60611

Stocks complete line of national brand merchandise normally in a chain supermarket (except fresh red meat). Investment: $25,000 and up.

CONVENIENT INDUSTRIES OF AMERICA, INC.
Louisville, Kentucky

Offers a unique retail food mart operation. Each store is open seven days a week. National and leading local brands sold. Investment: $25,000.

JITNEY-JUNGLE, INC.
440 N. Mill Street, Jackson, Mississippi 39207

Most stores are three dimensional: groceries, fast food, and self-service gasoline. Major concentration in rural communities. Investment: $17,000.

MAJIK MARKET
Atlanta, Georgia

Majik Markets offers individual and area franchises for convenience food stores. Self-service gasoline format also available. Investment: $5,000, plus inventory approximately $12,000.

OPEN PANTRY FOOD MARTS, INC.
3055 East 63 Street, Cleveland, Ohio 44127

Highly stocked miniature supermarkets open from early morning to midnight. Investment: $15,000.

ROCKVIEW DAIRIES, INC.
Downey, California

Drive-in dairy and related items, includes milk, butter, orange juice, punch, eggs, beer, gasoline, cleaners, photo-mat, etc., Investment: $10,000.

THE SOUTHLAND CORPORATION
2828 North Haskell Street, Dallas, Texas 75204

Convenience grocery stores. Investment: $15,000.

SUNNYDALE FRANCHISE SYSTEM, INC.
400 Stanley Avenue, Brooklyn, New York 11207

Sunnydale Franchise System, Inc., offers an ultra-modern, completely equipped retail convenience food store. Investment: $17,500.

SWISS COLONY STORES, INC.
Monroe, Wisconsin

Retail stores offering popularly priced, high quality domestic and imported cheeses, sausage, European-style pastries, candy, specialty foods, and gifts. Investment: Approximately $50,000, plus leasehold improvements.

TELECAKE INTERNATIONAI
Salt Lake City, Utah

National cake-by-phone service. Franchisee is usually a retail bakery. Investment: $210.

VIRGINIA HARDY'S OVEN, INC.
Milwaukee, Wisconsin

Baking specialty pies and breads. Investment: $21,500.

WHITE HEN PANTRY DIVISION
Jewel Companies, Inc.
Elmhurst, Illinois

Convenience-type food store. Product line includes delicatessen service. Investment: $8,000.

Food—Ice Cream/Candy/Popcorn/Beverages

BASKIN-ROBBINS, INC.
Burbank, California

Retail ice cream store. Franchisor selects site. Investment: Approximately $20,000.

BRESLER'S 33 FLAVORS, INC.
Chicago, Illinois

Multi-flavor specialty ice cream shops. Investment: Approximately $18,000.

CARVEL CORPORATION
Yonkers, New York

Retail ice cream shops, featuring both hard and soft ice cream, manufactured by the store owner in the shop. Investment: $35,000.

KARMELKORN SHOPPES, INC.
Rock Island, Illinois

Make and sell popcorn, popcorn confections, a variety of kitchen candies and related snack food items. Investment: $20,000 to $25,000.

MISTER SOFTEE, INC.
901 E. Clements Bridge Road
Runnemede, New Jersey 08078

Retailing soft ice cream products from a mobile unit. Investment: $25,000.

SWIFT DAIRY & POULTRY COMPANY
115 W. Jackson Blvd., Chicago, Illinois 60604

Dipper Dan retail ice cream shoppe. Investment: Approximately $30,000.

Foods—Pancake/Waffle/Pretzel

INTERNATIONAL HOUSE OF PANCAKES
6837 Lankershim Boulevard
North Hollywood, California 91605

Fast Food family-style restaurants—pancakes, steak and chicken dinners, sandwiches. Investment: $35,000 cash required.

PERKINS CAKE & STEAK RESTAURANTS
4917 Eden Avenue, Edina, Minnesota 55424

Family-type pancake specialty restaurant. Investment $125,000.

Food—Restaurants/Drive-Ins/Carry-Outs

A & W INTERNATIONAL, INC.
922 Broadway
Santa Monica, California 90406

Drive-in, walk-in restaurants. Investments: $50,000 and up.

AMERICAN DAIRY QUEEN CORPORATION
Minneapolis, Minnesota

High quality semi-frozen desert product, and "Brazier" fast foods consisting of hamburgers, cheeseburgers, chicken, hot dogs, fish sandwich, barbecue, etc. Investment: $25,000 liquid and $50,000 net worth.

ARTHUR TREACHER'S FISH & CHIPS, INC.
1328 Dubin Road, Columbus, Ohio 43215

A limited menu, quick service operation offering fish produced by a patented process. Investment: $300,000.

BURGER CHEF SYSTEMS, INC.
P.O. Box 927, Indianapolis, Indiana 42606

Limited menu restaurants. Investment: $75,000.

CHICKEN UNLIMITED FAMILY RESTAURANTS
1 Salt Creek Lane, Hinsdale, Illinois 60521

Quick service dining featuring fried chicken. Investment: $75,000.

COUNTRY KITCHEN INTERNATIONAL, INC.
7800 Metro Pkwy., Minneapolis, Minnesota 55426

Sit-down service restaurant; family-type, full line menu with home cooked meals. Investment: $53,000.

DAIRY SWEET COMPANY
610 Des Moines Street, Ankeny, Iowa 50021

Fast food drive-in and carry-out restaurants. Investment: $10,000 down payment.

FROSTOP CORPORATION
12 First Street, Pelham, New York 10803

Fast food drive-ins service Frostop Root Beer and limited American fast food menu. Investment: $25,000 to $50,000.

GOLDEN SKILLET CORPORATION
2819 Parkham Road, Richmond, Virginia 23229

Fried chicken and other items including hamburgers and seafood, prepared according to Golden Skillet's secret recipies. Investment: $30,000.

HARDEE'S FOOD SYSTEMS, INC.
P.O. Box 1619, Rocky Mount, North Carolina 27801

Fast food hamburger restaurants. Investment: $140,000 plus building.

JAPANESE STEAK HOUSES, INC.
Miami Springs, Florida

Japanese steak house restaurants. Investment: $30,000 to $90,000.

LONG JOHN SILVER'S, INC.
P.O. Box 11988, Lexington, Kentucky 40579

Fast food restaurants—self-service, carry-out, or seating in a wharf-like at-mosphere. Investment: $25,000 to $30,000.

LUM'S RESTAURANT CORPORATION
8410 N.W. 53rd Terrace, Miami, Florida 33166

Fast food family restaurant with waitress service and carry-out service. In-vestment: $50,000 cash.

MAID RITE PRODUCTS, INC.
100 E. Second Street, Muscatine, Iowa 52761

Fast food, limited menu, sandwich-type operation with various types of buildings and locations. Investment: $3,000 average for franchise fee.

MARYLAND FRIED CHICKEN MARKETING SYSTEM, INC.
P.O. Box 1139, Boca Raton, Florida 33432

Featuring fried chicken and seafood, eat-in and carry-out. Investment: $20,000.

McDONALD'S SYSTEM, INC.
Oak Brook, Illinois 60521

A successful nationwide chain of fast food restaurants. The menu consists of hamburgers, cheesburgers, fish sandwiches, etc. Investment: $190,000.

MR. STEAK, INC.
5100 Race Court, Denver, Colorado 80216

A family-type restaurant specializing in choice steaks, as well as seafood, chicken, and sandwiches. Investment: $48,000 to $55,000

ORANGE JULIUS OF AMERICA
3219 Wilshire Blvd., Santa Monica, California 90403

Fast food operation featuring the drink Orange Julius, made from fresh orange juice. Investment: $75,000 to $125,000.

THE PIZZA INN, INC.
P.O. Box 222247, Dallas, Texas 75222

Pizza restaurants seating 150 people. Investment: $50,000 to $75,000.

THE RED BARN SYSTEM, INC.
6845 Elm Street, McLean, Virginia 22101

Fast food operation service pressure-fried chicken and sandwiches. Investment: Approximately $75,000 not including cost of building and land.

SHAKEY'S INCORPORATED
5565 First Intl. Bldg., Dallas, Texas 75202

Resemble night clubs for the whole family featuring pizza, salads, marinated chicken, beer, soft drinks, live entertainment (piano and banjo), singing, and fun. Investment: $50,000 excluding real estate.

SIR PIZZA INTERNATIONAL, INC.
700 S. Madison Street, Muncie, Indiana 47302

Retail and commissary operations, selling pizza, sandwiches, etc., for both on-premise consumption and carry-out. Investment: $25,000 to $30,000.

STEWART'S DRIVE-IN
1420 Crestmont Avenue, Camden, New Jersey 08103

Drive-in restaurants, with or without dining room, with car-hop service. Investment: $35,000 to $70,000 cash.

SVENDEN HOUSE INTERNATIONAL, INC.
1200 Multifoods Bldg., Minneapolis, Minnesota 55402

A chain of smorgasbord restaurants. Investment: $500,000, includes land, building and equipment.

TACO TIME INTERNATIONAL, INC.
Eugene, Oregon

Mexican food restaurants. Investment: $32,000.

TASTEE FREEZ INTERNATIONAL, INC.
Chicago, Illinois

Year 'round fast food self-service drive-in restaurants. Investment: $10,000 to $15,000. Total investments for equipment and license run from $25,000 to $50,000, which does not include sales tax if applicable, or operating capital and food inventory.

WAFFLE HOUSE, INC.
Tucker, Georgia

Twenty four hour fast food operation. Breakfast foods, sandwiches, steaks. Investment: $30,000 plus financing for land, building, and equipment.

General Merchandising Stores

BEN FRANKLIN
Division City Products Corporation
Des Plaines, Illinois

A variety store operation. Investment: $50,000.

COAST TO COAST STORES
Minneapolis, Minnesota

Retail hard line outlets featuring national brands and private label merchandise in automotive, electrical, furniture, hardware, houseware, lawn-farm and garden, major appliances, paint and sundries, plumbing, sporting goods, toys and wheel goods. Investment: $20,000 to $100,000.

GAMBLE-SKOGMO, INC.
Minneapolis, Minnesota

A complete retail store operation; hardware, automotive, sporting goods, major appliances, furniture, electrical, housewares, paints and supplies, lawn and garden, plumbing, electronics, carpet and floor covering. Investment: $35,000 minimum. A total investment of $100,000 is recommended.

UNITED DOLLAR STORES, INC.
Dumas, Arkansas

Bantam Discount Variety Stores. Investment: $18,000 to $50,000.

Health Aids / Services

DIET WATCHERS FRANCHISE, LTD.
Spring Valley, New York

Lectures and group therapy motivation to obtain weight loss. Investment: Minimum of $3,000.

SMOKE WATCHERS INTERNATIONAL, INC.
New York, New York

Program to help people stop smoking. Investment: $1,000 to $10,000.

Home Furnishings/Furniture-Retail/Repair/Services

ABBEY CARPET COMPANY
6643 Franklin Blvd., Sacramento, California 95823

Specialty store, retail, carpets. Investment: $50,000.

AMITY, INC.
Madison, Wisconsin

A unique furniture stripping system to remove varnish and paint from wood and metal—effective on antiques. Investment: $2,900 to $3,585.

BIX SALES COMPANY, INC.
Lee's Summit, Missouri

Removing old finish from furniture. Investment: $3,000.

DELHI CHEMICALS, INC.
22 South Street, Stamford, N.Y. 12167

A community service to commercial, industrial, and family accounts in the removal of finishes from articles made of wood, metal, glass, marble, alabaster, tin, copper, brass, bronze, etc. Rust removal, tarnish removal metal cleaning, and rust prevention are included in the services offered. Investment: $15,000.

FLEX-COTE PRODUCTS CORPORATION
103 E. Hawthorne Avenue, Valley Stream, New York 11580

Reconditioning and re-coloring of upholstery finishes such as leather, vinyl, plastic, and cloth. Investment: About $375.

SPECIALTY COATINGS AND CHEMICALS, INC.
7360 Varna Avenue
North Hollywood, California 91605

Vinyl and leather repair, re-coloring, cleaning, and dressing. Investment: $198 to $1,285.

SPRING CREST COMPANY
La Habra, California

Retail draperies, drapery hardware, and accessories, Investment: $8,250 to $18,000.

STEAMATIC, INC.
1601 109 Street, Grand Prairie, Texas 75050

Steam carpet cleaning services and in-home dry cleaning process for upholstery and drapes. Investment: $10,000 to $50,000.

Laundries/Dry Cleaning Services

COIT DRAPERY & CARPET CLEANERS, INC.
897 Hinckley Road, Burlingame, California 90410

Supply, leasing, maintenance of draperies and other window furnishings. Investment: Minimum $15,000

COOK MACHINERY COMPANY, INC.
4301 S. Fitzhugh Avenue, Dallas, Texas 75226

Country Clean laundry and dry cleaning stores. Investment: $25,000.

FEDNOR CORPORATION
Woodbridge Avenue, Edison, New Jersey 08817

Laundry and dry cleaning stores. Investment: $15,000 to $35,000.

MARTINIZING FRANCHISE
5050 Section Avenue
Cincinnati, Ohio 45212

Fast service Martinizing cleaning stores. Investment: $20,000.

Lawn And Garden Supplies/Services

LAWN-A-MAT CHEMICAL AND EQUIPMENT CORP.
153 Jefferson Avenue
Mineola, New York 11501

Automated mobile garden center. Investment: $12,500.

LAWN KING, INC.
Fairfield, New Jersey

Automated lawn service: Investment $15,000.

LAWN MEDIC, INC.
Rochester, New York

Automated lawn service. Investment: $9,500.

Maintenance/Cleaning/Sanitation Services/Supplies

C.C.I., INC.
Janesville, Wisconsin

Specializing in heavy duty power vacuum, power washing, and catastrophe cleaning. Service is provided for all types of buildings, industrial, commercial, residential, governmental, and institutional. Investment: $7,900 or $13,990.

CROSSLAND LABORATORIES, INC.
Blissfield, Michigan

Products for maintenance, sanitary supply, and industrial fields. Investment: $10,000, which includes training and initial inventory.

DURACLEAN INTERNATIONAL
Deerfield, Illinois

On-location cleaning of carpet and upholstery fabrics, plus soil-retarding, spot removal, mothproofing, and minor carpet repair. Investment: $1,195 down payment.

MARK CHEMICAL COMPANY, INC.
Orange, California

Commercial dishwashing, pest control, and sanitation products. Investment: $15,000.

ROTO-ROOTER CORPORATION
West Des Moines, Iowa

Sewer and drain cleaning service. Investment: $5,000.

SERVICEMASTER INTERNATIONAL, INC.
Downers Grove, Illinois

Professional cleaning of homes, offices, plants, public buildings, and institutions, covering carpets, furniture, walls, floors, and fixtures. Investment: $3,500.

VON SCHRADER MANUFACTURING COMPANY
Racine, Wisconsin

Commercial cleaning of rugs, carpets, furniture, automobile interiors, and interior painted walls and ceilings with electrically operated automatic machines. Investment: $350 to $1,620.

Motels/Hotels

HOLIDAY INNS, INC.
3796 Lamar Avenue, Memphis, Tennessee 38118

Motels and restaurants. Investment: in excess of $1,500,000.

QUALITY INNS
10750 Columbia Pike, Silver Spring, Maryland 20901

Motor inns with food and beverage facilities. Investment: $275,000 plus land and financing.

RAMADA INNS, INC.
3838 East Van Buren Street, Phoenix, Arizona 85008

Motor hotels. Franchise fee: $15,000; other costs vary.

RED CARPET INNS OF AMERICA, INC.
444 Seabreeze Blvd., Daytona Beach, Florida 32015

Operation of motels. Investment: 20% of total cost.

RODEWAY INNS OF AMERICA
2525 Stemmons Freeway, Dallas, Texas 75207

Hotel/motel, recreational vehicle parks with food and beverage. Investment: Governed by size of project.

SHERATON INNS, INC.
470 Atlantic Avenue, Boston, Massachusetts 02210

Operate motor inns. Investment: $1,500,000.

TRAVELODGE INTERNATIONAL, INC.
El Cajon, California 92090

Motor hotels with full facilities. Investment: $1,000,000.

Paint And Decorating Supplies

DAVIS PAINT COMPANY
1311 Iron Street
North Kansas City, Missouri 64116

Retail paint and wallpaper stores. Also handles drapes, picture framing, unfinished furniture, floor coverings, and decorative gifts. Investment: $20,000 to $25,000.

MARY CARTER PAINT & DECORATING CENTER
1191 S. Wheeling Road, Wheeling, Illinois 60090

Retail stores handling paint, wallpaper, floor tiles, and do-it-yourself supplies. Investment: $10,000 to $20,000.

Pet Shops

DOKTOR PET CENTERS, INC.
Dundee Park, Andover, Massachusetts 01810

Retail pets, supplies, accessories, and grooming services. Investment: $50,000 to $60,000.

Printing

INSTY PRINTS, INC.
417 N. 5th Street, Minneapolis, Minnesota 55401

Instant printing. Investment: $42,000.

KOPY KAT INSTANT KOPY-PRINTING CENTERS
Executive Plaza, Ft. Washington, Pennsylvania 19034

While-you-wait copying service. Investment: $29,900 total cost.

POSTAL INSTANT PRESS
8201 Beverly Boulevard, Los Angeles, California 90048

While-you-wait printing. Investment: Total package $35,000.

SIR SPEEDY INSTANT PRINTING CENTERS
Newport Beach, California

Franchising of instant printing centers. Investment: $40,000.

Recreation/Entertainment/Travel Services/Supplies

AMERICAN AUTOMATED THEATRES, INC.
Oklahoma City, Oklahoma

Operates mini- and multi-auditorium theatres in shopping centers. Maintains central film buying and booking department. Investment: $10,000 to $16,500 theatre franchise; $50,000 area franchise.

COMPETITIVE SPORT SYSTEM
Cincinnati, Ohio

Operation of a number of recreational equipment devices patented by the franchisor and licensed to the dealer. Trademarks included are: football, match soccer, and flip match tennis. Investment: $745 minimum operational level.

FUN SERVICES, INC.
Elk Grove Village, Illinois

Professional Fun Fairs for the leisure time and recreational industries. The primary market is fund raising organizations, such as elementary school P.T.A.'s, religious institutions, youth and fraternal organizations. Investment: $9,950.

GOLF PLAYERS, INC.
Chattanooga, Tennessee

Miniature golf courses operated under the name "Sir Goony Golf." Investment: $25,000 and up.

LOMMA ENTERPRISES, INC.
Scranton, Pennsylvania

Prefabricated miniature golf courses that can be used indoors or outdoors with limited space. Investment: $5,000.

PUTT-PUTT GOLF COURSES OF AMERICA, INC.
Fayetteville, North Carolina

Franchised miniature golf facilities. Investment: $50,000.

TRAVEL GUILD OF AMERICA
Des Plaines, Illinois

T.G.A. is America's first shop-at-home travel service. Those selected are able to offer the traveling public the convenience of a door-to-door service at no additional charge. Investment: $3,000.

Security Systems

DICTOGRAPH SECURITY SYSTEMS
Florham Park, New Jersey

Complete line of automatic burglar, fire and smoke, hold-up, and security devices for residential, commercial, institutional, and industrial applications. Investment: Minimum $8,000.

THE NIGHT EYE CORPORATION
Iowa City, Iowa

Sale, installation, and service of burglar, hold-up, and fire alarm systems. Investment: Approximately $1,800.

Swimming Pools

CASCADE INDUSTRIES, INC.
Edison, New Jersey

Sell and install swimming pools. Investment: $6,600.

GLAMOUR POOLS BY AZTEC, INC.
Wyckoff, New Jersey

Two types of franchises are available: 1) dealership; 2) manufacturing franchise. Investment: $5,000 to $100,000.

Tools/Hardware

SNAP-ON TOOLS CORPORATION
Kenosha, Wisconsin

Sale of hand tools and equipment to garages and service stations. Dealer travels his territory using a truck or a similar vehicle. Investment: $10,000.

Water Conditioning

CULLIGAN INTERNATIONAL COMPANY
Northbrook, Illinois

Parent company is supplier to franchisee for water conditioning equipment. Franchisee sells, leases, maintains, and repairs water conditioning equipment for domestic, commercial, and industrial customers. Investment: $20,000 and up.

ECODYNE CORPORATION
St. Paul, Minnesota

Residential, commercial, and industrial water softening equipment with water conditioning. Investment: $5,000 minimum.

WATER REFINING COMPANY
Middletown, Ohio

Water conditioning sales, rentals, service. Investment: **$5,000 and up.**

Miscellaneous Wholesale / Retail And Service Businesses

ARTMASTERS LEAGUE, INC.
New York, New York

Setting up an art dealership to handle one-of-a-kind original American art that is registered, hand signed, matted under glass and distinctively framed. Dealer is trained to sell to all kinds of retail outlets, hold fund raising campaigns, auctions, art fairs, and he may also open his own gallery. Investment: $3,000 to $4,000.

FIREPLACE SHOPS, INC.
Walled Lake, Michigan

Specialized shop selling fireplaces, fireplace equipment and accessories, lighting fixtures, furniture items, wall decor, and decorative items. The shops are known as Kings Row Fireplace Shops. Investment: $25,000.

GIFTAMERICA, INC.
Upper Saddle River New Jersey

Offers a number of quality gifts for sale to callers to its national toll-free number. It has approximately 6,000 full service dealers throughout the continental United States who will deliver the gifts almost anywhere in the country within 24 hours. Dealers will also be able to make sales of these gifts from inventories in their own stores. Investment: $595 maximum fee.

GOLDEN DOLPHIN, INC.
29 E. Rawls Road, Des Plaines, Illinois 60018

Retailing of color coordinated bathroom accessories; towels, shower curtains, rugs, and a complete line of decorative accessories. The retail stores are generally classified as Bath Boutique Specialty Stores. Investment: $25,000 to $45,000.

LAFAYETTE ELECTRONICS SALES, INC.
P.O. Box L, Syosset, New York 11791

Retailing consumer and hobby electronics. Investment: $50,000 to $75,000.

MAGIC FINGERS, INC.
7800 Red Road
South Miami, Florida 33143

Manufacture and sale of Magic Fingers relaxation equipment—coin operated for motel installations. Investment: $7,500.

STRETCH & SEW, INC.
Eugene, Oregon

Teach the idea of sewing with knits. Sale of knit fabrics, patterns, and books. Investment: $30,000 to $50,000.

TEAM ELECTRONICS
720 29th Avenue S.E.
Minneapolis, Minnesota 55414

Establish retail electronics centers. Specializing in consumer-oriented home entertainment products such as stereos, television sets, and radios. Investment: $80,000 to $90,000.

THE TINDER BOX INTERNATIONAL, INC.
P.O. Box 830, Santa Monica, California 90406

Retail pipes, tobacco, cigarettes, and gifts, primarily in regional shopping centers. Investment: $15,000 to $30,000.

8.

MY "MILLION DOLLAR" SUCCESS SECRETS

I call this chapter "My 'Million Dollar' Success Secrets" for various valid reasons. The ideas herein can spell the difference between a business that's on a treadmill ... constantly piddling along ... as against one that keeps growing, and growing, and growing.

They can help to put you in control of your own business destiny. You no longer depend on customers who "just happen" to be passing by your place of business. You can now get customers to come to you—in large groups—and in constant flow.

The scope of business is no longer confined to the general area of your store or shop ... it can now encompass every single home and store in your community, with whom you can now get to deal on a one-to-one basis.

Among other things, this chapter will discuss:

● How To Get Your Products Displayed and Sold in the Finest Homes in Your Area—with possible sales as high as five hundred dollars a home!

● How To Have As Many As One Hundred (or more) "Branch Offices"—actively selling your product—with no cost to you.

● "Add On" Businesses That Add Big Earnings:
   —New Departments
   —Related Businesses
   —New Products, Services

217

- Shop-At-Home Techniques That Bring Your Store to Every Home

- Attracting Customers "In Groups" to Come to You . . . and Listen to Your Selling Story:
  —Through Seminars
  —Through Exhibits
  —Other Methods

- How Members of Virtually Every Club, Association, in Your Area Can be Recruited to Actively Promote and Sell Your Products Among Their Friends and Associates—with the potential of sales exceeding one hundred thousand dollars!

- Newcomers in Your Area—How To Mine This "Goldmine" of Potential Customers

- How To "Rent It!" and Multiply Your Sales and Profits

- The Excitement of Auctions—How To Apply It to Your Business

- 23 Ways Your Truck or Car Can Help Produce Sales

NEW SELLING CONCEPTS FOR THE 80'S

In presenting these "Million Dollar Success Secrets," the "Newest Selling Concepts for the 80's," I'm talking to *you,* the salesman of a product or a service . . . to *you,* the owner of a store, practically any kind of store whether small, medium, or large in size . . . to *you,* the owner of that corner gas station—rushed, harrassed, burdened with responsibilities, who just doesn't have the time to even think of new ideas—yet knows full well how vitally necessary they are to help him make more sales.

The ideas I'll give you are new, fresh concepts—concepts for the eighties. They have been tested on the firing line, and proved out. They are being used by dozens of enterprising individuals and firms who are making millions of dollars in sales from them. These ideas are actually working for them right now, day in and day out, and I'll show you, step by step, how they can be adapted to your business.

Let me stress that these are not fuzzy ideas . . . they're simple, clear, and easy to grasp. You need them to survive in today's competitive business world. In this era of chain stores, you, the small businessman, can easily fail unless you are shown how to "compete" with these giants . . . to do so effectively—and immediately—even though you have only limited funds, or none at all!

Let me begin with a thunderbolt that I'll call my first principle. It's this:

1. Stop depending on passerby patronage, walk-in patronage, telephoned-in patronage, advertising-induced patronage.

2. You're in the world of the 80's. It's a changing world, a mobile world. Think about your market. How it can be broadened and enlarged. Remember the market is greater than you believe. It is as large as you want to make it.

You must learn to do these basic things:

1. You must learn how to sell your product or service *away* from your home, or shop. You must *reach out* and contact your community by bringing your products directly to them—at their homes or place of business.

2. You must build the kind of programs that persuade your prospects to come to you . . . to seek you out . . . not one-by-one, but in *groups* . . . so that instead of one sale at a time, you can make many sales at a time.

To begin with, you have to visualize your business differently. Look at your shop or store as a *headquarters* for a great network of sales centers . . . stretching through every nook and cranny of your community. You can have five, ten, fifty, or even one hundred of such sales centers—all working for you, to make sales day-by-day—for your business!

Wherever you get your products discussed or displayed is the equivalent of a branch office, or a sales center. Your objective, then, is to find the places that will display and sell your products, and to make them into branch sales centers. It should come as no surprise to you to know that it's been done already by many merchants. Here's how they are doing this:

Mr. Smith walked past several banks one day. He noticed that they all had displays in their windows . . . one was guns; the other coins; a third, pictures of leading citizens. He reasoned that they might be willing to put a display of his products in their windows because they would be boosting local business. First, he approached his own bank and since he was an appliance dealer, suggested a display of antique radio sets. The bank was only too happy to help him. They were already looking for a new display. He then approached seven other banks with different display ideas . . . five of the seven agreed. Soon, his business was publicized in six banks—all prime locations!—and rent-free!

Mr. Bergson found other receptive exhibit locations in his city. These included all utility company offices—gas, electric, or phone companies—also bus and train terminals.

Mr. Jones had still another plan as to how to set up branch sales centers. He proceeded to contact about ninety different stores throughout his area . . . the ones that were non-competitive, of course. He asked each if they would permit him to place a quantity of his advertising brochures on their counter (contained in a specially designed box that said: "Take One"). He contacted practically every type of store: the grocer, the beauty parlor, the hardware store, the furniture store, practically every type you could think of. He gave them a good reason to cooperate . . . their own self-interest. He gave them a ten percent commission on all sales made through their store. He was able to do this by coding the brochures so that he could identify the stores which provided referrals. As a result, he found himself with eighty five branch offices in his community—*at no cost to himself.* Not only did the concept give him valuable advertising and public relations exposure, but something even more tangible: His sales tripled six months after his branch offices started to function.

Mr. Brown owned an appliance store. He added another wrinkle to the idea. He decided to let his catalog do the selling for him at branch sales centers. But he asked even more of those he selected: He looked for high traffic locations primarily. And he found many of them. They were bus, plane, and train depots and stores in the large shopping centers. These were places in which his catalog corners were installed. What are catalog corners? They are tables to which you attach a catalog and place it in a corner of the room. He, too, sweetened the pot for those storekeepers who cooperated with him. He gave them a commission on all referrals that came from them. Thus, Mr. Brown enlarged his market by some thirty six locations without increasing his overhead at all.

Such well-known stores as Sears-Roebuck, J.C. Penney, and even Macy's, have used catalog corners profitably. The term "catalog" is used in the widest sense. It can be your catalog, if you have one, or those of your supplier or suppliers. It can also be one or more of your advertising brochures, especially if they list a number of products or services.

Mr. Ferguson was a young merchant who sold boutique items. He placed "boutique exhibits" containing some ten selected boutique "specials" in local stores. These special displays took up little space, and were interesting to view. He placed them in all kinds of stores, including:

- Restaurants
- Dress Shops
- Beauty Salons
- Food Establishments
- Other places where people congregated

Once again, merchants were eager to cooperate as long as they had available space, and most of them did. He paid his commissions, too. The merchants got even more than they expected. The displays attracted traffic they wouldn't ordinarily get, and they earned fifteen percent commission for normally unproductive space.

Another idea: Why not promote *related* products? If you sell cosmetics, why not place cosmetic displays in other types of stores, for example, drug stores. It is an old idea and a good one. There are new ways to apply this same idea. A wig maker enlarged the scope of his market many times by contracting every barber and beauty salon in a three-state area. He added hundreds of "branch offices." A pipe shop installed a large display of its expensive pipes in hotel lobbies. The perfect location since hotels are filled with people who often have time on their hands in the evening. Hotel lobbies were also used by a boutique dealer for displays. An art supply store searching for a way to enlarge its market, found art galleries glad to show its paints. A wine shop set up "Wine Cellars" in small department and other type stores. The same idea can be applied in an infinite number of ways. How does it apply to your business?

There are other roads to Rome, and many other ways to enlarge your market. Take department stores. They offer the smart merchant many ways to tie in with their advertising. As everyone knows, department stores send out regular mailings to thousands of customers. They also take large ads in the local papers. Question: How do you turn that to your advantage? Answer: You try to work out an arrangement to your mutual benefit. If your products do not conflict with theirs, these stores are often receptive to including your ad in their promotions. They will be providing their customers with an additional service, and earning profits for it. Here is a list of various types of businesses that are cooperatively promoted with department stores:

- Automotive services
- Home security systems
- Termite control
- Shoe repair stores
- Reupholstering
- Lawn service
- Photographers
- Home modernizations
- Sauna bath installations
- Employment services
- Home cleaning
- Roofing
- Travel agency

Let's return to our earlier concept: finding branch sales centers. The department store is an ideal branch sales center. It is a high traffic location. It eagerly seeks displays, even one-time displays that attract traffic. Just think what a pet show could do for department store traffic. Just think what it could do for you and your sales if you owned a pet shop.

When we talk of department stores, we also include the very important Five-and-Dime Store. These stores have changed over the years. They are now, for the most part, general variety stores. They often will permit many kinds of product or service displays. These can vary "all over the lot," including pizza-makers, bakeries, even key-making, and shoe repair. They are, of course, looking for ideas to build traffic.

But if department stores will permit displays, what about other kinds of establishments—banks, for example? Today many banks actually set up complete departments of products or services that will appeal to their customers. These include such diversified offerings as: insurance, travel, ticket agencies (for community recreational programs), and even such an unrelated service as photography. These banks have the interior space which, in most cases, is not being fully used; they have the customer traffic and they can gain a fine continuing income, too. Moreover, the banking business, too, has become very competitive. How can your product or your service qualify as an "add-on" business for your local bank?

In considering new ideas to enlarge your market, consider old ideas, too. Have you been taking the Yellow Pages of your phone book for granted? Do you think its value is limited? Not all merchants do. Some believe it can provide them with a very inexpensive equivalent of branch offices. Motels do, as one example. They place ads in the Yellow Pages of *surrounding* communities. We also know an exterminating firm which placed ads in the Yellow Pages of some fifteen surrounding communities. Thus, the Yellow Pages reaches areas and prospects not ordinarily covered by other advertising or by competitors—each of which becomes, in effect, another branch sales center for you!

Telephones can also be used to broaden the market. Let's mention "telephone squads." There are literally hundreds of women in your area who are eager to fill in spare time—by telephoning prospective customers for you, opening many doors to huge potential sales. They will work for a commission, or a small guarantee—such as three dollars an hour—plus commissions on sales made. Each of these "telephone homes" that you've appointed becomes, in effect, another branch sales center for you—giving you total market coverage.

There is still another way to cultivate your garden at a minimum cost. If you don't want to open up a branch permanently, why not do it for a day or two. Rent hotel rooms in a number of cities and exhibit your merchandise. This can increase your local and regional sales penetration; and if you are very ambitious, you can even go national. The cost is small: room, travel, expenses, and promotion.

Is this "branch office" concept too novel, too unorthodox for you? Consider this fact: Brooks Brothers is one of New York's most prestigious men's apparel stores. Its patronage is so highly selective that, it has been humorously stated, one needs to show proof of a ten thousand dollar bank account and impeccable character references before you are even permitted to buy from them. Yet recently, this firm rented hotel rooms throughout the country to display and sell its merchandise. Brooks Brothers thus gained the benefits of branch offices on a nationwide scale for a rather minor investment.

Let's now discuss "Bird dogs." We're not referring to "birds" nor are we discussing "dogs." It is a term that describes people who make it their business to hunt up prospect leads for you. They canvass their friends, relatives, and other associates. They send you a list of these prospective customers—on a regular basis—and you then contact them to make sales. Many "bird dogs" are available in any community—as it gives them a means of utilizing their contacts and, consequently, earning nice commissions from the sales that you subsequently make to these prospect leads. The better the lead, the more the sales, the greater their commission . . . hence, they're motivated to give you the most selective leads obtainable.

We haven't mentioned still another way to reach your customer. Give your business "mobility," the kind that enables you to cover your entire market. It will give you the equivalent of mobile branches in virtually every nook and cranny of your market area. It can be done very simply. Equip your auto, van, or truck with your products and bring them directly to the customer. Here are illustrations:

• A hardware store established a Handyman Mobil van that cruised around the community fixing things. The van was greeted with enthusiasm by housewives who had so many appliances that needed repair.

• There's the pet store that created a Poodle-Van, to groom the animals directly in their homes. Most of the dog owners found it a great service because of the time and trouble it saved them.

• And there's the bookstore that traveled around with its bookmobile, displaying the newest books, and thus created many new readers.

• And let us give credit to the ingenious businessman who sold tools to literally hundreds of garages and service stations. He equipped a truck for this purpose and sent it around on a regular weekly basis.

• Another enterprising firm had its truck equipped to "spray paint" homes in its area, and thus to sell its paint.

Now I present another fundamental principle: Cultivate the *Group Sale* wherever possible. Let me explain what I mean by group selling. I look at it two ways: either you sell to groups, or you have groups selling for you. Both ways mean bigger profits. You have more people working for you, or buying from you. It means using a shotgun, not a rifle, for your big game.

Here's how it will work: Practically every club and organization has a fund raising program. They need money to help finance their worthwhile activities. Either these funds are earned somewhere, or their programs must be ended. I'm talking about such respected organizations as the Lions, Elks, Kiwanis, Eagles, Jaycees, Rotary, even Boy and Girl Scouts—and practically every other public service organization you've heard of. These organizations comprise, as members, the solid citizens in your community. They are the people with the contacts. They can open doors which are normally closed to you.

Let's talk about case histories:

I know about a lamp shop . . . a small business you'd say . . . which got the cooperation of the Kiwanis Club in its area. The product was a mundane one: a "long-life" light bulb. Members sold more than ten thousand bulbs to help their club's fund raising program.

Here's another: A local seed store enlisted the assistance of the local Boy Scout Council to help increase sales. The 104 members of this Council went door-to-door peddling seed packets and sold two thousand. And a store which sold ornamental candles got a local women's club to sell specially matched candle sets by giving them a commission of twenty five cents a box. The women's club earned three hundred twenty five dollars which means that thirteen hundred boxes were sold through their efforts.

The same idea has many variations. An aggressive hosiery store sold the local PTA on conducting a women's pantyhose sale. In addition to commission, it offered a "Free Evening on the Town," dinner and theatre tickets to the most successful saleswoman. The results exceeded expectations. Even alumni groups of various universities participate in this type of fund-raising program—many times on a national basis.

There are other ways to work with institutions and clubs. I'm referring now to the sponsoring of exhibits or fairs. An antique shop persuaded a local church to present an antique fair to benefit its building fund. A service-type business specializing in cleaning homes held a "Good-Bye Pollution" Fair to dramatize the need for constant home cleaning to help combat pollution . . . and gave a trophy award to that section of its community that acted to become most "pollution free." A stamp dealer held a stamp and coin fair. Even a gas station (and you'd offhand think they would have no "theme" for sponsoring a fair) conducted one on the subject of "Proper Care for Your

Auto To Help Prevent Accidents." Money was raised from admission fees, commission on sales, and receipts from refreshments. Needless to say, the sponsoring merchants also profited.

There's another simple idea waiting for you to apply. It's the Hostess Plan. Many businesses recruit housewives to invite their friends, relatives, and neighbors to their homes to display and sell their products and services. It can be for an informal afternoon at which tea and cookies are served. The housewife, of course, receives a commission or a discount on the merchandise. Many of those attending make purchases; others are exposed to sales pitches which ultimately may turn into purchases. Most important, they are being exposed to your merchandise under pleasant, relaxed conditions. Sales can be as high as five hundred dollars in a single afternoon. The party hostess idea is an old one. Tupperware has built a massive international sales organization selling cookware and other products through the Hostess Plan.

One firm in Florida achieved sales of over one hundred million dollars in two years through the use of a variation of the Hostess Plan. So the plan has worked . . . and today it should work even better than ever! There are many housewives ready and eager to find ways to supplement their incomes. Practically every kind of business can use this plan. The beauty salon can demonstrate new hair-do styles and collateral products; the upholsterer, new fabrics and upholstery techniques. It is particularly valuable for stores that sell merchandise; e.g., women's apparel, linens, etc. Parties can be created for both the spring and fall when new fashions are introduced. Here are a few examples of more unusual ways the Hostess Plan was used:

- A dancing school demonstrated new dances before younger couples.
- An antique store brought a collection of Meissen china.
- A garden shop held an outdoor party at which new bulbs from Holland were displayed.
- A local tile shop showed how to use colored tile to decorate homes.
- A bank gave a mini-course in money management and signed up many new depositors.
- A tobacco shop, fighting the drop in sales because of anti-cigarette propaganda, introduced little cigars and minipipes to an audience which knew little about these products.

Another idea is the "Seminar." The purpose of a Seminar is to bring people with similar interests together. That interest is education and information. You furnish them with the information and education they want while they're relaxed, eager to listen, and you are talking to them under prestigious circumstances. This is truly the best concentrated group of prospective customers you can find anywhere! Here are a few examples of Seminars that have been conducted with highly profitable results:

● An interior decorator held one on "The Newest Methods for Decorating Your Home," attended by sixty five people. Many became customers.

● A jeweler struck gold when he held a Seminar on: "When and How To Wear Jewelry—and How To Select Diamonds." He had happened upon a subject dear to the heart of the average woman. The attendance was very large.

● A gourmet shop had a Seminar on "How To Prepare Gourmet Meals," and to its surprise, the attendance by men was almost as great as by women.

● An infants wear shop rendered its community a great service when it conducted a Seminar on "Better Care for Babies." The two chief speakers were a pediatrician and a child psychologist. The advice they gave the mothers who attended was much appreciated by them.

You'll be surprised at how easy it is to obtain local experts to participate in your Seminar program—for example, professors at the local university, and many others. In most instances they'll be glad to cooperate. Your suppliers, also your manufacturers and wholesalers, will be glad to participate in the Seminar, because the more sales that you make, so do they. Moreover, there are many films available which not only minimize the need for expertise, but also expand interest in the Seminar.

There is yet another way to enlarge the scope of your market beyond the four walls of your shop or store, and to get your products and services before *many* new prospects. Some of these are groups, some individuals. You can create exhibits. These exhibits can be placed in conventions, trade shows, state and city fairs, associations, trade unions, and clubs. They should be pinpointed to reach your exact prospects, and in the exact areas you want to reach them. You've probably seen bank exhibits on "Counterfeit Coins and How To Detect Them." Here are a few other exhibit ideas that have succeeded:

● A shoe store displayed "Shoes From the Revolutionary War Until Now," at the Knights of Columbus headquarters in its city.

● A paint store displayed a photo montage of "Prize Homes of Suburbia," at the largest women's club in its area. Along with this exhibit, it conducted a Seminar on new colors and improved types of paint for beauty, durability, and easy application.

● A book shop exhibited "Original Manuscripts of Famous Authors," as well as rare books, first editions, and new titles with pictures and biographies of the authors.

The trade or professional convention can be a very valuable location for your exhibits. Large numbers of people from throughout the entire country gather at these conventions. Many may have leisure time to spend and, therefore, are easily approachable. Take the case of the salesman who sold computerized invoicing systems for the medical profession. He went to a medical convention and instead of selling one system at a time to a doctor, had the opportunity to contact groups of them. He was able to talk and sell to as many as one hundred prospects at a time.

Volume sales can be made to "unexpected" groups, for example, trade unions. They have been often looked at as unapproachable—non-commercial—and their sales potential has been largely ignored. Yet union members comprise many, many millions. One salesman we know saw the tremendous potential offered by the desire of unions to help to "uplift" the status of their members. He contacted unions and sold them his motivational programs that reached six thousand of their members. This was another highly profitable GROUP sale.

Salesmen and merchants can also increase business through Tip Clubs. My suggestion is to contact ten or more "non-competitive" salesmen or businessmen. As members of the Tip Club, you tip each other off to business leads. One hand washes the other. You give them tips and they give you tips. And you reap mutual benefits. The idea here is that any businessman or salesman knows the needs of the people he contacts beyond the products and services he sells. You can do more than just tip off each other. You can set up interviews and demonstrations. Suppose you're a plumber and you're called on to fix a radiator leak. You see that the carpet is ruined. You realize they'll have to buy a new one soon. Naturally, you tell her about your friend Herman, the carpet merchant. You set up an interview for him. He can come and show them different kinds of carpets. Now Herman owes you one. You can be sure he's going to reciprocate. Other examples comprise:

- The insurance salesman who "tips" the salesman of cash registers of his customer's need for his product . . . the cash register salesman who, in turn, knows of prime insurance prospects.

- The towel service salesman who knows which individuals or companies are planning to move, and can "tip" off a great variety of businesses. For example:
—the real estate firm
—the moving company
—the decorating service merchant
—the office furniture and machinery merchant
—and many other such examples!

These Tip Clubs have worked very successfully . . . and literally hundreds of thousands of dollars in sales have thus been achieved. Each member gets you into the "front door" of a customer—usually by invitation!

Have you considered the "gold mine" of orders that you can get—practically for the asking!—from the people whom you buy things from? One merchant made a list of those from whom he purchased things regularly. He came up with twenty four in all. He reasoned that since he bought from them, they'd like to accommodate him . . . and he was right. His contacts paid off, both in direct sales and in referral sales. His list included:

● Grocer	● Insurance Agent
● Doctor	● Bank
● Newsstand	● Radio & TV Shop
● Gas Station	● Liquor Store
● Jeweler	● Tobacco Store
● Car Dealer	● Appliance Store
● Dry Cleaner	● Hardware Store
● Electrician	● Optician
● Men's Apparel	● Bakery
● Women's Apparel	● Drugstore
● Dairy	● Fuel Supplies
● Dentist	● Auto Service

Yes, he came up with a list of twenty four prospects that provided a gold mine of sales returns. He found them to be the easiest, most receptive group of prospects to approach and to sell.

And, before leaving the subject of Group Sales, let's discuss AUCTION PROMOTIONS. There is an excitement and challenge about an auction that stirs and strokes the imagination and invites participation and patronage. Many merchants have profitably utilized auctions to promote sales for their business. Here are a few examples:

● The art dealer, who conducted regular Art Auctions—generally in conjunction with charitable activities of local churches, temples, etc.

● White Elephant Auctions—held to auction off "unwanted" merchandise.

● Automobile Auctions—usually conducted through the auspices of a used car dealer.

One merchant we know had his own Auction Dollars printed up and gave them—very much like trading stamps—for purchases of one dollar or more. Twice a year, auctions were held, either at his home or a nearby hall, and merchandise was bid for with the auction dollars.

Here's another powerful idea for your consideration—shop-at-home selling. Some of the largest department stores and major merchandisers of consumer products have profited from the effectiveness of direct to consumer sales. These include such department store chains as Macy's, Gimbel's, and many others. The slogan, "Avon Calling," has become a part of Americana, and the company, the darling of Wall Street through this shop-at-home business. You can sell in-home service for practically any product or service—for interior decoration, upholstery, draperies, home modernization, furniture, apparel, and dozens of other items. A recent ad by Gimbel's even offered shop-at-home termite protection service. Shop-at-home selling is unique. It offers you a chance to utilize your time and that of your salesmen when business may be slow. Let me illustrate:

One salesman sold water softeners on a "shop-at-home" basis for three hundred dollars each. In the same community, a department store also sold similar equipment at a lower price. Yet the business of this salesman was three times that of the department store. Why? In this case, there was no passive waiting for customers to come by and ask for the product. The approach he used *demonstrated* the benefits of the water softener to prospects who previously were not aware of it. They were being sold in their own homes, an important additional service.

An upholstery store sends its salesmen to suburban homes with swatches of its goods. These are color-blended within the prospect's own living room and she can see how they look against her other furniture.

A roofing contractor made a survey of the roofing needs of homes in his area. Then armed with this information, his salesmen informed the house-holders of their roofing needs. This idea can be improved on. A tailor of custom-made clothes made the rounds of top corporations with swatches of fabric. The tailor thus acted to familiarize executives and other personnel with his services. In many instances, the sale was made immediately.

One major characteristic of American society is that it is a mobile society. In our affluent society, people are always moving—to new jobs, to new homes, to warmer or colder climates, from the city to the suburbs and back again. They are, most often, in need of new products and services. Remember, if you serve them well in the beginning, you can have their repeat business for many, many years. A few of the services they need are electrical, plumbing, heating, and automotive of all kinds. Here are a few of the products they will buy: furniture, appliances (major and minor), food and drugs, clothing, etc. The list is virtually endless. This is one of the great gold mines you may be over-looking. Nearly 350 million dollars is spent annually by these newcomers.

In most instances, they constitute ideal ready-to-buy prospects for your shop-at-home services. In many cases, they are looking for advice as to their needs. They are eager for your help, eager to buy. Go out of your way to greet these newcomers on arrival. Do it in person or by mail. A free gift and a discount offer is very much appreciated. A gas station often presents a free car wash; a florist, a free floral "Welcome Bouquet"; an electrician, a five dollar discount on his initial services.

There are, of course, many ways to learn the names of newcomers. These include the utility companies, realtors, movers, and your local county clerk. Two organizations, "Welcome Wagon" and "Getting To Know You," specialize in getting lists of newcomers and contacting them on your behalf. Remember that the initial contact is merely half the job. Follow-through is very important. They must be recontacted to show your interest continues— to provide you with a host of opportunities to sell other services and products.

I've spoken often of the need for you to look at your resources—at the gold underneath your feet. Too often we don't know the gold, even when we see it. We get complacent and tired. We adopt many of the attitudes our prospects do toward our products. You've got to shake yourself by the scruff of the neck. You've got to convince your customers you're selling them rare jewels, not just another product. You've got to dramatize your sale.

I remember walking through the famous "push cart" district of New York City. As I walked through, I passed push cart after push cart with goods piled high. Much of it was shabby and undesirable. I remember one push cart in particular. Its merchandise defied description . . . it was really a pile of junk —an old razor, a rusty handle for a drawer, an old key, a broken toy, and so on. I looked and looked again. Who would ever buy these things? I wouldn't have had them free. But I didn't own the push cart. The owner didn't think his merchandise was junk. I watched him as he handled each piece; I marveled. Each piece seemed as if it were a rare jewel to him. When he picked up a rusty razor, he cradled it in spotlessly white tissue paper—almost like a jeweler showing off a rare diamond. In some mysterious fashion his attitude communicated itself to those people congregated around the stand. They actually started buying the rusty nail, the razor, the old picture frames. He had dramatized his goods. They weren't buying his products; they were buying the dream of what they *could be!*

I also remember a barber I patronized. At that time he charged two dollars for a haircut. It was a large sum and business was poor. He seemed to be struggling along on a treadmill. He had five chairs in his shop. There were never more than two occupied at one time. One day after I had been out of the country for several months, I passed the shop. I stopped. Something new must have been added! The store was choked with customers. Upon entering, I was surprised to see my previously impoverished barber is a formal suit, striped trousers and all. Even more astonishing—he now charged the colossal sum of five dollars for a haircut! The sign in the shop read: "Luxurious *Gold Comb* Haircuts—$5." When you asked for the "Gold Comb Haircut," the gold comb would be taken out of a small locked safe where it was placed on velvet. It was carried to the customer as if it were a rare jewel. The patron was made to feel as if he were some king in a palace being given a haircut befitting to royalty! The same two dollar haircut was now a five dollar haircut because patrons were buying a dream, an elevated status in life, not a mundane reality. My barber friend took something commonplace and made it rare—he dramatized it.

One of the most successful merchants I know attributes his success to "daze-crashing." What in the world is "daze-crashing"? I asked this man. How does that help sales? He answered, "Daze-crashing" is the knack of being able to dramatize the benefits of your product in your very first words. People normally have a "dazed" or unthinking reaction to sales pitches. They're usually on the defensive if you ask them to buy anything. If you're selling a wrench, you'd get a quick "No" if you asked them whether they were interested in buying a wrench. But if you asked them whether they'd like to buy one thousand tools for the price of one, you'd get a receptive ear. Well, my "daze-crashing" friend had the right idea, and the success to prove it. He knew how to dramatize his merchandise. You've got to take another look and see how you can sell your dreams, too.

Here are a few other examples of "daze-crashing" that helped to dramatize the benefits of a product or service, and to multiply sales:

- The typewriter salesman offered the sale of an "idea-manufacturing" machine instead of just another typewriter.

- The shoe salesman offered one thousand miles of "blissful walking" instead of just another pair of shoes.

- A travel magazine offered a "glorious trip around the world"—for only six dollars!

While you're taking a look at your products and services, take a look at your entire business. There's a way to link these products together so they have a totally new look. This is being done often today. Companies sell systems, not products, anymore. And you do, too, but quite often you don't know it. For example: If you're a hardware salesman you can become a "Store for Better Living," that offers:

- increased home conveniences
- durability, safety, security
- better equipped kitchens
- increased home value

No longer will you be just another hardware store, competing with many other similar ones. You won't have to worry about price wars, building neighborhood loyalty, and going through the competitive rate race. By selling systems, you dramatize the effect of your products—the things they can do, rather than the things they are. You can sell your products in clusters—a number at a time—instead of one by one. You're now offering a concept that none of your competitors have. Think about the idea! What systems can you offer?

Let me illustrate: A salesman in the lighting field who sold lamps of all kinds offered his customers a *complete lighting system* for homes and offices. He was selling "better vision," and "better working efficiency," not just products. A seller of door locks began to sell a "Home Security System"—a complete line of locks and other security precautions for the entire home—front and back doors, patios and windows, etc. A salesman of recordkeeping books offered a complete "Business Management System." It included all books and forms needed to assist the businessman in keeping proper records and managing his business.

I repeat in summation: expand and enlarge your markets. Leave the narrow confines of the four walls of your shop or store . . . open branch outlets . . . get after the big game—the group sale. Seminars, fund-raising programs, and hostess parties will produce that business for you . . . build your shop-at-home business . . . woo newcomers to your area . . . build your instant conglomerate. These things are easy to do. They are the new highways you must learn to drive. They produce the difference between profit and loss. That profit must be yours!

9.

ACHIEVING THE PROPER START IN YOUR SELECTED BUSINESS

There is a tide in the affairs of men, which, taken at the flood, leads on to fortune; omitted, all the voyage of their life is bound in shallows and in miseries; and we must take the current when it serves, or lose our ventures.

—Shakespeare

How To Achieve the Proper Start In Your Business

- A journey of one thousand miles starts with a single step forward

- Forming a plan

- Preparing a schedule—keeping it

- Avoiding distractions:

    —Mr. Deflector
    —Mr. Advice-Giver
    —Mr. Devil's Advocate

- Importance of starting immediately

- Progress in "steps"—gain momentum

The most critical phase of your new business operation is its very beginning. The first ninety days can well spell the difference between success and failure.

The stage is set during this initial, crucial period. It's the momentum you establish at the very outset that can set the pattern for your entire new career. That is why it is most important that you start with determination, energy, and enthusiasm. Don't allow yourself to be sidetracked by meaningless distracting procedures.

Bear in mind that what you do and how you do it at the beginning can be most effective in putting you on the high road to success. Your energies and efforts should be immediately directed onto the following paths:

1. Familiarize yourself fully with your operation.
2. Familiarize yourself with your community.
3. Devise a workable plan and set it into operation.

Familiarizing Yourself With Your Operation

Become thoroughly conversant with all aspects of your business, your competition, etc.

Familiarizing Yourself With Your Community:

From the day you start business in your area, you are wed to the economy of your community. From that day on, this is your territory, your hunting grounds for prospective referral sources.

It is now vital that you take immediate steps to get to know and become known in your community. It is essential that you set out instantly to create a favorable image while you develop an ever-widening circle of friends and acquaintances. You thus set the stage for a constantly increasing sales potential and the opportunity for bigger and bigger profits.

Here is how this is done:

1. *Contact Influential Community Leaders:* Seek out and cultivate important people and institutions in your area. Make friends of people who influence people, and who are in a position to assist you, advise you, and help you establish that so-important image . . . and who can give you enthusiastic references and recommendations.

Such influential contacts would include:

● president of the Chamber of Commerce
● local banks and bank officials

- editors of local papers
- Better Business Bureau
- community industrial leaders
- civic and poltiical leaders
- educational leaders
- community clubs (Kiwanis, Lions, Rotary, Eagles, Elks, etc.)
- leaders of church groups and organizations

Make as many such contacts as you can, and do it promptly. Acquaint these people with your operation, and with the product or service you are offering. Make your field sound as interesting as possible, and enlist their cooperation and solicit their referrals. You will be agreeably surprised at the extent to which these community goodwill contacts pay off.

2. *Be a Joiner:* Join as many clubs in the community as you conveniently can. This will bring you into direct social contact with important people who represent a cross section of your community groups.

3. *Arrange for Publicity:* Seek to place articles in local papers and newsletters which will publicize your business and acquaint people with your operation. Start out with about three such articles. The first should contain your picture and a notice stating that you are now in business for your particular area. The second should inform readers about your "grand opening." The third should give interesting and unusual "human interest" sidelights about your business, such as unusual prospects you have met, and interesting problems you have faced, etc.

4. *Send Out Mailings:* These should go to prospects in your area and be directed to lists pertinent to your product or service. If your product appeals to home owners, you might want to consider "occupant" mailings. These mailings serve to invite residents to your "grand opening" (if your business comprises a store, shop, showroom, etc.), or to notify them of your service and offer some special first-customer inducement.

Devise a Good, Workable Plan

Every business should have a plan. If you are in a service business, you should plan to make a fixed number of contacts each day and a fixed number of repeat contacts. Once you set up this schedule, stick to it steadfastly and do not permit yourself to deviate from the plan.

You should also have a territorial plan. Map out the streets (and prospects) in your community. Cover a section of your community each day, massing together prospects in a given area so as not to waste valuable time and make every moment of your "contact" time count to the utmost.

You should also have a promotional plan. Establish a schedule for the placement of advertising . . . also a schedule for direct mail advertising.

Importance of Good Records

It is estimated that over 60% of those who start in business on their own fail (and often within the first year) because of poor recordkeeping. Your business records constitute the arithmetical "eyes and ears" of your business; they provide you with signals as to what you're doing right and what you're doing wrong . . . enabling you to conform your procedures accordingly.

With an adequate, simple bookkeeping system you can answer such questions as:

- How much business am I doing?
- What are my expenses? Which expenses appear to be too high?
- What is my gross profit margin; my net profit?
- How much am I collecting on my charge business?
- What is the condition of my working capital?
- How much cash do I have on hand and in the bank?
- How much do I owe my suppliers?
- What is my net worth; that is, what is the value of my ownership of the business?
- What are the trends in my receipts, expenses, profits, and net worth?
- Is my financial position improving or growing worse?
- How do my assets compare with what I owe? What is the percentage of return on my investment?
- How many cents out of each dollar of sales are net profit?

35 WAYS TO MAKE PEOPLE WANT TO DO BUSINESS WITH YOU: Positive Methods That Are Used By Most Successful Businessmen

Unless you act to let people know of the product or service that you have to offer, that product or service will certainly not get up and sell itself. And to carry that still further, the way you impress your customers . . . the kind of image you create and portray . . . can well make the difference between a prospective customer buying from you instead of from a competitor—or the difference between eager, constant, repeat business instead of a casual, occasional sale.

This elusive, hard-to-pinpoint, and almost indefinable something—the *you* of your business—is just about topmost among your assets, and represents an amount of goodwill practically beyond measure and virtually impossible to evaluate.

- *Remember Names and Faces.* You yourself know how you like to have people stop you on the street and show recognition with a friendly, "Hello, Mr. ...." You are pleased and perhaps a little flattered at this display of personal recognition. Your customers will be similarly pleased, and flattered, by such recognition and greeting on your part. And you will find that this simple friendliness and attention will help get additional orders.

- *Be a Joiner.* Socializing and mingling with people in itself is fun. In addition, it's good business to join various clubs and organizations in your community and get to be known.

- *Be a Good Listener.* Act interested when people want to talk to you. If they feel they can "get your ear" you'll find that you'll "get their business."

- *Play Up the "You" Appeal.* When explaining your product or service, be sure to emphasize the benefits in the light of your prospect's interest . . . how it can best help and serve him.

- *Be Helpful.* Your helpfulness will be reciprocated in the added business you get. As an example, we know of a salesman who ingratiated himself with telling results by clipping news items he considered of importance and interest to his prospects, and turning these items over to them.

- *Give Service.* Show a little extra interest through special attention and personalized service. This extra interest will pay off in extra business.

- *Demonstrate Your Integrity.* Let people know that you keep your word. Live up to promises made. You'll find that you don't have to force sales . . . that your reputation for honest dealing will spread quickly by word of mouth, and will result in considerable repeat and referred business.

- *Be Consistent . . . in the Prices You Quote, and in the Claims You Make.* Don't tell one customer one thing and another customer something else. People compare notes, and such inconsistencies will do damage to your image.

- *Be Creative.* Keep thinking up new "angles" and new benefits your customers can derive through your product or service. Think of your customers' special problems and how your product or service can help in relation to them.

- *Be Systematic.* Pre-arrange the coverage of your territory from day to day, and plan your contacts so as to cover the maximum number of prospects.

- *Be Self-Motivating.* Don't allow sporadic adversities to get you down. View yourself in proper perspective, and set your business course with conviction and determination.

• *Be Affirmative, Not Negative.* Don't go about knocking competitors. Emphasize the "positive"—what you can do, not what others, or competitive products, cannot do.

• *Be Thoughtful and Considerate.* A follow-up thank you note . . . a birthday remembrance . . . an occasional friendly phone call are just good public relations. Thoughtfulness of this kind will not only bring you business, but will give you personal satisfaction.

• *Be Alert.* Keep on the watch for new ideas and developments in your field and think of how they can be turned to your customers' advantage.

• *Be Neat.* Maintain neatness in dress and in your presentation. Nothing can be more discouraging or distracting to your prospect than furled-up and soiled pages carelessly included in your presentation material.

• *Be Patient.* Remember that your prospects don't know your product or service as well as you do. What you consider elementary may appear complex to them. Develop your sales pitch in "stages"—with valid "reasons why" . . . to be absorbed and digested a little at a time.

• *Be Logical.* Appeal to your prospect's intelligence. Make your approach believable, and avoid evasive answers to your prospect's questions.

• *Be Specific.* Avoid generalities. Wherever possible, give specific figures . . . and supply documentation to prove your point.

• *Be Authoritative.* Read up on all the instruction material furnished you by your company. Familiarize yourself thoroughly with your company's product and sales methods. In this way you can speak with confidence, and gain the respect and loyalty of your customers.

• *Show Humility.* As stated in the last point, answer all questions with authority. But when you haven't got the answer, admit it frankly rather than "bull" your way through. In such cases, merely say, "This I do not know— but we have highly paid experts in our company, and I'll be glad to consult them for the answer."

• *Be Generous.* If you are selling a service, small attentions like treating the prospect to a lunch or a cocktail will be appreciated, and will pay off.

• *Be Punctual.* Keep appointments on time. Not to do so may be regarded as an insult by your prospect, and an indication that you consider your time worth more than his.

- *Display Good Manners.* This may certainly seem elementary, yet it is of vital importance in building a proper "image." Little things like asking permission to smoke . . . being considerate of the prospect's time . . . apologizing for outside interruptions, etc.—help establish you as a person with whom it's nice to do business.

- *Be Original.* Don't allow yourself to become dull or monotonous with the same, unchanged sales talk and approaches.

- *Keep Analyzing Yourself.* Think of how you can improve your approach and procedures and change those thoughts into actions.

- *Be Cheerful.* Maintain a cheery demeanor. Dejection communicates itself and dampens both your sales efforts and your prospect's interest. Keep your chin up, and keep your troubles out of your sales efforts.

- *Be a Graceful Loser.* Even if you don't get the order, show the same amount of cordiality as you did at the outset of your sales effort, and don't display any irritation. Your prospect will continue as a prospect, and chances are you'll have better luck the next time.

- *Respect Time.* Time is valuable—especially your time. Don't waste it. Keep your sales pitch and visits as brief as possible. Your prospect will respect you for it.

- *Don't Be a Lecturer.* Don't deliver your sales pitch as a monologue. Make it conversational and invite your prospect's participation. Encourage your prospect to ask questions as you go along . . . and answer those questions patiently.

- *Be an "Anticipator."* Before seeing your prospect, anticipate the personal factors, the problems . . . the questions that may arise. Through this form of anticipation, you can bypass and make short shift of the negatives, and can concentrate on the positives.

- *Be a Note Taker.* Jot down the results of your visit with the prospect as soon as possible, and be sure your notes don't get lost. Being able to refer back to your notes will help assure correct follow-through.

- *Be Friendly, But Not Over-Familiar.* Friendship begets friendship. But a prospect feels pressured by over-familiarity, and resentment can ruin the sale.

• *Get Fun Out of Your Work.* Learn to enjoy your work, and your prospects will enjoy doing business with you, rather than with your competitor.

• *Display Self-Respect.* Put yourself on an equated level with your prospect. Be polite, but not over-polite.

• *Be Forthright.* Answer each of your prospect's questions "on the bull's eye." Don't give inadequate half answers. When your prospect sees that you are not trying to avoid any issues, he will respect you and he will respect your product or service.

• *Exercise Polite Persistence.* Don't let a turn-down deter you from trying again. A "polite" renewal of your sales effort, after a "polite" waiting period, won't offend, and may well turn a prospect into a customer.

10.

CREATING IDEAS

How To "Create" Ideas

Whatever you do, whatever you aspire to do, there's always the need to be creative, to generate new ideas covering practically every need, inclusive of:

- how to advance in your present job or business
- how to increase salability of your products or services
- how to overcome competition
- how to be a happier person

Ideas don't just "happen." They can be manufactured, practically at will. The formula contained in this chapter can help you accomplish this.

Ideas are all-important to business creativity and success. For example, my friend, Marty Sugar, thought of the idea of "leasing" television sets to hotels and institutions. He thus pioneered a distinctive merchandising approach to a "usual" product—most hotels were happy to have these sets placed in each room, at a cost of five dollars a week per room. In a comparatively short time, he had placed thousands of these sets in thousands of rooms, and collected very substantial weekly dividends year-in and year-out.

Mort Sobel also took an ordinary product—attached a "uniqueness idea" to it, and struck it rich. The product was perfume. Rather than trying to sell a bottle at a time, which everyone was doing, he had the idea of offering "20 world famous perfumes for $1.00." A virtual flood of orders came in, and kept coming and coming.

He had another idea. He recognized the appeal Disneyland had to children. What could he offer that would please children and, simultaneously help promote Disneyland? Idea! He produced children's records (with Disneyland advertising on the jacket) to be sold both inside and outside of Disneyland. Thousands were sold.

Master the idea formula in this book. See if it helps unlock previously locked doors—both personal and business—leading to both increased profits and self-contentment.

This chapter is intended to expedite creative thought—and to do so in a clearly-explained, workable manner.

It is based on a technique for idea-conception, developed by the author after twelve years. The term "idea," as used here, includes the abstract form (any idea on any subject) or the concrete form (a specific idea on a specific subject).

The suggestions in this chapter are also intended for business persons seeking business-improvement ideas—e.g., retailers, wholesalers, jobbers, industrialists, specialty firms, etc.

Second-person approach is used in the writing of this chapter. This, to simplify explanation and to avoid becoming academic and "text-bookish." Further, the reader may better understand the step-by-step development of this technique, and best apply it to his own problems.

Adherence to the suggestions contained herein will, I am convinced, help you to increase the quantity and the quality of your ideas to a substantial extent. They have helped me.

You are, let us say, a copywriter for an advertising agency.

Or . . . you are responsible for the development of new business for a manufacturing concern, a wholesale enterprise, a laundry, a department store, a specialty shop, a bank, an insurance company, etc.

Or . . . you head your own business and take personal charge of all sales promotion and advertising.

Now let us say that you have a problem. A specific problem that requires a specific answer. And fast!

As an advertising copywriter, perhaps your problem is to complete three advertisements by the following morning. As a businessman, perhaps *your* problem is how to better your enterprise (through advertising, merchandising, marketing, publicity, etc.).

Your quest is identical: you want an idea.

Your task is also identical. Broadly speaking, you must find the correct answers to these two simple but "oh so irritating" problems: first, what to say, do, or write; second, how to do or say it—successfully.

The first sensation (when starting to think) is usually that of mental "chaos." You have a mess of raw, ungoverned facts and figures. You'd like to mold them into some recognizable pattern—yet you do not know what kind of pattern it should be. In other words, you want an idea, but you do not know what kind of an idea you are seeking!

There are two different ways you can go about "tackling" your problem. First, the wrong way. Second, the right way.

The wrong way is often the usual way. The procedure is something like this: You first stare, then glare, at the material before you. Your thoughts are unguided, helter-skelter; your mind tends to wander. You get to reflect on many irrelevant subjects—say, the things you did yesterday...plan to do tomorrow.

But no idea *now*.

You may then vary the procedure by gazing into space (or at the wall) hoping, vaguely, for some kind of heavenly guidance. This failing, you subsequently "take it out" on your brain. You cudgel it, coax it, torment it. Alas, that idea has still failed to arrive.

Finally, with a deadline closing in, mentally fatigued, or plum disgusted, you'll throw deliberation to the winds and deliberately grab some half-acceptable idea. One you're not completely satisfied with.

You acknowledge defeat.

Method Two—which we shall call the "right way"—acts to avoid mental confusion. It seeks to focus in your mind the things you want to think about, to cleanse your mind of nonessentials. It strives to boil the business of thought into some sort of one-two-three formula.

Here are your prerequisites:

First: equip yourself with all the relevant facts.

Second: clearly understand your problem.

Third: apply *relevant* facts to a *specific* problem.

Let us explain it via an analogy. An invading army: First, it has an "objective." Second, it prepares the kind of forces that may best achieve this objective. Third, it "applies" these forces to the objective in the most compact, forceful manner—meanwhile avoiding unrelated moves that may dissipate strength.

So, in thinking, you must have your "objective"—that is, know what kind of problem you want to solve. Second, you must have the kind of facts at your "command" that may best attain this objective. Third, you must apply these facts in a systematic, effective way—avoiding all mental distraction.

Your resulting idea is as good, or as bad, as the relevant facts you have absorbed. Hazy facts, half facts, unrelated facts, breed weak, inadequate results.

Generally speaking, you should proceed through five separate stages in gathering and organizing your material, and in guiding your thought processes:

1. The Assimilative stage
2. The Organizational stage
3. The Eliminative stage
4. The Inspirational stage
5. The Percolation stage

First, the *Assimilative Stage:* Collect all the material you have, and can obtain on the subject—whether through library research, interviews, consulting your competitors' ads, etc. Write down everything you can possibly say in favor of the product. This is preferably done on 4 x 6 inch index cards.

Second, the *Organizational Stage:* Classify this information into topic-groups. Difficult? Not at all! For, in reviewing your data, you will find that every fact you have listed—confused as the original list may appear—is divisible into clearly defined general-topics, such as construction, operation, installation, appearance, convenience, economy, durability, etc. Simply jot down all the facts under their respective headings; classify them.

Now . . . consider these topics according to importance. Which is *most* important? Is it operation (simplicity); is it economy (either in the original purchase price or in use); is it appearance; is it taste, beauty? Or is it a combination of advantages? Decide, at this point, the advantage (or advantages) you would like to feature in your ad, or in your business-promotion campaign.

Third, is the *Eliminative Stage:* Study your facts. Extract the *most outstanding* point (or points) about your product or service, the one you'd like to feature. Summarize it into a single word, phrase, or sentence. Write it down; memorize it. *This* is the fact you're going to think *with;* it's the "vehicle" that carries you to your ultimate idea.

See—you've hacked through the jungle maze of your facts, tree by tree. Instead of thinking about a mumble-jumble of things, you are now thinking about a specific thing—the most important thing to your immediate problem!

Thus, you are ready for the fourth stage, the *Inspirational Stage.* This acts like a thought-catapult. It projects new experiences into your mind. It introduces a series of "sensations" to excite your imagination, prod your intellect. Gradually . . . you obtain *several* ideas from which you may select the *exact* one that *exactly* fits your problem.

How? Through the Words-and-Pictures procedure (similar to that employed for Abstract Ideas, related in the foregoing portion of this book).

You do this: You equip yourself with a list of "thought-nudgers." These may consist of many different things. For example, advertisements (of competitors and others); magazine and newspaper write-ups, pertinent research, effective ideas of any kind; interesting photos, illustrations, cartoons. The test is: Are they imagination-stirring?

The kind of things that act to "nudge" thought varies with different people—hence, no specific formula can be presented as to the kind of thought-nudgers you should gather for your specialized needs. Experiment with various types of data; decide which achieve the best results for *you.* Keep adding to your collection.

Remember, the subject need not relate to your own product or business. The *idea* it conveys is the all-important gauge of its value to you.

Thumb through your list of thought-nudgers. Let them bounce up against your senses—like so many ping pong balls. Lo, your imagination is heated. A flow of thoughts surge through your mind. You get "loads" of ideas.

For example, you are advertising a finance plan. You have decided (after organizing your facts) that "flexibility" is your most important sales point— that is, a loan plan to fit every budget.

Scanning your idea-nudgers, you see a picture of a tailor measuring a customer for a suit. You "associate" your facts with this picture. You perceive that "flexibility" can also be described as "tailor made." Soon, you create the heading "Tailor Made Loans—*You* Select The Plan!" Perhaps you encircle the heading with a tape measure for better visual effect.

Or . . . say you want to increase the sale of your book—a directory of the paper industry. The outstanding point (you have decided) is that this directory provides the salesman with more sales prospects. You see a picture of chain links in your idea-nudgers. An idea! . . . . Your ad is illustrated with a chain link—the picture of your book in one link, the copy, "Links You To A Bigger Selling Market," in the second link.

Or . . . you are advertising the merits of a newspaper in Podunk, Iowa. The outstanding point is its "exclusive coverage" of that area. Sight of a beverage bottle (in your idea-nudgers) may inspire the headline, "A Bottled-Up Market, Opened Only By The Podunk Times"—(a map of the area is contained in the bottle).

Perhaps you'll get many other ideas on the same subject. A picture of locked doors, or a gate, gives you the idea of illustrating a map of the area behind locked doors, with the headline, "Opened Only By The Podunk Times." Or you may show a picture of the town, cover it with the newspaper. headline it, "Blanket Coverage Of The Podunk Area"—and you got this idea by simply noting a picture of such a prosaic, unrelated thing as a blanket!

Not only advertising ideas, but also sales promotional and merchandising ideas, may be produced in this manner. For example—you want an idea to sell more packaged goods. You note something about "treasure hunt" in your idea file. You reflect: "Why not a treasure hunt with *my* product?" This gives you the idea of inserting money in a number of packages as an incentive to purchase.

Again, you read about the popularity of "personalized" items. You wonder how you can "personalize" your own product. This helps create a novel promotional idea—sending flowers to women customers on Mother's Day.

Or . . . you're selling razor blades. You read about the "Book of the Month Club." "Associating" your own business—you think of the idea of sending razor blades through the mail, at regular monthly intervals, to "subscribing" customers.

Or . . . you're selling radios. You had, some time past, jotted down in your idea file a "reminder" of a novel billboard idea you had seen, showing a coffee pot cooking and actual smoke issuing from the sign. You wonder how you can contrive a similar "live" tie-up for your own billboards. You have it! You place an actual radio in your billboard ad, playing audible music.

Or . . . you're selling hand lotion. Your idea file contains a write-up about "spending habits" of the public. You read that some $2,000,000 a year is spent for palmistry readings, indicating the popularity of this subject. You associate "palmistry" (concerned with hands) with your product (also concerned with hands). Thus you get an idea: You offer palmistry readings as a premium to purchasers of your product.

Or . . . you are an executive in a bank. You read an ad regarding canned goods that recommends ways for women to budget their kitchen labors. Applying this idea to your own problem, you get the idea of a book showing how people may budget their money.

YOU CAN UNFAILINGLY PRODUCE IDEAS, AGAIN AND AGAIN, WITH THESE NUDGERS!

Here's why:

First of all, they provide a "beach-head" for your thoughts, give you a mental foothold from which you may expand . . . think ahead.

Second, they surround you with a multitude of ever-handy stimulating *experiences* which are all-important for creative thought.

Experiences act to stir the "senses" (giving you an "awareness" of GENERAL relationships to your own problem). Thereafter, it acts upon the intellect (prompting you to "reason out" SPECIFIC relationships). The idea ensues . . .

You'll recall that most of your best ideas came through experiences—talking to friends, seeing a movie, traveling, reading, feeling some deep emotion, etc. Your imagination was aroused, your brain was subsequently put to work.

Normally we do not have the opportunity to accumulate all the experiences that we need. Certainly, we can't leave the office to absorb new experiences whenever we must think up an idea. Hence, the effectivensss of this file, giving you a mass of experiences in vest pocket form—at your beck-and-call, at the exact moment that you need them!

Our fifth, and last stage is the *Percolation Stage*. At this point you have filled your mind with several alternative ideas to fit your problem. Now, relax—

Get away from your problem. Take a walk, go out to lunch, listen to the radio, chat with friends, work on something else, read the newspapers. Put your mind at rest.

Yet ... you *have not* abandoned your problem!

All this time your pre-conceived ideas are going through a "drip ... drip ... drip" process within your mind, working on your subconscious self. Gradually, invariably, the very idea you want sprouts forth in your mind. You can see it clearly, precisely!

And this idea was not achieved through "happenstance"—it was inevitable ... the product of organized and methodical thinking. For the essence of this idea-technique is that it helps you to become master rather than slave of thought. It equips you to produce ideas scientifically, as you want them, on the assembly-line principle.

Prove it for yourself. Make it a habit to follow through on the foregoing plan for "thinking up" more and better ideas. It will yield dividends!

Ways To Use "Creativity"

Everything you sell requires creative selling. Creative selling comprises more than merely demonstrating a product or service and its uses. It requires wrapping the product with excitement, drama—with living, breathing *benefits*—that make the prospect look beyond the product itself to his own welfare ... how this product can do something to "better his life" for him— starting right now!

Jed Burton was one of our favorite creative salesmen. His product was a very, very ordinary one—a wrench. Practically everyone had a wrench, few felt they needed one. Hundreds—perhaps thousands—of other salesmen competed with him to sell wrenches.

What made Jed different? Before he started to sell, he sat down to think: How could he "stop" prospects to listen to him? What could he say or do that would get across the wrench benefits as quickly and dramatically as possible? Suddenly—he had it! He used this approach: "I'm here to sell you a thousand tools for the price of one ...."

The fantastic bargain value of this offer stopped the prospect. Jed received an audience—in fact, every prospect he saw gave him a receptive hearing. He could now get into his sales pitch, explaining how the wrench he sold was capable of one thousand uses.

Within this one simple approach, Jed compressed these selling benefits: First, he "stopped" the prospect to listen. Second, he grabbed his interest. Third, he dramatized the benefits of his product—all the things it could do for the prospect. Needless to say, Jed's sales soared. Just one single sentence—and his income jumped to fifteen times what it was formerly.

Another example: Bob Henderson sold typewriters. This, you'll agree, is also a very ordinary product. He, too, recognized that he'd make a few sales just asking people if they wanted a typewriter. He had to dramatize some benefit that his typewriter would give them . . . do for them . . . that the prospect never realized before.

Suddenly—it came to him! He said:

"I have something sensational to show you—an actual IDEA-MANU-FACTURING MACHINE!"

Every prospect stopped to listen, and look. Bob had the relaxed, responsible audience to explain the smoothness of the typing, enabling easy "idea-manu-facturing" . . . how the prospect could type and express so much more with this typewriter than others, etc.

Still another example is a friend of ours, George Cole. George sold subscriptions to a travel magazine. On the surface you'd say this is a tough item to sell—who reads travel magazines? Yet—George earned upwards of ten thousand dollars a year.

His approach: "How would you like to buy a trip through Europe for only six dollars?" This stopped people, they listened. He then explained how the current issue takes them on a "fascinating, romantic" trip through Europe—"almost as if you were there in person." The next issue would take them through South America. And so on. All for the subscription price of only six dollars.

It's easy to see why George's income was so high.

Another of our favorite creative selling approaches was that used by Dolph Stonehill. His product was a photo-copying machine to reproduce letters, office forms, etc. He analyzed the "benefits"—that the machine saved business firms a great deal of money each year over usual duplicating methods. He now created an approach that would best get this across. He said:

"I have something to show you that will interest you very much—a MONEY-MAKING MACHINE!"

People listened. A money-making machine! . . . this, they had to see! Dolph now found it easy to get into his sales pitch, demonstrating how the machine actually "made money"—lots of it! for business firms each year (in savings they achieved)—and could do so for the prospect's firm, also.

Creative selling isn't always symbolized by the first words of an approach. It takes on other forms. However, the goal is always the same, to demonstrate and dramatize how the product will benefit the prospect.

For example, Gene Stern sold creatively by performing a useful service for his prospects. Gene sold industrial lighting (a highly competitive field). He analyzed: "Why do people buy lighting from salesmen—rather than from the corner hardware store? Why should they buy it from me?"

He recognized that lighting was (a) an expense, not an income—hence, he had to justify the expense, to show how it could be an income, (b) that few people have "technical" knowledge of lighting needed for the various operations in a business establishment.

As a result of this analysis, he transformed himself from a lighting salesman into a "scientific lighting consultant." He equipped himself with a pad of Lighting Survey sheets . . . and an impressive, professional-looking lighting meter. As his new approach, he offered to take a "scientific" lighting survey of the business firm—exposing lighting inadequacies He used his light meter to measure foot-candles of light, and the survey pac to to down his findings. He pointed out lighting needs, room-by-room

He went still further: He showed the prospect a chart (that he had previously prepared) listing actual savings that the prospect would make per year through longer lighting . . . and lesser maintenance costs . in addition to getting better work from employees, and attracting more store traffic. Thus, the lighting now represented a "savings" and "profit' to the prospect rather than an expense!

Needless to say the prospect was impressed—listened respectfully to Gene's recommendations. The result? Where, previously, his sales (when he made them) averaged ten dollars, they now averaged one hundred twenty five dollars! And he made sales more frequently.

A similar "survey" approach was used by Howard Holmes, a printing salesman. Few prospects had responded when he had asked whether they needed printing. Practically all responded when he offered to give them a "free, scientific analysis of their office forms . . . and letterheads."

Another firm—selling shrubbery—built up a thirty million dollar a year business offering prospects a sketch of how their landscape should look. (They sold "beauty," not shrubbery!)

11.

FINANCING YOUR BUSINESS: 126 SMALL BUSINESS FINANCING SOURCES

GETTING FINANCING FOR YOUR BUSINESS

Being "undercapitalized" is one of the biggest reasons for business failure. Often, the entrepreneur believes he has enough capital, and is astounded when—in midstream—unforeseen expenses cause him to "run dry" and to forfeit a business that otherwise could have a good potential.

In deciding to enter a business, you must first decide:

1. What are the anticipated operating expenses that you must cover until expected cash flow from your new business comes through?

2. How much income do you need, during this initial period (normally six months) to cover your usual living expenses?

3. The difference between your answers to numbers one and two above and the amount of your available capital, indicates the amount of financing that you must seek prior to entry into the business.

Start-up expenses usually comprise.

- cost of rented space
- office equipment and furniture
- inventory
- supplies
- renovations
- advertising and promotions
- wages and salaries

Have you decided that you need financing? Seeking a financial source? There are normally two broad categories of financing sources, as follows:

1. Collateral Financing: based on iron-clad security that you provide to assure loan repayment; e.g., home, fixed property, etc. This type of financing usually carries lowest interest rates.

2. Venture Capital Financing: wherein you may not have such iron-clad security . . . and the investor "takes a chance" on you based on what he projects to be your potential, and the potential of your planned business. This type of financing usually carries highest interest rates . . . and often, too, an "equity interest" in your business.

In approaching a financing source for a loan, you should have a detailed Estimated Financial Statement that shows:

1. projected expenses of your business
2. projected income of your business (usually over a five-year period)
3. your own "track record"—your background, business ventures you've entered, your successful accomplishments
4. a personal financial statement

Thus, you provide a Financial Statement that shows both where you are now, and where you intend to be within the next five years as a result of your new business. The investor judges both in determining your eligibility for a desired loan.

Types of loan sources include:

● Banks: Your local bank is usually most receptive to providing a loan under normal circumstances. This type of of loan is normally preferable, since interest rates are usually lower. Also, the local bank is usually acquainted with you and the potential for your type of business in their locality. There are a variety of possible bank loans: short-term loans (sixty to ninety days), or long-term (as long as ten years).

Popular types of bank loans are:

● *Straight Commercial Loans:* (usually thirty to sixty days) based on submitting financial statement. This loan is generally used for seasonal financing or inventory expansion purposes.

● *Installment Loans:* These are usually long-term loans, repaid on a monthly basis. These loans can be tailored to the business needs, for example, heavier repayments during peak months and smaller repayments during off-season periods.

- *Term Loans:* Such loans have maturities of one to ten years and may either be secured or unsecured. Loan repayments may be made on almost any agreed-upon basis—monthly, quarterly, semi-annually, annually. Early repayments are often relatively small, with a large final payment. Although many term loans are backed by collateral security ... the lender ordinarily requires that current assets exceed current liabilities in at least a two-to-one ratio.

- *Bills or Notes Receivable:* Promissory notes are often given for purchase of goods. These notes are called "accounts receivable," or "notes receivable." These receivables can usually be discounted—that is, purchased by the bank at a discount. Your account is credited with the amount of the note less the discount to due date. The bank will collect from the note-makers when it's due.

- *Warehouse Receipt Loans:* Under this form of financing, goods are stored in warehouses and the warehouse receipt is given to the bank as security for a loan to pay off the supplier. As fast as the borrower is able to sell his merchandise, he buys back portions of the inventory.

- *Equipment Loans:* Loans are made to finance the purchase of machinery or equipment. The lender usually retains title until installment payments have been completed.

- *Collateral Loans:* Based on such collateral as chattel mortgages on personal property, real estate mortgages, life insurance (up to cash surrender value of the property) or stocks and bonds. If your banker says "No," then contact your local Small Business Administration Office. They are geared to expedite loans (that are justifiable) for small businesses like yours. They request, as your first step, that you initiate your loan request via your local bank. If the bank turns you down, SBA will undertake, in many instances, to "share" your loan with the local bank, assuming responsibility for 50% or more. The majority of banks (even those refusing your initial loan request) usually cooperate with SBA sponsored loans.

Small Business Investment Companies

Another "prime" source is small business investment companies. SBIC's use partly private, partly federal money to provide capital for small businesses —through loans, direct stock purchases, or debentures convertible into stock. This gives you a loan-permanent opportunity formerly available only to bigger companies. These SBIC's are generally assisted by the Small Business Administration (authorized to buy up to $1,000,000 in debentures of an individual SBIC). There are more than four hundred eighty SBIC's now in operation. Financing costs are generally higher than banks' but often lower than other outside "private" sources. To obtain names and addresses of SBIC's in your area, write to Small Business Administration, Investment Division, Washington, D.C., or to National Association of SBIC's, 537 Washington Bldg., Washington 5, D.C.

- *Mortgage Companies, Savings & Loan Associations:* Where real estate is involved, mortgage companies and savings and loan associations are receptive to providing "mortgage" loans. This can apply to business or personal real estate holdings.

Private Capital

Insert an ad in your local newspaper under "Capital Wanted." Through this medium you may attract private investors who regularly consult this column for investment opportunities.

Factors

In each community there are factoring firms who make loans of all types to businesses. Their standards are lower than banks', hence, they are more inclined to extend you your desired loan (even though turned down by banks and government sources). Factors are recommended only as a "last resort" since their interest rates are often excessive.

Veterans Administration Loans

If you are a veteran (either of World War II or the Korean War) you may be eligible to obtain a loan via your local Veterans Administration Office. Write to them to obtain their detailed pamphlet on types of loans offered and controlling conditions.

Commercial Investment Companies

There are many investment companies, privately constituted, that grant loans. You will find them listed in your local telephone directories (Yellow Pages). Their rates are generally on a par with rates of factoring organizations.

Leasing Firms

"Leasing" has become more and more prominent in recent years. Almost any type of product or equipment can now be leased. Thus, it acts to:

- Finance many aspects of your business—e.g., furniture, fixtures, machinery, equipment—giving you a period of three to five years to pay back (via small monthly payments).

● Finance your customers (particularly if the product cost is comparatively high). You, as the seller, are paid the full amount due, immediately. The customer pays the leasing company monthly—over a period of years.

● Franchise "Package" Financing: Often your franchise "package" comprises products or equipment that are financeable (usually to the extent of 60% of the wholesale cost).

● Floor Plan Financing: These are usually short-term loans applicable to merchandise in your store (on the floor). For example: boats, autos, appliances, etc.

FINANCING FOR "MINORITY" GROUPS

This type of financing has been provided by:

● SBA (and other governmental agencies), to help minority businesses.

● Private-fund organizations—e.g., Ford Foundation, Urban League, etc.

● Industrial organizations—foremost industrial organizations have participated in financial aid programs for minority enterprises (particularly in those cities where their main plants are located).

When should you seek a loan? Do not seek a loan if you do not need the money for specific business purposes (otherwise you are paying the penalty of high interest rates without obtaining proportionate benefits). Your rule of thumb should be: Will this money that I am borrowing help me to earn more money (in excess of interest rates incurred)?

Do borrow money if it does help you establish yourself in business, quicken your progress, and expand your profits. Bear in mind that it's always good "economics."

Below are listed possible financing sources . . . companies that have, at some period, indicated their receptivity to the financing of viable businesses. This list has been compiled from various sources. Because of the frequent "fluidity" characterizing the financing field in general—especially during recent years—there is no assurance of the current applicability of some of the names on this list.

SMALL BUSINESS LOAN SOURCES

Frederick R. Adler
817 Fifth Avenue
New York, N.Y.

Allen & Company
40 Broad St.
New York, N.Y.

Amco Capital Corp.
703 Market St.
San Francisco, Calif.

American Commercial Finance Corp.
26 Fellowship Rd.
Cherry Hill, N.J.

American-European Assoc., Inc.
640 Fifth Avenue
New York, N.Y.

American Fidelity Corp.
P.O. Box 217
Bristol, Ind.

A.J. Armstrong, Inc.
2618 Guardian Bldg.
Detroit, Mich.

Associated Financial Services Corp.
1030 E. Jefferson Blvd.
South Bend, Ind.

Bank of America
485 California St.
San Francisco, Calif.

Bankers Investment Company
Bankers Investment Bldg.
Hutchinson, Kans.

Bankers SBIC
301 20th St.
Oakland, Calif.

Bankers Trust Company
New York, N.Y.

Basic Capital Corp.
40 W. 37th St.
New York, N.Y.

Bayside Capital Corp.
706 One Main Plaza East
Norfolk, Va.

A.G. Becker & Co.
55 Water St.
New York, N.Y.

Bessemer Securities Corp.
245 Park Avenue
New York, N.Y.

Blair & Company
Stamford, Conn.

N.A. Bogdan Company
245 Park Avenue
New York, N.Y.

Boston Capital Corp.
535 Boylston St.
Boston, Mass.

W.A.M. Burden & Co.
630 Fifth Avenue
New York, N.Y.

Burnham & Company
60 Broad St.
New York, N.Y.

Business Capital Corp.
636 Meadows Bldg.
Dallas, Texas

C.I.T. Corp.
650 Madison Avenue
New York, N.Y.

California-Northwest Capital Co.
2210 "S" Street
Eureka, Calif.

Capital For Future
635 Madison Avenue
New York, N.Y.

Capital Investment, Inc.
238 W. Wisconsin Avenue
Milwaukee, Wis.

Carr Management Company
445 Park Avenue
New York, N.Y.

Casady Capital Corp.
2625 Britton Rd., Northwest
Oklahoma City, Okla.

Catawba Capital Corp.
P.O. Box 3121
Charlotte, N.C.

Central Florida Investments, Inc.
125 South Court Avenue
Orlando, Fla.

Charleston Capital Corp.
19 Broad St.
Charleston, S.C.

Chase Manhattan Capital Corp.
One Chase Manhattan Plaza
New York, N.Y.

City Capital Corp.
9255 Sunset Blvd.
Los Angeles, Calif.

Clark Dodge & Company
140 Broadway
New York, N.Y.

Colony Credit Corp.
6326 Marlboro Pike
District Heights, D.C.

Commercial Credit Corp.
300 St. Paul Pl.
Baltimore, Md.

Consolidated Technical Capital Corp.
121 So. Broad St., Ste. 620
Philadelphia, Pa.

Construction Capital Corp.
c/o Medical Center Bank
6631 South Main St.
Houston, Texas

Creative Ventures
71 W. Cambridge Avenue
Phoenix, Arizona

Louis Cristoforo
8009 Westchester Avenue
Bronx, N.Y.

Dawnlee Investment Company
P.O. Box 6233
Alexandria, Va.

Diablo Capital Corp.
350 20th St.
Oakland, Calif.

Dial Finance Company
410 Kilpatrick Bldg.
Omaha, Neb.

Diebold Venture Capital Corp.
430 Park Avenue
New York, N.Y.

Anthony Earl
34 Ashgrove Pl.
Don Mills, Ontario, Canada

Eastern Capital Company
185 Devonshire
Boston, Mass.

Edifice Realty
15 Herzog Pl.
Hicksville, N.Y.

R. Elvain
P.O. Box 65
Eufaula, Ala.

Empire SBIC
57 W. 57th St.
New York, N.Y.

Empire Capital Corp.
109 Oak St.
Greenwood, S.C.

Equal Opportunity Finance, Inc.
1202 S. Third St.
Louisville, Ky.

Equitable SBIC
350 Fifth Avenue
New York, N.Y.

Exchange Capital Corp.
134 S. LaSalle St.
Chicago, Ill.

Federal Street Capital Corp.
535 Boylston St.
Boston, Mass.

Federated Capital Corp.
122 E. 42nd St.
New York, N.Y.

Ferguson Funding Corp.
10111 North Western
Oklahoma City, Okla.

Field Investments Company
1980 Cold Water Canyon
Beverly Hills, Calif.

Financial Corp. of America
737 N. LaSalle
Chicago, Ill.

Financial Investors Svces. of Pacific
745 Fort St., Suite 2106
Honolulu, Hawaii

First Carolina Capital Corp.
First Citizens Bank & Trust Company
4th & Tryon
Charlotte, N.C.

First Midwest Capital Corp.
703 Northstar Center
110 S. 7th St.
Minneapolis, Minn.

First National Bank of Denver
Terminal Box 5808
Denver, Colo.

First Texas Investment Corp.
South Houston, Texas

First Wisconsin Investment Corp.
735 N. Water St.
Milwaukee, Wis.

First SBIC of Los Angeles
611 N. Alvarado
Los Angeles, Calif

Floco Investment Company
South Aceline Ave.
Lake City, S.C.

W.E. Fox
P.O. Box 420
Hazelwood, Mo.

Garden State SBIC
385 N. Field Ave.
West Orange, N.J.

Garvin, Bantel & Company
120 Broadway
New York, N.Y.

GEICO (Military/Gov't. Employees)
Vermont Avenue & "K" St., N.W.
Washington, D.C.

General Acceptance Corp.
1105 Hamilton St., W.
Allentown, Pa.

General Business Investment Corp.
9 S. High St.
West Chester, Pa.

General Electric Credit Corp.
570 Lexington Avenue
New York, N.Y.

General Equities Corp.
23880 Woodward Avenue
Pleasant Ridge, Mi.

General Investment Corp.
1301 Central St.
Evanston, Ill.

Harvard SBIC
33 E. Hunting Dr.
Arcadia, Calif.

Investment Capital, Inc.
Main St. at 13th
Duncan, Okla.

Medical Capital Corp.
1041 E. Grand Avenue
Decatur, Ill.

Mid-Tex Capital Corp.
104 North Avenue, E.
Clifton, Texas

Jesse E. Mocorro
8801 121st St., S.W.
Tacoma, Wash.

David Morgenthaler
1414 Union Commerce Bldg.
Cleveland, Ohio

Motor Enterprises, Inc.
3044 W. Grand Blvd.
Detroit, Mich.

Mutrusco Management Corp.
4722 Broadway
Kansas City, Mo.

National Property Consultants, Inc.
6100 Dutchman's Lane
Louisville, Ky.

Newton Capital Corp.
733 Third Avenue
New York, N.Y.

Northwestern Investment Corp.
1919 Record Crossing Rd.
Dallas, Texas

Postal Thrift Loans, Inc.
703 Douglas St.
Sioux City, Iowa

Quaker City Investment Corp.
6701 N. Broad St.
Philadelphia, Pa.

Sherman Mortgage Company
877 Frederick Blvd.
Akron, Ohio

State Loan & Finance Corp.
1320 Fenwick Lane
Silver Spring, Md.

Walter Stephens
1005 McKinney
Arlington, Texas

Edward Swartz
177 Newbury St.
Boston, Mass.

Trans-Western Acceptance
1018 Live Oak Blvd.
Yuba City, Calif.

Trinity Capital Funds, Inc.
3636 Lemmon, No. 308
Dallas, Texas

Union Commerce Capital, Inc.,
P.O. Box 5876
Cleveland, Ohio

Union SBIC
572 Madison Avenue
New York, N.Y.

United Oil Management Svce.
2451 W. Locust St.
Eldorado, Ill.

Western Group, Inc.
P.O. Box 1273
Weston, Conn.

Western Urban Redevelopment Corp.
1472 Russ Bldg.
San Francisco, Calif.

Weikort & Associates
P.O. Box 1495
Rapid City, S.D.

World Finance Company
620 Symes Bldg.
Denver, Colo.

Vanguard Mortgage Company
7100 Biscayne Blvd.
Miami, Fla.

GOVERNMENT FINANCIAL ASSISTANCE PROGRAMS
(For Minority Groups)

Office Of Minority Business Enterprise

The Office of Minority Business Enterprise (OMBE) was established within the Department of Commerce to be the focal point of the Federal Government's efforts to assist the establishment of new minority enterprise and the expansion of existing ones.

To provide local assistance to prospective and existing minority businessmen, OMBE has affiliated with local business development organizations in cities with substantial minority populations. These organizations serve as a central information source on business opportunities in addition to providing assistance to minority businessmen. A list of these organizations follows:

ALABAMA

Magic City Economic Dvlpmnt. Corp.
1417 N. 4th Avenue
Birmingham, Ala. 35203

ARIZONA

Guadalupe Organization, Inc.
8810 S. 56th St.
Guadalupe, Ariz. 85281

Indian Dvlpmnt. District of Ariz. (IDDA)
1230 E. Camelback Rd.
Phoenix, Ariz. 85014

National Economic Dvlpmnt. Assn.
2034 N. Third St.
Phoenix, Ariz. 85004

Progress Assn. for Economic Dvlpmnt.
1525 N. Central Avenue, Ste. 206
Phoenix, Ariz. 85004

National Economic Dvlpmnt. Assn.
100 E. Alameda
Tucson, Ariz. 85701

Navajo Small Business Dvlpmnt.Corp.
P.O. Drawer "L"
Fort Defiance, Ariz. 86504

ARKANSAS

Arkansas Business Dvlpmnt. Corp.
(This organization has 11 branches
serving the Arkansas area.)
Union National Plaza, Ste. 105
P.O. Box 1467
Little Rock, Ark. 72203

CALIFORNIA

National Economic Dvlpmnt. Assn.
2607 Fresno St., Ste. 2
Fresno, Calif. 93721

CALIFORNIA (Cont'd.)

Asian American Natl. Bus. Alliance, Inc.
The Olympic West Bldg., Suite 332
1543 W. Olympic Blvd.
Los Angeles, Calif. 90015

Interracial Cncl. for Business Opportunity
4801 S. Vermont Avenue
Los Angeles, Calif. 90037

National Economic Dvlpmnt. Assn.
5218 E. Beverly Blvd.
Los Angeles, Calif. 90022

National Economic Management Assn.
5059 W. Pico Blvd.
Los Angeles, Calif. 90019

So. Central Imprvmnt. Action Cncl., Inc.
8557 S. Broadway Avenue
Los Angeles, Calif. 90003

The East Los Angeles Community Union
1330 S. Atlantic Blvd.
Los Angeles, Calif. 90022

United Indian Dvlpmnt. Assn.
1541 Wilshire Blvd., Rm. 307
Los Angeles, Calif. 90017

Golden State Business League, Inc.
13 Eastmore Mall, Professional Bldg.
Oakland, Calif. 94605

Western Economic Dvlpmnt. Corp.
4000 Broadway
Oakland, Calif. 94611

Pasadena Urban Coalition
118 S. Oak Knoll
Pasadena, Calif. 91101

National Economic Management Assn.
2210 "K" St., Ste. C
Sacramento, Calif. 95816

Operation Second Chance
Technical Assistance Center
1653 N. Vernon Avenue
San Bernardino, Calif. 92405

National Economic Management Assn.
1736 N. Euclid St.
San Diego, Calif. 92115

National Economic Dvlpmnt. Assn.
2223 El Cajon Blvd., Ste. 314
San Diego, Calif. 92104

CALIFORNIA (Cont'd.)

Tri County Mexican American Unity Cncl.
607 S. Main
Salinas, Calif. 93901

Asian, Inc.
1610 Bush St
San Francisco, Calif. 94109

United Indian Dvlpmnt. Assn.
1390 Market St.
Fox Plaza, Ste. 911
San Francisco, Calif. 94102

Latino Local Dvlpmnt. Company
2959 Mission St., Ste. 303
San Francisco, Calif. 94111

Plan of Action for Challenging Times, Inc.
635 Division St.
San Francisco, Calif. 94117

National Economic Dvlpmnt. Assn.
100 Park Center Plaza, Ste. 325
San Jose, Calif. 95113

National Economic Management Assn.
235 E. Santa Clara St., #1009
San Jose, Calif. 95121

COLORADO

Colorado Economic Dvlpmnt. Assn.
735 Curtis St.
Denver, Colo. 80204

Denver Coalition Ventures, Inc.
4849 E. 32nd Avenue
Cure D'Ars Bldg.
Denver, Colo. 80207

Upland, Inc.
777 Main Avenue, P.O. Box 1909
Durango, Colo. 8130⁴

CONNECTICUT

National Economic Dvlpmnt. Corp.
1475 Barnum Avenue, Ste. 333
Bridgeport, Conn. 06610

Ebony Business League
703 Albany St.
Hartford, Conn. 06112

Puerto Rican Businessmen's Assn.
96 Wadsworth St.
Hartford, Conn. 06106

CONNECTICUT (Cont'd.)

Greater New Haven Business & Professional Men's Assn.
226 Dixwell Avenue
New Haven, Conn. 06511

Southwestern Equal Economic Council of Connecticut, Inc.
One Bank St.
Stamford, Conn. 06901

DELAWARE

Wilmington Business Opportunities & Economic Dvlpmnt. Corp.
915 Washington St.
Wilmington, Del. 19801

DISTRICT OF COLUMBIA

Anacostia Economic Dvlpmnt. Corp.
2200 Martin Luther King, Jr., Ave., S.E.
Washington, D.C. 20020

Community Learning Corp.
1026-28 6th St., N.W.
Washington, D.C. 20001

Interracial Council for Bus. Opportunity
735 15th St., N.W., Ste. 240
Washington, D.C. 20005

Model Cities Economic Dvlpmnt. Corp.
1325 Massachusetts Avenue, N.W.
Washington, D.C. 20005

One American (LBDO Support)
1330 Massachusetts Avenue, N.W., Ste. 205
Washington, D.C. 20005

Spanish Speaking Economic Enterprise Dvlpmnt.
917 15th St., N.W., Ste. 202
Washington, D.C. 20005

Washington Black Economic Union Dvlpmnt. Corp.
1025 Vermont Ave., N.W., Ste. 1025
Washington, D.C. 20005

Washington Business Dvlpmnt. Center
733 15th St., N.W., Ste. 1026
Washington, D.C. 20005

Washington Cncl. for Equal Bus. Oppor.
1211 Connecticut Avenue, N.W.
Washington, D.C. 20036

FLORIDA

Gate City Advertising & Public Relations,
    Inc. (BDO Support)
412 Broad St.
Jacksonville, Fla. 32202

Jacksonville Urban League Business
    Dvlpmnt. Center (NUL)
225 W. Ashley St., Rm. 201
Jacksonville, Fla. 32202

National Economic Dvlpmnt. Assn.
2994 N.W. 7th St.
Miami, Fla. 33125

Florida A & M University
Business Development Center
Tallahassee, Fla. 32307

GEORGIA

Atlanta Business League
571 Ashby St., S.W.
Atlanta, Ga. 30310

C.S.R.A. Business League
624 Greene St.
Augusta, Ga. 30901

ILLINOIS

Breadbasket Commercial Assn.
10842 S. Michigan Avenue
Chicago, Ill. 60619

Chicago Economic Dvlpmnt. Corp.
162 N. State St.
Chicago, Ill. 60601

National Economic Dvlpmnt. Assn.
343 S. Dearborn, Ste. 1500
Chicago, Ill. 60604

Rockford Metropolitan Minority Business
    Dvlpmnt. Corp.
P.O. Box 706, 524 Kent St.
Rockford, Ill. 61102

Minority Business Dvlpmnt. Corp.
1003 9th St.
Rock Island, Ill. 61201

INDIANA

Indianapolis Bus. Dvlpmnt. Foundation
320 N. Meridian St., Ste. 317
Indianapolis, Ind. 46204

Indianapolis Urban League Business
    Dvlpmnt. Center (NUL)
3326 Clifton St.
Indianapolis, Ind. 46208

KANSAS

National Economic Dvlpmnt. Assn.
Two Gateway Center
4th St. & State, Ste. 130
Kansas City, Kan. 66101

Kansas State Office of Minority
    Business Enterprise
402 Jackson St.
Topeka, Kan. 66603

Kansas State Office of Minority
    Business Enterprise
2210 E. 13th St.
Wichita, Kan. 67214

Life, Inc.
1 Gateway Center
Kansas City, Kan. 66101

LOUISIANA

Capital Eco. Dvlpmnt. District, Inc.
Old State Capital, P.O. Box 2786
Baton Rouge, La. 70821

Acadiana Bus./Eco. Dvlpmnt. Corp.
603 Jefferson Blvd.
Lafayette, La. 70501

Interracial Cncl. for Bus. Opportunity
2138 St. Bernard Avenue
New Orleans, La. 70119

National Economic Dvlpmnt. Assn.
100 Howard Avenue
New Orleans, La. 70119

National Information, Research and
    Action League, Inc.
1532 B Milam St.
Shreveport, La. 71103

MARYLAND

Community Enterpr. Dvlpmnt. Assn., Inc.
142 South St.
Annapolis, Md. 21401

Baltimore Cncl./Equal Bus. Opportunity
1925 Eutaw Place
Baltimore, Md. 21217

MASSACHUSETTS

The Small Bus. Dvlpmnt. Center
    The Circle, Inc.
90 Warren St. (Roxbury)
Boston, Mass. 02119

United South End Settlements
20 Union Park
Boston, Mass. 02118

MICHIGAN

Inner City Bus. Imprvmnt. Forum
6072 14th St.
Detroit, Mich. 48208

Metropolitan Contractors Assn.
4450 Oakmond Blvd.
Detroit, Mich. 48238

MINNESOTA

The Minnesota Chippewa Tribe
Box 672
Cass Lake, Minn. 56633

Metropolitan Economic Dvlpmnt. Assn.
2021 E. Hennepin Avenue
Ste. 370, Hennepin Square Bldg.
Minneapolis, Minn. 55413

MISSISSIPPI

Jackson Business League
1904 Valley St.
Jackson, Miss. 39204

Community Economic Dvlpmnt., Inc.
P.O. Box 379
Natchez, Miss. 39120

MISSOURI

Black Economic Union
2502 Prospect
Kansas City, Mo. 64127

Community Solutions
3232 Olive St.
St. Louis, Mo. 63103

Interracial Cncl. for Bus. Opportunity
4144 Lindell Avenue, Rm. 401
St. Louis, Mo. 63108

St. Louis Minority Economic Dvlpmnt.
    Agency
2024 Olive St.
St. Louis, Mo. 63103

NEBRASKA

Urban Business Dvlpmnt. Center
3231 Decatur St.
Omaha, Neb. 68111

NEVADA

Nevada Economic Dvlpmnt. Co., Inc.
618 E. Carson
Las Vegas, Nev. 89101

NEW JERSEY

Project Bold of South Jersey
1623 Arctic Avenue
Atlantic City, N.J. 08401

Black People's Unity Movement
201 S. Broadway
Camden, N.J. 08103

Joint Enterprise & Trusteeship Corp.
239 Central Avenue
East Orange, N.J. 07018

Interracial Cncl. for Bus. Oppor. (CBO)
24 Commerce St., Ste. 524
Newark, N.J. 07102

National Economic Dvlpmnt. Assn.
1180 Raymond Blvd., Ste. 802
Newark, N.J. 07102

Progress Assn./Eco. Dvlpmnt. (NPAED)
123 E. Hanover St.
Trenton, N.J. 08608

NEW MEXICO

National Economic Dvlpmnt. Assn.
1801 Lomas Blvd., N.E.
Albuquerque, N.M. 87104

Corporation in Action for Minority
        Bus. Industrial Oppor. (CAMBIO)
Rte. 2, Box 114, 437 Onate, N.W.
Espanola, N.M. 87532

National Economic Dvlpmnt. Assn.
1405 Luisa St., Ste. 7
Santa Fe, N.M. 87501

NEW YORK

Brooklyn Local Eco. Dvlpmnt. Corp.
1519 Fulton St.
Brooklyn, N.Y. 11216

Minority Mgmnt. Assistance Program
S.U.N.Y., School of Management
Crosby Hall, Rm. 125A
Buffalo, N.Y. 14214

Capital Formation, Inc.
5 Beekman St.
New York, N.Y. 10038

Capital Formation, Inc.
215 W. 125th St., Rm. 313
New York, N.Y. 10027

NEW YORK (Cont'd.)

Harlem Commonwealth Cncl., T/A Ctr.
44 W. 143rd St.
New York, N.Y. 10027

Interracial Cncl. for Bus. Opportunity
2090 Seventh Avenue, Ste. 108
New York, N.Y. 10027

Minority Bus. Information Inst., Inc.
295 Madison Avenue
New York, N.Y. 10017

National Economic Dvlpmnt. Assn.
19 W. 44th St., Ste. 407
New York, N.Y. 10036

National Puerto Rican Forum, Inc.
214 Mercer St.
New York, N.Y. 10012

New York Urban League Local Bus.
    Dvlpmnt. Center
261 W. 125th St., Ste. 210
New York, N.Y. 10027

P.R. Plus, Inc.
120 W. 44th St., Ste. 502
New York, N.Y. 10036

Hispanic Business Assn.
21 Essex St.
Rochester, N.Y. 14611

NORTH CAROLINA

Business Dvlpmnt. Center (NPAED)
Cavalier Inn, Rm. 1230
426 N. Tryon St.
Charlotte, N.C. 28202

Durham Bus. & Prof. Chain, Inc.
511 Grant St., P.O. Box 1088
Durham, N.C. 27702

Forsyth County Eco. Dvlpmnt. Corp.
The Pepper Bldg., Ste. 305
Fourth & Liberty Sts.
Winston-Salem, N.C. 27107

Midwest Piedmont Area Business
    Dvlpmnt. Organization, Inc.
623 Waughton St.
Winston-Salem, N.C. 27107

OHIO

Victory Economic Dvlpmnt. Corp.
Harvard Bldg., Rm. 216
203 Central Plaza, South
Carlton, Ohio 44702

OHIO (Cont'd.)

Determined Young Men
3880 Reading Rd.
Cincinnati, Ohio 45229

Greater Cleveland Growth Corp.
690 Union Commerce Bldg.
Cleveland, Ohio 44115

Minority Economic Dvlpmnt. Council
10518 Superior Avenue
Cleveland, Ohio 44106

ECCO Dvlpmnt. Corp.
    Technical Assistance
595 E. Broad St.
Columbus, Ohio 43215

Youngstown Area Dvlpmnt. Corp.
1616 Covington St.
Youngstown, Ohio 44510

OKLAHOMA

United Indian Tribes of Western
    Oklahoma & Kansas
OK Indian Bus. Dvlpmnt. Program
10½ N.W. First St., P.O. Box 668
Anadarka, Okla. 73005

Oklahomans for Indian Opportunity, Inc.
555 Constitution Avenue
Norman, Okla. 73069

Progress Assn. for Economic Dvlpmnt.
1707 N. Broadway, Rm. 110
Oklahoma City, Okla. 73103

OREGON

Valley Migrant League
P.O. Box 7334
Salem, Ore. 97303

PENNSYLVANIA

Entrepreneurial Dvlpmnt. Training Ctr.
1501 N. Broad St.
Philadelphia, Pa. 19122

Philadelphia Urban Coalition
1512 Walnut St.
Philadelphia, Pa. 19102

Spanish Merchant Assn. of Philadelphia
2852 N. Fifth St.
Philadelphia, Pa. 19133

Business & Job Dvlpmnt. Corp.
Manor Bldg., Ste. 501
564 Forbes Avenue
Pittsburgh, Pa. 15219

PENNSYLVANIA (Cont'd.)

University of Pittsburgh
Office of Urban & Community Services
606 Bruce Hall
Pittsburgh, Pa. 15219

SOUTH CAROLINA

Columbia Urban League for Business
    Dvlpmnt. Organization (NUL)
2530 Devine St., Ste. 205
Columbia, S.C. 29250

PENN Community Services, Inc.
Box 126
Frogmore, S.C. 29920

Spartanburg Minority Businessmen's
    Dvlpmnt. Corp.
124 W. Hampton Avenue
Spartanburg, S.C. 29301

TENNESSEE

Chattanooga Chapter Natl. Bus. League
1408 McCallie Avenue
Chattanooga, Tenn. 37404

Memphis Natl. Business League
348 E.H. Crump Blvd.
Memphis, Tenn. 38127

Progress Assn. for Economic Dvlpmnt.
2209 Buchanan St., Ste. B-100
Nashville, Tenn. 37208

TEXAS

Mexican-American Cncl./Eco. Progress
404-A W. 15th St.
Austin, Texas 78701

Corpus Christi Eco. Dvlpmnt. Corp.
1801 S. Staples
Palm Plaza North
Corpus Christi, Texas 78404

Dallas Mexican-American Chamber of
    Commerce
4343 Maple Avenue, Ste. 202
Dallas, Texas 75219

Interracial Cncl. for Bus. Opportunity
3219 Gaston Avenue
Dallas, Texas 75226

Venture Advisors, Inc.
2828 Forest Avenue, Ste. 203
Dallas, Texas 75215

National Economic Dvlpmnt. Assn.
6960 Gateway East
El Paso, Texas 79915

TEXAS (Cont'd.)

National Economic Dvlpmnt. Assn.
202 E. Jackson, Ste. 201
Harlingen, Texas 78550

National Economic Dvlpmnt. Assn.
Kallison Tower, Ste. 916
1222 N. Main Avenue
San Antonio, Texas 78212

VIRGINIA

Community Improvement Council
608 Upper St.
Danville, Va. 24541

Hill City Minority Eco. Dvlpmnt. Corp.
801 Main St.
First & Merchants Bank Bldg.
Lynchburg, Va. 24501

Tidewater Business League
415 St. Paul Blvd., Ste. 700
P.O. Box 1943
Norfolk, Va. 23501

Metropolitan Business League (NBL)
615 N. Second St.
Richmond, Va. 23219

Roanoke Valley Business League
720 Fairfax Avenue
Roanoke, Va. 24016

WASHINGTON

United Inner City Dvlpmnt. Fndtn. (NBL)
4718 Rainier Avenue, South
Seattle, Wash. 98118

WEST VIRGINIA

Progress Assn. for Economic Dvlpmnt.
426 Shrewsbury St.
Charleston, W. Va. 25301

WISCONSIN

Afro Urban Institute
2200 N. Third St., Ste. 406
Milwaukee, Wis. 53212

Milwaukee Urban League
532 E. Center St.
Milwaukee, Wis. 53206

PUERTO RICO

Puerto Rican Dvlpmnt. Fndtn., Inc.
Housing Investment Bldg., Ste. 930
416 Ponce deLeon Avenue
Nato Rey, P.R. 00918

National Economic Dvlpmnt. **Assn.**
Banco Popular Center
San Juan, P.R. 00918

SMALL BUSINESS ADMINISTRATION

The Small Business Administration renders assistance in various ways to those planning to enter business as well as to those in business. This assistance includes counseling and possible financial aid.

Counseling may be by SBA specialists or retired executives under the Service Corps of Retired Executives (SCORE) program, and could include various seminars or courses, or a combination of services including reference publications.

Financial assistance may take the form of loans or the participation in, or guarantee of, loans made by financial institutions. Such assistance can be given only to those eligible applicants who are unable to provide the money from their own resources and cannot obtain it on reasonable terms from banks, franchisors, or other usual business sources.

A list follows of Small Business Administration field offices (and the names and telephone numbers of SBA franchise representatives as of September 1, 1973) where more detailed information regarding the various services available can be obtained.

Regional Offices

Region 1 (Connecticut, Maine, Massachusetts, New Hampshire, Rhode Island, Vermont)
   John F. Kennedy Federal Bldg., Rm. 2113, Boston, Mass.
   (617) 223-2100

Region 2 (New Jersey, New York, Puerto Rico, Virgin Islands)
   26 Federal Plaza, Rm. 3930, New York, N.Y. 10007
   (212) 460-0100

Region 3 (Delaware, District of Columbia, Maryland, Pennsylvania, Virginia, West Virginia)
   1 Decker Square, East Lobby, Ste. 400, Bala Cynwyd, Pa. 19004
   (215) 597-3311

Region 4 (Alabama, Florida, Georgia, Kentucky, Mississippi, North Carolina, Tennessee)
   1401 Peachtree St., N.E., Rm. 441, Atlanta, Ga. 30309
   (404) 526-0111

Region 5 (Illinois, Indiana, Michigan, Minnesota, Ohio, Wisconsin)
   Federal Bldg., 219 S. Dearborn St., Rm. 437, Chicago, Ill. 60604
   (312) 353-4400

Region 6 (Arkansas, Louisiana, New Mexico, Oklahoma, Texas)
   1100 Commerce St., Rm. 300, Dallas, Texas 75202
   (214) 749-5611

Region 7 (Iowa, Kansas, Missouri, Nebraska)
   911 Walnut St., 24th Floor, Kansas City, Mo. 64106
   (816) 374-7000

Region 8 (Colorado, Montana, North Dakota, South Dakota, Utah, Wyoming)
   721 19th St., Rm. 426A, Denver, Colo. 80202
   (303) 837-0111

Region 9 (Arizona, California, Hawaii, Nevada, Pacific Islands)
   Federal Bldg., 450 Golden Gate Ave., San Francisco, Calif. 94102
   (415) 556-9000

Region 10 (Alaska, Idaho, Oregon, Washington)
   710 Second Ave., 5th Floor, Dexter Horton Bldg., Seattle, Wash. 98104
   (206) 442-0111

District Offices

Region 1
 1326 Appleton St., Holyoke, Mass. 01040 - (413) 536-8770
 Federal Bldg., 40 Western Ave., Rm. 512, Augusta, Me. 04330 - (207) 622-6171
 55 Pleasant St., Rm. 213, Concord, N.H. 03301 - (603) 224-4041
 Federal Bldg., 450 Main St., Rm. 710, Hartford, Conn. 06103 - (203) 244-2000
 Federal Bldg., 87 State St., Rm. 210, Montpelier, Vt. 05602 - (802) 223-7472
 57 Eddy St., Rm. 710, Providence, R.I. 02903 - (401) 528-1000

Region 2
 225 Ponce deLeon Ave., Hato Rey, P.R. 00919 - (809) 765-0404
 970 Broad St., Rm. 1635, Newark, N.J. 07102 - (201) 645-3000
 Hunter Plaza, Fayette/Salina Sts., Rm. 308, Syracuse, N.Y. 13202
   (315) 473-3350
 Chamber of Commerce Bldg., 55 St. Paul St., Rochester, N.Y. 14604
   (716) 546-4900

Region 3
 109 N. 3rd St., Rm. 301, Lowndes Bldg., Clarksburg, W. Va. 26301
   (304) 624-3461
 Federal Bldg., 1000 Liberty Ave., Rm. 1401, Pittsburgh, Pa. 15222
   (412) 644-3311
 Federal Bldg., 400 N. 8th St., Rm. 3015, Richmond, Va. 23240 - (703) 782-2000
 1030 15th St., N.W., 2nd Fl., Washington, D.C. 20417 - (202) 382-4901

Region 4
 908 S. 20 St., Rm. 202, Birmingham, Ala. 35205 - (205) 325-3011
 222 S. Church St., Rm. 500, Addison Bldg., Charlotte, N.C. 28202
   (704) 372-0711
 1801 Assembly St., Rm. 117, Columbia, S.C. 29201 - (803) 765-5376
 Petroleum Bldg., Ste. 690, Pascagoula/Amite Sts., Jackson, Miss. 39205
   (601) 948-7821
 Federal Bldg., 400 W. Bay St., Rm. 261, Jacksonville, Fla. 32202
   (904) 791-2011
 Federal Bldg., 600 Federal Plaza, Rm. 188, Louisville, Ky. 40202
   (502) 582-5011
 Federal Bldg., 51 S.W. 1st Ave., Rm. 912, Miami, Fla. 33130 - (305) 350-5011
 500 Union St., Rm. 301, Nashville, Tenn. 37219 - (615) 749-9300
 502 S. Gay St., Rm. 307, Fidelity Bankers Bldg., Knoxville, Tenn. 37902
   (615) 524-4011

Region 5
 502 E. Monroe St., Ridgely Bldg., Rm. 816, Springfield, Ill. 62701
   (217) 525-4200
 1240 E. 9 St., Rm. 5524, Cleveland, Ohio 44199 - (614) 469-6600
 Federal Bldg., 550 Main St., Cincinnati, Ohio 45202 - (513) 684-2200
 1239 Washington Blvd., Rm. 1200, Book Bldg., Detroit, Mich. 48226
   (313) 226-6600
 36 S. Pennsylvania St., Rm. 108, Century Bldg., Indianapolis, Ind. 46204
   (317) 633-7000
 122 W. Washington Ave., Rm. 713, Madison, Wis. 53703 - (608) 256-4441
 12 S. 6th St., Plymouth Bldg., Minneapolis, Minn. 55402 - (612) 725-4242

Region 6
 Federal Bldg. & Courthouse, 500 Gold Ave., S.W., Albuquerque, N.M. 87101
   (505) 843-0311

808 Travis St., Rm. 1219, Niels Esperson Bldg., Houston, Texas 77002
(713) 226-4011
Post Office & Courthouse Bldg., W. Capital Ave., Rm. 377, Little Rock, Ark.
72201 - (501) 378-5871
1205 Texas Ave., Lubbock, Texas 79408 - (806) 747-3711
219 E. Jackson St., Harlingen, Texas 78550 (Lower Rio Grande Valley)
(512) 423-8933
505 E. Travis St., Rm. 201, Travis Terrace Bldg., Marshall, Texas 75670
(214) 935-5257
Plaza Tower, 17th Fl., 1001 Howard Ave., New Orleans, La. 70113
(504) 527-2611
30 N. Hudson St., Rm. 501, Mercantile Bldg., Oklahoma City, Okla. 73102
(405) 231-4011
301 Broadway, Rm. 300, Marion Bldg., San Antonio, Texas 78205
(512) 225-5511

Region 7
New Federal Bldg., 210 Walnut St., Rm. 749, Des Moines, Iowa 50309
(515) 284-4000
Federal Bldg., 215 N. 17 St., Rm. 7419, Omaha, Neb. 68102 - (402) 221-1221
Federal Bldg., 210 N. 12 St., Rm. 520, St. Louis, Mo. 63101 - (314) 622-8100
120 S. Market St., Rm. 301, Wichita, Kans. 67202 - (316) 267-6311

Region 8
Federal Bldg., 100 E. "B" St., Rm. 4001, Casper, Wyo. 82601 - (307) 265-5550
Power Block Bldg., Main/6th Ave., Rm. 208, Helena, Mont, 59601
(406) 442-9040
Federal Bldg., 653 2nd Ave., N., Rm. 218, Fargo, N.D. 58102 - (701) 237-5771
Federal Bldg., 125 S. State St., Rm. 2237, Salt Lake City, Utah 84111
(801) 524-5500
National Bank Bldg., 8th & Main Ave., Rm. 402, Sioux Falls, S.D., 57102
(605) 336-2980

Region 9
149 Bethel St., Rm. 402, Honolulu, Hawaii 96813 - (808) 546-8950
849 S. Broadway, Los Angeles, Calif. 90014 - (213) 688-2121
112 N. Central Ave., Phoenix, Ariz. 85004 - (602) 261-3900
110 W. "C" St., San Diego, Calif. 92101 - (714) 293-5000

Region 10
1016 W. 6th Ave., Anchorage Legal Center, Anchorage, Alaska 99501
(907) 272-5561
503 3rd Ave., Fairbanks, Alaska 99701 - (907) 452-5561
216 N. 8th St., Rm. 408, Boise, Idaho 83701 - (208) 342-2711
921 Southwest Washington St., Portland, Ore. 97205 - (503) 221-2000
Courthouse Bldg., Rm. 651, Spokane, Wash. 99210 - (509) 456-0111

INTERNAL REVENUE SERVICE, DEPARTMENT OF THE TREASURY

The Internal Revenue Service offers a number of services designed to assist new businessmen in understanding and meeting their Federal tax obligations. For example, a *Mr. Businessman's Kit* (Publication 454) which contains informational publications, forms, instructions, and samples of notices which the IRS issues to business concerns is available free.

The kit is a convenient place for storing retained copies of tax returns and employee information. It also contains a checklist of tax returns and a tax calendar of due dates for filing returns and paying taxes identified on the folder. Copies of the kit may be obtained from local offices of the Internal Revenue Service. Employees of the IRS are available to explain items in the kit and answer questions about the tax forms, how to complete them, requirements for withholding, depositing, reporting Federal income and social security taxes, and the Federal unemployment tax. Copies of the kit may also be obtained by writing to the District Director who will have it delivered and explained at a mutually convenient time.

The Tax Guide for Small Business (Publication 334) may also be obtained at local offices of the IRS, the District Director, or the Superintendent of Documents, U.S. Government Printing Office, Washington, D.C. 20402. Price: 75¢.

Conclusion and Summation

If this book has achieved its purpose, you should now know how to find the answers to these basic questions:

- Should I go into business for myself?
- What business should it be?
- How do I make my selection?
- How do I judge the suitability of the business?
- What financing is needed? How and where can I obtain it?
- How do I get started?
- How can I achieve success in my business?

In addition, the chapter on "Creating Ideas" has shown you how to think innovatively, how to come up with winning ideas that can make your business distinctive *and* successful.

More important, this book can help you avoid the usual time-consuming and highly expensive "trial and error" method of selecting and operating a business. That route so often leads only to loss of financial liquidity . . . loss of years of effort . . . loss of all your hopes and aspirations.

But now, instead of drift, you have direction. Instead of aimlessness of outlook, you have purposefulness. Instead of constant hit-or-miss experimentation, you can proceed directly to your targeted goals and achieve the success you seek.

This book was not designed, however, to simply get you on the right road. Properly used, it can serve you as an enduring friend and sagacious counselor, always available to provide constructive answers to recurring business and personal problems.

The rest, of course, depends on you—on your willingness, your dedication, your optimism, and your tenacity.

Whatever business you do select, please accept my sincere wishes for continuing success.

The Author

Index